MOTIVES IN CHILDREN'S DEVELOPMENT

The contributors to this collection employ the analytic resources of cultural-historical theory to examine the relationship between childhood and children's development under different societal conditions. In particular they attend to relationships between development, emotions, motives and identities, as well as the social practices in which children and young people may be learners. These practices are knowledge-laden, imbued with cultural values and emotionally freighted by those who already act in them.

The book first discusses the organising principles that underpin a cultural-historical understanding of motives, development and learning. The second part foregrounds children's lives to exemplify the implications of these ideas as they are played out – examining how children are positioned as learners in pre-school, primary school and play environments. The final part uses the core ideas to look at the implementation of policy aimed at enhancing children's engagement with opportunities for learning, by discussing motives in the organisations that shape children's development.

Mariane Hedegaard is professor in developmental psychology and head of the Centre for Person, Practice, Development & Culture at the University of Copenhagen.

Anne Edwards is professor of educational studies and director of the Department of Education at the University of Oxford.

Marilyn Fleer holds the foundation chair for early childhood education at Monash University, Australia, and is the research director for the research group Child and Community Development.

Motives in Children's Development

CULTURAL-HISTORICAL APPROACHES

Edited by

Mariane Hedegaard
University of Copenhagen

Anne Edwards
Oxford University

Marilyn Fleer
Monash University

CAMBRIDGE
UNIVERSITY PRESS

CAMBRIDGE UNIVERSITY PRESS
Cambridge, New York, Melbourne, Madrid, Cape Town,
Singapore, São Paulo, Delhi, Tokyo, Mexico City

Cambridge University Press
32 Avenue of the Americas, New York, NY 10013-2473, USA

www.cambridge.org
Information on this title: www.cambridge.org/9780521767422

© Cambridge University Press 2012

First published 2012

A catalog record for this publication is available from the British Library.

Library of Congress Cataloging in Publication data
Motives in children's development : cultural-historical approaches / [edited by] Mariane
Hedegaard, Anne Edwards, Marilyn Fleer.
p.   cm.
Includes bibliographical references and index.
ISBN 978-0-521-76742-2
1. Child development.   2. Developmental psychology.   I. Hedegaard, Mariane.
II. Edwards, Anne, 1946–   III. Fleer, Marilyn.
HQ772.M68   2011
155.4–dc23   2011022033

ISBN 978-0-521-76742-2 Hardback

CONTENTS

FIGURES

Introduction: Cultural-Historical Understandings of Motives and Children's Development

How to engage children, whether pre-school or adolescents, with what is culturally valued is a universal challenge for educators and for parents. Adults expend considerable energy trying to align what matters to them and what matters to children so that cultural patterns endure and children learn to participate as productive members of society within them.

All too often these attempts at alignment are seen as a problem of how to motivate children, and the impact of such efforts is frequently short-term. However, this book is not simply about motivation. It is far more ambitious: It unravels how children's longer-term development is interconnected with why and how they take part in everyday practices.

The contributors discuss how children develop in relation to what matters for them as they are with their families, go to child-care or school and play with their friends. The central concern across the chapters is the motives that give shape to children's development as they take an active part in the practices they encounter at home, in more formal education settings and at play.

The authors come from Australia, Europe – including Russia – South America and the United States. They therefore bring together analyses of relationships between childhood and children's development under quite different societal conditions. As such, it is possible to gain a more global view of how the concept of motives has been used to solve specific cultural and local community research problems. Taken together, the country-specific studies provide a strong focus on the interplay between development, emotions, motives, identities and the social practices in which children and young people may be learners. Collectively, these chapters bring together both a historical and a contemporary view of these concepts, giving a more expansive meaning to motives.

The book has the term *cultural-historical approaches* in its title to indicate its origins in the cultural-historical approach of Lev Vygotsky, a

Russian researcher who studied the intertwining of learning, development and culture and who produced his main work between 1924 and 1934. His death, at age thirty-eight, put an end to this productive research period, which yielded an impressive collection of manuscripts. Much of his work was first published in Russian after his death and then later in English and other languages. Over the intervening period, his ideas have led to a rich vein of cultural-historical research which has continued his examination of the interplay of learning, development and culture. Much of this diversity and development is reflected in the writing of the authors of the chapters contained in this book, giving a fuller account of the concept of motives.

After eighty years, there are, of course, differences in how his analyses have been developed. Nonetheless, within this diversity, considerable coherence remains among the cultural-historical research approaches which have built on his work. Hence we have long believed that it would be fruitful to bring together researchers from these approaches to discuss the key concepts of *motives* and *emotions* in relation to children's development and to examine their interconnections with the conditions that family and professional practices provide for their development.

Many authors of chapters in this volume have drawn upon Leontiev's idea of motive in relation to the problems they are working on. Leontiev was one of Vygotsky's co-workers and has been a central figure within the cultural-historical tradition with his introduction of the concepts of activity and the object-motive. Leontiev has a particular view of motive, which he explained in relation to activities and what matters in those activities: 'The main thing that distinguished one activity from another, however, is the difference in their objects. It is exactly the object of activity, that gives it a determined direction. According to the terminology I have proposed, the object of activity is its true motive' (Leontiev, 1978, p. 17).

The idea of an object-motive within a system of concepts in activity theory is used throughout this book in connection with its historical roots which commenced with the theoretical writings of Vygotsky. In this volume, object-motive is critiqued (see Kravtsova and Kravtsov), elaborated upon (see Gonzalez Rey), but has also inspired well-known Russian (e.g. Elkonin, Zinchenko) and Danish (e.g. Hedegaard) scholars to put forward contemporary works which others in this volume have used to frame or analyse their scientific investigations (see, Fleer, Sanchez Medina and Martinez Lozano, Stenild and Sejer Iversen, Wardekker and Boersma, Winther-Lindqvist). Many authors in this volume have also drawn upon a range of cultural-historical theories (e.g. Daniels, Edwards, Hedegaard,

Wardekker and Boersma, Winther-Lindqvist, Zinchenko) to better understand the theoretical problems they are examining. Taken together, these ideas have allowed contributors to connect the activities that arise in the practices of the home, child-care, school or playground with the thinking and actions of children so that their engagement in activities in practices is open to scrutiny. Through this empirical and theoretical activity, many challenges, possibilities, and opportunities arise for scientific research (see Chaiklin, this volume).

AN OVERVIEW OF THE CHAPTERS

The book consists of three parts. Part One draws on studies of children and young people to explain the organising principles that underpin a cultural-historical understanding of motives, emotions, development and learning. Part Two foregrounds children's lives to exemplify the implications of these ideas as they are played out in how children are positioned as learners in home, child-care, school and play environments. The two chapters in Part Three then take the core ideas to an examination of the institutional conditions for children's engagement with opportunities for learning, by discussing motives in the organisations that shape children development. The final chapter by Seth Chaiklin draws on themes discussed in a workshop of the first edition of the chapters. He points out central topics in this discussion and the challenge for future research.

The cultural-historical research traditions that Vygotsky inspired draw particularly on the idea that children are social from birth and that children's individualities develop into their personalities through becoming members of society. In this way children come to reflect the society they have grown up in, both by how their primary functions of need and perception are transformed and by how what matters in the culture influences their emotional and motivational orientation to the world.

In Chapter 1, Mariane Hedegaard proposes that this view of development has to be nuanced with the concept of institutional practice. Children's everyday lives are lived across institutional practices as they move, for example, between home and school, and the objectives in these practices influence the development of children's motives. Hedegaard argues that the dynamic of children's activities and development has to be analysed at several planes, for example, at the levels of institutional practices, activity within the practices and children's actions. Such an analysis recognises that children's intentional actions within activities have to be the core object of enquiry when researching the development of children's motives while they are participating in institutional practices. Elena Kravtsova and Genady Kravtsov in Chapter 2 make a case similar to Hedegaard's, suggesting that children's perspectives have to be central to our understanding of their activity. These views, they remind us, reflect Vygotsky's analyses of human will, which for him functioned as a mediating device which links personal actions. Kratsova and Kratsov propose that children's will has a central role in how they live their lives and should be a primary focus in attempts at understanding the development of children's play and learning.

The remaining chapters in the collection build on Hedegaard's premise that institutional practices mediate children's learning and development. The authors therefore all recognise that the various forces emanating from cultural settings, social relations and a child's needs are interwoven to mediate a child's actions. They also work with the view that differences between institutions can be conceptualised as differences in the practices that are at the core of these institutions. Importantly for child development, these practices influence what Vygotsky termed 'the leading activity' for a child in a given period of their development and which is reflected in the child's motives, feelings, values and identity.

In Chapter 3, Fernando González Rey picks up these Vygotskian ideas by examining emotion and the part it plays in the formation of personality through the complex configurations of the emotions that constitute a child's subjectivity. In Chapter 4, Vladimir Zinchenko indicates an important gap in psychology, arguing that whereas language has been seen as central in children's cognitive development, there has been a lack of consideration of language as a cultural medium for emotions. Zinchenko observes that language mediates what matters in a culture through communicating feelings from the moment that the child is born, and language thereby becomes a cultural medium that influences a child's emotional and motivational relation to the world from the first moments of life.

Illustrating these points, in Chapter 5, Marilyn Fleer shows, through her comparative case studies of young children, how kindergarten practices can be diverse and provide different possibilities for children to be actively engaged. Her research shows that the opportunities that children have for structuring their imitation and their creation of rules for play in the activity settings of early education can influence the development of their learning motives.

José A. Sánchez Medina and Virginia Martínez Lozano in Chapter 6 show that peer interactions, even in early childhood, exhibit a marked cultural component. The way in which peer groups are organised, the type of activity they develop, and even the conflicts issues and the way of nego- tiating and resolving them reflect values and norms of the adult cultures in children's motives for interacting in play. Children rebuild, in their acts, this world of reference. They re-create these values and norms conforming to a *peer culture* where those cultural issues play an important role as motives that guide and organise their own acts.

The importance of practices to the development of motives means that transitions between practices can be demanding. Examining the transition from kindergarten to school, Ditte Winther-Lindqvist in Chapter 7 dem- onstrates that both continuity and discontinuity in children's experiences take place. Her study reveals in detail the restructuring of what matters for children as they enter school and how this influences their engagement. Establishing engagement across situations and institutionalised practices is also a theme in Harry Daniels' contribution (Chapter 11) in Part Three of the book. He points to the importance of the re-contextualisation of soci- etal motives within concrete situations to change the situations. In this process, changes in the local arrangement of power and control are import- ant so that children can engage in new ways and develop motives for learn- ing in school.

Part of the educational process in school involves engaging children with what is to be learnt. In Chapter 8, Kåre Stenild and Ole Sejer Iversen in their project demonstrate that mobile phones and IT technology can be used in this process. They also argue, however, that the motivational advan- tage of using mobile phones and IT technology in school will be evident at first as an educational tool when this technology motivates children's use of the subject matter knowledge in their everyday activities.

In Chapter 9, Wim Wardekker, Annoesjka Boersma, Geert Ten Dam and Monique Volman also examine school practices. They draw on their study of motives and adolescents to discuss the mutual aligning of school motives and those of young people through an innovative curriculum development. They suggest that motivation has to relate both to the child's earlier knowledge and what is meaningful knowledge for the child in the future to achieve a 'use value' which is recognised by the child.

The importance of what matters for people in practices is also found in the final section of the book in Chapter 10, where Anne Edwards's focus is the professional practices of the children's workforce, which create the con- ditions for children's engagement as learners. She discusses the weaknesses of practices, and therefore the experiences of children, where what matters for practitioners does not include distinct professional knowledge which is open to scrutiny. She argues that responsible and responsive practice with children involves attention to working on and with the knowledge to be found in professional practices. In Chapter 11 Harry Daniels argues that reconceptualisation of societal motives within specific situations provides an important approach to formulating a theory of how to change situations. In this conceptualisation he draws on Basil Bernstein's sociology of cultural transmission. Seth Chaiklin brings the the contributions together in Chapter 12 locating motives within the wholeness approach in Cultural-Historical theory and discussing the concept of motives in relation to problems in the theory.

REFERENCE

Leontiev, A. N. (1978). *Activity, consciousness, and personality*. Englewood Cliffs, NJ: Prentice-Hall.

PART ONE

MOTIVES, EMOTIONS AND DEVELOPMENT

1

The Dynamic Aspects in Children's Learning and Development

MARIANE HEDEGAARD

Over the years I have pondered about the relation between Jerome Bruner's study of infants' intentional orientation to the world and Marx Wartofsky's philosophical conceptions of human's dynamic relation to objects, and how to relate this to A. N. Leontiev's activity theory. Bruner (1972) and his co-workers studied experimentally how infants from one month to seven months of age transform intention-oriented movements into the intentional act of reaching for objects. From this research Bruner proposed that what characterizes humans is that we are born with 'pre-adaptive structures that make a possible comparison of what is intended in an activity and what is accomplished' (Bruner 1972, p. 34). Wartofsky in his theory questioned the notion that human perception is 'natural' and argued that human perception is an activity that is mediated by artifacts such as tools and language. These mediating artifacts, Wartofsky argued, have to be seen as objectifications of human needs and intentions '*already* invested with cognitive and affective content' (Wartofsky, 1979, pp. 205–206).

What is special in Bruner's and Wartofsky's conceptions of the dynamic between persons and the world is that they do not conceptualize the dynamic of children's relation to the world starting with the child's primary needs. Rather, it is a characteristic in humans' general relation to the world, that can be seen as demands from the world onto the person. The aim in this chapter is to integrate this conception of how demands of being in the world can be related to the cultural-historical approach of children's development and Leontiev's theory of motives.

Leontiev's (1978) theory draws attention to how children's needs, through participating in collective activities, become attached to objects (in the form of material objects such as different kind of foods, or ideal objects such as the value of studying or religious beliefs) and thereby can turn into a person's motives. Theoretically this is conceptualised so that a human, born as an individual, becomes a person through acquiring collective motives.

This chapter formulates a more comprehensive understanding of the dynamic which includes not only human activity, but also demands by both objects and persons in different types of institutional practice. Institutional practice will be used to extend Leontiev's conception of activity and its motives.

The objectives of institutional practices, and how they create demands for children's activities, will be the central focus in the analyses. A central argument will be that on the one hand, children learn and develop through their orientation towards the demands in institutional practices for competences, motives and values; on the other hand, children's activities personalise practice in their realisation and contribution to the activity settings of practice; thereby children create conditions for their own learning and development of personal competences and motives.

In this chapter I draw on an earlier model (Hedegaard, 1999, 2009) of the relation between children's activities, institutional practices and societal conditions. The model is extended here by the concept of activity setting. Children's activities in this version (see Figure 1.1) are seen as located within activity settings that can be found in specific practices such as family or school. Demands in these settings by objects or persons can be seen as conditions for as well as motivating children's activities. For home practices this can be the meals, homework and preparation for going to bed. In school it can be the different subject matter sessions and recess. The model in Figure 1.1 illustrates a dynamic where a child concurrently should be seen as participating in several institutional practices in her/his everyday life – for instance, in the family, school or day-care.

The following section contains a short introduction to a wholeness approach to learning and development, that allows us to anchor the dynamic of children's learning and development in a theoretical frame. This is followed by an overview of the main theoretical approaches to the dynamic aspects in children's learning and development. The discussion then, from these premises, focuses on the dynamic relations in children's everyday life in institutional practices, discussed in relation to a concrete example. From this example the relation between children's intentional actions and motive-oriented activities is discussed.

A WHOLENESS APPROACH

In cultural-historical approaches a salient aim is to move beyond an empirical-research approach of combining elements, and instead to

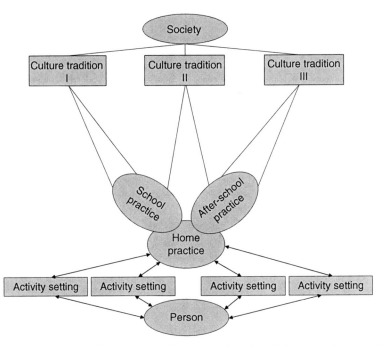

FIGURE 1.1. Model of the relations between cultural tradition, practice, activity settings and children's activities as the core in a cultural-historical approach to children's learning and development.

define the area of study as a whole, anchored in historical values where the processes are in focus (such as practices, social situations, activities and actions) (Bozhovich, 2009; Hedegaard, 2002; Iljenkov, 1977; Leontiev, 1978; Vygotsky, 1998; Zinchenko, 2002). Therefore a theoretical outline of learning and development which can be seen as a wholeness approach will focus on children's activities in activity settings located in institutional practices that have a history embodied in traditions and framed by societal conditions.

In Vygotsky's and Leontiev's theories the focus is on how societal objects are mediating between the child and the world in his/her social situation, and how this mediation leads to the individual's learning and development as a personality. Vygotsky's wholeness approach to children's development relates the emergence of different development periods to changes in the child's social situation. The concept of the social situation of development is the key to understanding this dynamic and how the world is seen from a specific child's perspective in a given age period. It is important to note that Vygotsky did not refer to biological age in itself, but rather to age periods defined by societal traditions which then become reflected in the child's experiental relation to the world: 'The social situation of development represents the initial moments for all dynamic changes that occur in development during a given [age] period.... The social situation of development specific to each age [period] determines strictly regularly the whole picture of the child's life or his social existence' (Vygotsky, 1998, p. 198).

Leontiev similarly pointed to the necessity to overcome the nature-nurture split which in different theoretical refinements has dominated psychology as a two-factor model of children's development – either inner factors or outer factors (or both) determining development. He wrote:

> Of course, no development directly comes from what comprises only the prerequisites necessary for it, no matter in what detail we might describe it. The method of Marxist dialectics requires that we go further and investigate the development as a process of 'self movement', that is, investigate its internal moving relations, contradictions, and mutual transitions so that its prerequisites appear in it as its own changing moments. (Leontiev, 1978, p. 105)

To extend Vygotsky's and Leontiev's points I will introduce the concepts of practice. The relation between institutional practice and its objective and the person's motivated activity within his/her social situation of development can be seen as the core in conceptualisation of the developmental process as self-movement. By distinguishing between practice and activity one can better see the inner relation between a child's activities and the societal conditions as mediated by the institutional objectives of practices and thereby get deeper into the analyses of a self-movement of development which is cultural and historical.

I conceptualise Vygotsky's and Leontiev's concepts of the collective and the social as institutional practices which are created and re-created by a person's activities in the activity settings of the practices (such as breakfast in the family, lessons in school), while at the same time the collective institutional practices are the social conditions for a person's activities. People learn when their activities change their social relations in a practice and thereby give them possibilities for new activities. Development occurs when a person's learning takes place across institutional practices and changes the person's relation qualitatively across all the practices in which the person participates. This is what Vygotsky meant when he wrote: 'The social situation of development specific to each age determines strictly regularly the whole picture of the child's life or his social existence' (1998, p. 198).

DRIVES, NEEDS, MOTIVATION AND MOTIVES AS DYNAMIC FORCES IN CHILDREN'S LEARNING AND DEVELOPMENT

The role of drives, needs, motivation and motives has been formulated in different theories as forces giving rise to how persons relate to the world and how this relation develops. Broadly they can be divided into theories which conceptualise these dynamic aspects of a person's relation to the world (1) as building on inborn drives and needs and modification of these drives and needs (psychoanalytical, humanistic and behaviourist approaches); (2) as societal demands which become appropriated as motives for cognitive conduct (cognitive anthropological and sociological approaches); and (3) as forces, both in the person and in the environment, that together create a dynamic field which accounts for a person's activity and learning (wholeness approaches).

Drives, Needs and Their Transformation into Motivation as Dynamic Explanations for Human Activity

Theories within the drives-and-needs approach focus on drives, needs and motivation as explanations for human activity, and especially on problems in a person's activities and conduct. The psychoanalytic tradition, with Freud (1983) as the main figure, belongs to this category. To understand human activity Freud used drives (sex and death/aggression) to explain human activity. The theory points to the modification of these drives, especially in early childhood, through children's relations with their parents. In this modification culture is seen as a burden which regulates the development of a human's relation to the world.

The humanistic tradition in psychology, with Murray (1938) as well as Maslow (1955), also falls within this category, conceptualising the dynamic aspects of human conduct as coming from the person. They both argued that the concept of drives is too simple and supplemented biological drives and needs with learned needs. Murray conceptualised that humans are characterised by two types of need – primary biological needs and psychological learned needs – that are derived from primary needs. The problem with Murray's list of learned needs is that one could suggest a need for every type of a person's activity, so instead of explaining activity, the list becomes more of a circular conceptualisation of needs nested in the American-Western societal tradition. Maslow pointed out that physiological need gratification as the origin for human conduct is too simple. He therefore introduced the concept of growth-motivated perception and the motive of self-actualisation. Growth-motivated perception introduces variations in how timid or positively oriented different people are towards life and other persons (Hoffman, 1988; Maslow 1955).

The conceptualisation of needs as learned was refined in the behavioural and cognitive traditions into the concept of motivation. This conception has been important in learning theory and cognitive theory (Ames & Ames, 1984; Covington, 1992; Maehr, 1983; McClelland, 1965; Pintrich, 1991, 2000; Pintrich, Marx, & Boyle, 1993; Weiner, 1990). The core in these theories is how children appropriate motivation for learning. The research within this tradition has focused on achievement and mastery motivation. In principle children's appropriation of achievement and mastery motivation has been conceptualised as a process based on success and failure from children's early experiences. In principle these theories could also be categorised as forces both from within and from the environment, but they are included here because they are conceptualised as forces directed at the person's relation to the world, basically oriented towards reducing harm or attaining pleasure.

Societal Demands as the Primary Forces

Theories in the second approach to explaining the dynamic in human learning and development have conceptualised the forces for human actions and conduct as societal demands that persons in a given society gradually internalise. In this category we find cognitive anthropology and sociological approaches. In cognitive anthropology motives have been connected to cultural models, schemas or scripts where these are seen as forces for people's conduct (D'Andrade, 1992; Holland, 1992; Strauss, 1992). In this theoretical approach the dynamic comes from appropriating cognitive schemas. Goal schemas are treated as motives. It is a theory of motives as located in the person's cognitive representation of the world (D'Andrade, 1992, p. 30).

Societal demands as the primary forces of human conduct can also be found in the sociological approach of C. Wright Mills. Mills (1940) formulated a theory of motives as values of public conduct. In this meaning motives are related to practices and values in a society; therefore, motives are seen as coming from the collective: Rather than fixed elements 'in' an individual, motives are the terms with which interpretation of conduct by *social* actors proceeds (Mills, 1940, p. 904).

Mills argues that there is a stable repertoire of motive vocabularies connected to different practices. Business practices have one set, religious practices have another set and school practices have a third set, which means that traditions of each practice have their own vocabulary of motives which are evaluated as 'good and bad', although there will be overlap: 'Motives can be seen as "social instruments" by which the agent will be able to influence [himself or others]. The motivational structures of individuals and the patterns of their purposes are relative to societal frames' (Mills, 1940, p. 911).

Campbell (1991, 1996, 2006) re-examines Mills's theory of motives. He supports Mills's ideas of motives as ideologies but criticises the way other sociologists have interpreted Mills's concept of motives primarily as societal vocabularies for human conduct. This interpretation, Campbell writes, has influenced the sociological tradition, so the institutional aspect in Mills's theory of motives has not had a serious impact; instead Mills's ideas have been restricted to social interactions.

D'Andrade's and Mills's 'script' approaches are important to take into consideration in relation to Vygotsky's and Leontiev's cultural-historical and activity theories, so that not only the social and societal but also the institutional dynamic aspects of people's learning and development become explicit. This means one has to see motives as something which exists in institutional practices that a person confronts through the activity settings in his/her everyday life.

Mills's conception of motives points to the importance of relating institutional demands to the situated activity of persons. The institutional aspect will, in the next part of this chapter, be related to persons' perspectives, where both the institution and the person are seen as important for understanding the role of motive for how people learn and develop.

Motives as an Integration of Demands from Environment and Children's Conditions into Psychological Forces in Children's Activities

The third approach to theorising the dynamic of person's actions and conduct is called a wholeness approach and covers both the tradition from Kurt Lewin and the cultural-historical and activity traditions from Vygotsky and Leontiev. How the person-environment dynamic integrates into forces giving rise to human activity is not understood in the same ways in the Lewin tradition and in the cultural-historical and activity traditions, and will be refined here. However, both Vygotsky and Lewin are central to a wholeness approach to children's learning and development of motives.

Lewin argued that one should see children's activities as related to the complexity of the actual social field. The psychological forces here must be seen as integrating demands from the environment with the child's physiological and psychological conditions. In Lewin's theory psychological forces thereby were seen as part of the social world and not conceptualised only as the person's inner forces. It was important to conceptualise the person's actual social field to understand the person's activities. It is this lead from Lewin – to focus on the social field as the ways a person relates to his/her actual social world – that in this chapter will be developed further into the concept of activity setting. However, Lewin did not take into account the historical construction of a person's social field. To bring the historical and societal dimensions into conceptualising the dynamic in humans' relations to their world I build on Vygotsky's (1998) concept of 'the social situation of a child's development' and Leontiev's (1978) concept of 'motive' to conceptualise both the dynamic of children's development and how to create motivation in the dynamic field of an activity setting (i.e. homework in a family or native-language teaching in a classroom).

Using the concept of motive that he developed, Leontiev (1978) created a tool for microanalysing how the dynamic in human activities evolves. Leontiev's theory of children's activities starts with the concept of primary needs, but when a child's need 'finds' its object, the object becomes the need. From the newborn being an individual he/she becomes a personality through acquiring the object motives of society (Levitin, 1982). The concept of an object, however, is not to be associated with a 'thing', as pointed out by Davydov, Zinchenko and Talyzina (1983, p. 31): 'An object is not however, understood as a thing that exists in itself and acts upon the subject, but as "that toward which an act is directed … i.e., something to which a living being relates, as the *object of his activity* – regardless of whether the activity is external or internal."' Thus, human activity is characterised not only by its objectiveness, but also by its *subjectiveness*: The activity of the subject is always directed towards the transformation of an object that is able to satisfy some specific need (Davydov et al., 1983). Then the relation is turned around from being *need – activity – object/motive* and becomes *object/ motive – activity – need*. It is through the child's inclusion in social relations that this turnaround takes place.

Vygotsky's theory can be seen as encompassing the dynamic in not only the child's social field, but also in the child's relation to the field over time. Vygotsky's theory (1998) about children's age periods is a concept which locates children's relation in specific societal and historical conditions and at the same time in specific periods within the child's own ontogenetic development that reflects the societal and historical conditions. Vygotsky divides the dynamic transformation of a child's age period into three phases. With the beginning of each age period there is a specific and unique relation between the child and reality; Vygotsky characterises this relation as the child's social situation of development:

> Toward the end of a given age, the child becomes a completely different being than he was at the beginning of the age. But this necessarily also means that the social situation of development which was established in basic traits toward the beginning of any age must also change since the social situation of development is nothing other than a system of relations between the child of a given age and social reality. (Vygotsky, 1998, p. 199)

According to Vygotsky, this change takes the form of crises in the child's social situation of development. Daniel Elkonin (1989) continues Vygotsky's conceptions of crises in a child's social situation of development. He suggests that crises and changes in the child's motive orientation can be initiated by the child entering a new practice or acquiring a new competence.

In what follows, Leontiev's and Vygotsky's theories of the dynamic of children's activities and development will be extended, with the inspiration from Mills, to include the demands in institutional practice in the conceptualisation of motives. Thereby it becomes possible to analyse the dynamic between the environment and the child as a relation between institutional demands and values and a person's activities within his/her social situation of development.

How cultural-historically developed values become personalised needs cannot be understood as a straightforward shift from primary biological needs. The values exist as historically developed in the different institutional practices. The child's own activities do not explain how an individual person acquires and creates the cultural-historically developed values. To understand how emotions and motives related to values become personal, one must conceptualise how values that have developed historically in different institutional practices also exist as demands on persons participating in these practices. Mills's concept of motive relates to institutionalised societal demands that include the values by which a person will be able to influence his/her own or others' situated activity.

THE SOCIETAL AND INSTITUTIONAL DIMENSIONS IN A CULTURAL-HISTORICAL APPROACH TO MOTIVES

The Relation between Children's Activities and Institutional Practices

Children's learning and development have to be conceptualised as well as studied by focusing on their activities and the demands they meet in institutionalised practices. Traditions for practice frame the actual practice but also transcend the actual situated practice and make the practice surpass its situated local realizations. The demands children meet in their everyday social practice can be seen as located in different activity settings.

The inspiration to look at children's activities within activity settings comes from Lewin's tradition of field analyses. Barker and Wright (1954), inspired by Lewin's field studies in their study of 'One boy's day', have conceptualised their units of study as behavioural settings. Replacing the concept of behaviour with the concept of activity, the cultural-historical aspect of a human's activities in settings will become explicit, because activity settings can be seen as structured both by the person and by the traditions that constrain institutional practice.[1]

From the *institution's perspective*, activity settings are recurrent structures of traditions for activities that take place in an institutional practice. Eating breakfast, for instance, is an example from the institutional perspective of a recurrent activity setting in many Danish families. From the *person's perspective*, activity settings are recurrent social situations in which the child takes part together with other persons. A proposal to integrate the outlined different planes of dynamics in children's learning and development can be seen in Table 1.1.

Each plane presented in Table 1.1 depicts the relation between entity, process and dynamic. These planes are interrelated: Society creates the conditions for institutions with its activity settings and persons do so with their specific biological conditions.

The activity setting, such as breakfast or homework in a family practice, is framed by societal traditions and can be quite different in different societies. In a specific family the activity setting takes a special form that family members create together. Depending on the child's social situation

---

[1] Gallimore, Goldenberg and Weisner (1993) and Galimore and Tharp (1988) have also used the concept of activity setting inspired by Barker and Wright, but they do not relate this to institutional practice.

TABLE 1.1. *Planes of analysis of the dynamic relations in children's learning and development*

Entity	Process	Dynamic
Society	Tradition	Societal needs/conditions
Institution	Practice	Value motive/objectives
Activity setting	Situation	Motivation/demands
Person	Activity	Motive/intentions
Human's biology	Neurophysiological processes	Primary needs/drives

of development, the child will be influenced and also contribute to the families' activity settings, as I will illustrate in the following observation of mother and children creating a homework setting. By influencing the activity settings, a child contributes to the conditions for her/his own learning and development. The children were observed thirty-one times across different practice over a period of nine months.

Homework in the Living Room

It is 10 A.M. on a Saturday morning. There are four children in the family: Kajsa (aged four years), Emil (six years), Lulu (eight years) and Laura (ten years). Together with Mother they create the activity setting of homework. The three younger siblings have been watching TV while Mother and Laura read a book about the Egyptian pyramids. Mother had told the three younger children to turn off the TV.

MOTHER: sits down at the dinner table and reads the newspaper.

LAURA: places herself next to her and, on her own initiative, starts to prepare her homework. Laura writes a draft for her horror story [drawing on the story she read earlier with Mother] and explains to Mother that because it is a draft it is okay to be a bit sloppy.

LULU: joins Mother and Laura at the table and takes out her homework. She wants to do her math homework. She starts with multiplication tasks in which she has to use the nine-times table. She cannot remember the table by heart so she uses a written version of it.

MOTHER: tells Lulu that she has to know the table by heart.

LULU: responds by putting the booklet with the table over her heart and makes Mother laugh. Then Lulu starts the next task in her math book, which involves subtraction. The task is difficult for her. She has particular difficulty figuring out how to borrow while subtracting.

MOTHER: notices that Lulu's attention wanders and that homework is posing a problem for her, so she tries to give Lulu a task that resembles the one in her math book. Lulu has to figure out how old her grandmother is when she was born in 1938. Despite Mother's attempts to keep Lulu's attention on the task by formulating steps in the problem, Lulu says shortly after that she does not want to do homework right now.

MOTHER: tells Lulu that sometimes you have to do things you do not want to do.

   Although Lulu accepts this, she finds it hard to keep her focus throughout the activity and is not really working on her math tasks.

   While the interaction is going on between Mother and Lulu, Emil enters the room, finds some stickers and asks Mother if he is allowed to play with them. She confirms. Emil goes into his room to get some extra stickers, but returns with a toy cash register. He sits down at the table and starts to play with the cash register.

EMIL: starts to make money by writing different numbers on small pieces of paper, that he puts into the drawer of the cash register.

MOTHER: watches and notices that he is not writing the numbers correctly to represent money. She explains to Emil that there is a difference between writing 100 and 001.

KAJSA: has also entered the living room and tells Mother that she wants to put on her pink blouse.

MOTHER: leaves the table to help Kajsa, opening the closet with her clothes in Kajsa's room. She then re-enters the living room.

KAJSA: then enters the living room again and shows Mother that she had put on her blouse.

Homework in this family is a well-known situation, and together the mother and children create the activity settings in which all children join. In the example the setting is initiated by the oldest child, perhaps because she wants to have her homework finished for the weekend or perhaps because she wants to demonstrate her competence in writing the essay for the mother and the observer; she also seems to like doing her homework. The other children join when they see what is going on. Lulu starts doing her homework, but rather soon wants to leave, and is not allowed to. Emil has just started school and does not have homework, but he joins and plays with numbers – an activity which can be considered preparation for school. The youngest child, Kajsa, just flows around the setting doing her own thing.

   It seems that being together and mother's attention are important for creating this setting for all children. The demands for the activity of doing homework are created by the school and are directed at the two oldest children. This demand and the challenge presented by the homework do not engage Lulu, but it seems obvious from following Laura in other homework settings in the family that the demand has become a motive for her. We can interpret that the demands have become a motive through Laura's repeated intentional acting in the homework situation over several observations.

In the 'homework' example, several persons participate in the activity setting and each from their specific social situation of development act according to their experience. The personalising of each person's activity links the social situation of development in the form of the person's emotional experience to the social demands in the activity setting (Bozhovich, 2009). In this way, persons' activities in their social situations realise their motives in the activity setting.

Through anchoring the child's social situation in activity settings in institutional practice, a double perspective can be put on the child's activity. From the perspective of the child's social situation of development, it is how the child experiences the activity emotionally and acts in the situation, whereas from the institution's perspective, it is how the activity takes place in recurrent activity settings. This dialectic is the key to understanding the dynamic of a specific child's learning and development through participating in a specific practice. Motive development can then be seen as a movement initiated by the child's emotional experience related to the activity setting. To catch this movement, the tradition of practice within which person's activities takes place has to be analysed as encompassing activity settings that contain recurrent demands for activities.

Researching Children's Intentions and Motives within the Cultural-Historical Wholeness Approach

To focus on the social situation of development brings the child's experience of his or her situation into the analyses of motives. Bozhovich (2009) – one of Vygotsky's original students – writes that in Vygotsky's last works, the child's experience became the central unit in his conceptualisation of children's development. The emotional aspect is central in this conceptualisation of experience and reflects the dynamic aspects of a person's relation to the world.

Experience should be understood as a relation between the person and the world and not only as something in the person. Drawing on Alfred Schutz (1970), this can be followed further, given that he shares the same preconceptions as the cultural-historical approach presented here. That is, people are born into a world of human practices and through their actions create their own relations to this world, as well as modifying their world through their actions (Schutz, 1970, p. 73). Schutz writes that the unconditioned experiences a person has are present for him in the form of typification. This means that the person will relate these experiences to earlier experiences, but will also be open to new experiences (Schutz, 2005, p. 27 ff). Typifications of experiences mean that people's expectations will be reflected in their relation to other persons and will make sense to them. This is because knowledge has a social origin, and thereby there can be interrelatedness between persons' perspectives. This means that parents or teachers can take the child's perspective and from what make sense for the child motivate the child to act in relation to values in their shared practice.

The Danish phenomenologist Franz From (1953) demonstrated that people always see other persons' acts as intentional. If a small child is running away from something, this is seen as the child acting intentionally (that he/she is afraid of something, or he/she is playing). The point is that we see the child's acting intentionally directly in relation to something in the world. Children are acting from their social situation of development in relating to what is important to them. This can, according to Bozhovich (2009, p. 75), be seen in relation to two factors: the child's motives[2] and the child's position in the social system of relations.

To focus on the child's motives is to take a child's perspective and to analyse the child's intentional actions. Davydov et al. (1983, p. 32) point out that action is the basic unit to analyse motives and their activities. It is only through the analyses of the child's intentional actions that we can catch the child's activities and motives: 'As the act of practical and theoretical activity, "an action, as unit of activity, taken in its psychological sense, is an act that derives from specific motives and is aimed at a specific goal; taken into account the conditions under which this goal is achieved, an action is a solution of a problem the individual encounter"' (Davydov et al. 1983, p. 37).

Boris Elkonin has formulated a theory of actions' double character through which actions give the researcher the possibility of capturing intention in action. He explains:

> A human action is only apparently the transformation of things. In whatever form (individual and collective) it might be realised, its essence and its purpose consist in the construction of another action.... It is for this reason that a human action is two dimensional and has two objects. The schema by which an action unfolds in a given set of circumstances prescribes and constructs another schema and other circumstances: the product of an action itself does something and has no meaning outside its function, which is the designing of another action. (Elkonin, 1989, p. 33)

[2] Bozhovich used the term 'need' not in the organic meaning but as a motive factor.

Elkonin explains that the genesis of children's development from the very beginning is mediated by models of actions through adults' bodily manipulation, which transcends into intentional interactions between the child and the caregiver.

Observing a child's acting within an activity setting allows one to see how the child in interaction with other partners contributes to creating the settings that both include the demands from the institutionalised practice as formulated by Mills and the child's social situation of development as formulated by Vygotsky. Activity settings combine the relation between the actual child's actions and activities and the demands the child meet in the practice.

To interpret a child's motive, an observer has to follow the child's actions in the same activity setting over time to follow what leads the child's activities. From this, an interpretation of what is the most important motive in a specific activity setting can be made. In the homework example, Laura's social situation of development is characterised by a leading motive – doing what you should do in school – that subordinates other motives. In this homework setting, school learning can be seen as a dominant motive which one can expect gradually the other three children will acquire.

The second aspect which Bozhovich points out is that a child's social situation of development has to be seen in the daily practice where it takes place, and in this practice a child acquires a position:

> Children's positions are determined by two conditions: first by the demands of the social environments that have developed historically and are placed on children of a particular age (from this perspective we can talk about the position of the preschooler, the schoolchild, the working adolescent, the dependent, etc.); second by the demands the people around them place on children based on their individual developmental features of a particular child and on the specific circumstances for the family. (Bozhovich, 2009, p. 78)

For example, children's positions within the family and in school are created by the attitudes of other children and members of the family as well as the child's own assessment.

Bozhovich writes that because there are expectations related to most children, by the end of preschool age they begin to strive towards the new social position as a school child and towards performing the socially new significant activity of learning. In light of these findings, it becomes clear why school children's attitude towards learning depends primarily on the degree to which learning turns out to be a means for them to realise their striving towards this new social position. In the earlier example of the homework setting, Emil's participation illustrates how he prepared to live up to a position as a school child doing homework.

When a child enters school, the motives for learning are coming to the forefront in the child's understanding of the social situation of development. There is a qualitative difference between preschool children's social situation of development and their motive orientation and those of school children. Bozhovich points out the importance of the child's positioning in school practice, both by the other participants and by the child him- or herself in the activity setting. The value-laden demands in an activity setting also influence children's activity, but here it is important to point out that the demands are going both ways, from the practices and other persons to a child, but also from the child to the other persons and the practice.

CONCLUSION

In this chapter I have tried to elaborate Vygotsky's cultural-historical approach and Leontiev's activity approach to theorising the dynamic in children's learning and development. The presentation of Vygotsky's ideas has centred on his concept of the social situation of development and Leontiev's conceptualising of motives in relation to human's activity. Missing from their theories is the analyses of dynamic forces from institutional practices, a conception which has been developed here with inspiration from Mills' concept of institutional demands for conduct. Motive can then be seen both as relating institutions and children. From the institutional perspective, motives are seen as object motives or objectives that build on institutional values and purposes. From the child's perspective, motives reflect the child's social situation of development, which also implies the child's position in the institutional practice. The relation between the child's activity and institutional practice is found in the concrete activity settings defined both through traditions and the participants' activities. To understand and research children's motives, we have to follow the child in his or her activities as intentional actions and interactions with others in activity settings.

Intellectual debts to be paid in my arguments are to Bruner's conception that infants' actions are intentionally oriented to the world, and to Wartofsky's conceptions of how human experiences are always mediated by the objectification of human need and intentions. To study human activity, Davydov, Zinchenko, and Talyzina pointed out that the focus has to be on actions, whereas Boris Elkonin contributed is his analysis that it is the effect actions have on further actions both by others and themselves that influence the child's development.

In this chapter the concept of motive has become related to institutional values and demands, motivation in activity settings, and person's motives and intentions; however, there are still many nuances about the dynamic factors in children's learning and development that need to be unfolded. They include, for instance, the sociological aspect of societal needs and conditions and the relations between children's engagement, interests, intentions and motive orientation. In this short chapter I hope I have begun to suggest what a fruitful field of enquiry this can be.

REFERENCES

Ames, C., & Ames, R. (1984). Systems of student and teacher motivation: Toward a qualitative definition. *Journal of Educational Psychology, 76,* 535–556.

Barker, R. G., & Wright, H. (1954). *One boy's day – a specimen record of behavior.* New York: Harper & Brothers Publishers.

Bozhovich, L. I. (2009). The social situation of child development. *Journal of Russian and East European Psychology, 47,* 59–86.

Bruner, J. (1972). *Processes of cognitive growth: Infancy.* Vol. 3, Heinz Werner Lecture Series. Worcester, MA: Clark University Press.

Campbell, C. (1991). Reexaming Mills on motive: A character vocabulary approach. *Sociological Analyses, 52,* 89–97.

(1996). On the concept of motive in sociology. *Sociology, 30,* 101–114.

(2006). Do today's sociologists really appreciate Weber's essay *The protestant ethic and spirit of capitalism? Sociological Review, 54,* 207–223.

Covington, M. V. (1992). *Making the grade: A self-worth perspective on motivation and school reform.* Cambridge: Cambridge University Press.

D'Andrade, R. G. (1992). Schemas and motivation. In R. D'Andrade & C. Strauss (Eds.), *Human motive and cultural models* (pp. 23–44). Cambridge: Cambridge University Press.

Davydov, V. V., Zinchenko, V. P., & Talyzina, N. F. (1983). The problem of activity in the work of A. N. Leontiev. *Soviet Psychology, 24*(1), 22–36.

Elkonin, B. D. (1989). The nature of human action. *Journal of Russian and European Psychology, 31*(3), 22–46.

Elkonin, D. B. (1999). Toward the problem of stages in the mental development of children. *Journal of Russian and East European Psychology, 37,* 11–29.

Freud, S. (1983). *Kulturens byrde* [The burden of culture]. Copenhagen: Hans Reitzels.

From, F. (1953). *Om oplevelsen af andres adfærd* [The experience of others' behaviour]. Copenhagen: Nyt Nordisk Forlag.

Gallimore, R., Goldenberg, C. N., & Weisner, T. S. (1993). The social construction and subjective reality of activity settings: Implications for community psychology. *American Journal of Community Psychology, 21,* 537–559.

Hedegaard, M. (1999). Institutional practice, cultural positions, and personal motives: Immigrant Turkish parents' conception about their children's school life. In S. Chaiklin, M. Hedegaard & U. Juul Jensen (Eds.), *Activity theory and social practice* (pp. 276–301). Aarhus: Aarhus University Press.

(2002). *Learning and child development.* Aarhus: Aarhus University Press.

(2009). Children's development from a cultural-historical approach: Children's activity in everyday local settings as foundation for their development. *Mind Culture and Activity, 16,* 64–81.

Hoffman, E. (1988). *The right to be a human.* Los Angeles: Jeremy P. Thatcher.

Holland, D. C. (1992). How cultural systems become desire: A case study of American romance. In R. D'Andrade & C. Strauss (Eds.), *Human motive and cultural models* (pp. 61–89). Cambridge: Cambridge University Press.

Iljenkov, E. V. (1977). The concept of the ideal. In *Philosophy in the USSR* (pp. 71–99). Moscow: Progress Publishers.

Leontiev, A. N. (1978). *Activity, consciousness, and personality.* Englewood Cliffs, NJ: Prentice-Hall.

Levitin, K. (1982). *One is not born a personality.* Moscow: Progress Publishers.

Lewin, K. (1946). Behavior and development as a function of the total situation. In L. Carmichael (Ed.), *Manual of child psychology* (pp. 791–844). New York: Wiley.

Maehr, M. L. (1983). On doing well in science: Why Johnny no longer excels; why Sarah never did. In S. G. Paris, G. M. Olson & H. W. Stevenson (Eds.), *Learning and motivation in class room* (pp. 179–210). Hillsdale, NJ: Erlbaum.

Maslow, A. (1955). Deficiency motivation and growth motivation. In Marshall R. Jones (Ed.), *Nebraska symposium on motivation* (pp. 1–30). Lincoln: University of Nebraska Press.

McClelland, D. C. (1965). Toward a theory of motive acquisition. *American Psychologist, 20,* 321–333.

Mills, C. W. (1940). Situated actions and vocabularies of motive. *American Sociological Review, 5,* 904–913.

Murray, H. (1938). *Explorations in personality.* New York: Oxford University Press.

Pintrich, P. R. (1991). Editor's comment. *Educational Psychologist, 26,* 199–250.

(2000). An achievement goal theory perspective on issues in motivation terminology, theory, and research. *Contemporary Educational Psychology, 25,* 92–104.

Pintrich, P. R., Marx, R. W., & Boyle, R. A. (1993). Beyond conceptual change: The role of motivational beliefs and classroom contextual factors in the process of conceptual change. *Review of Educational Research, 63,* 167–199.

Schutz, A. (1970). *On phenomenology and social relations.* Chicago: University of Chicago Press.

(2005). *Hverdagslivets sociology* (transl. from Collected works, vol 1, 1972). Copenhagen: Hans Reitzels.

Strauss, C. (1992) Models and motives. In R. D'Andrade & C. Strauss (Eds.), *Human motive and cultural models* (pp. 1–20). Cambridge: Cambridge University Press.

Tharp, R. G., & Gallimore, R. (1988) *Rousing minds to life.* Cambridge: Cambridge University Press.

Vygotsky, L. S. (1998). *The collected works of L. S. Vygotsky. Volume 5. Child psychology.* New York: Plenum Press.

Wartofsky, M. (1979). *Models: Representations and the scientific understanding.* Dodrecht and Boston: D. Reidel.

Weiner, B. (1990). History of motivational research of education. *Journal of Educational Psychology, 82,* 616–622.

Zinchenko, V. P. (2002). From classical to organic psychology: In commemoration of the centennial of Lev Vygotsky's birth. In D. Robbins & A. Stetsenko (Eds.), *Voices within Vygotsky's non-classical psychology: Past, present, future* (pp. 3–26). Hauppauge, NY: Nova Science.

2

The Connection between Motive and Will in the Development of Personality

ELENA KRAVTSOVA AND GENNADY KRAVTSOV

THE PROBLEM OF MOTIVATION – AN HISTORICAL PERSPECTIVE

The concept of motive is foundational to psychology. Generally, motive can be defined as the basis for one's acts and as a fundamental force of actions. That is why the questions of motivation is a central attraction for psychological science. There are many different research projects which focus on motive and motivation. It can be argued that motive holds a firm place in general psychology and psychology directed at the study of personality. It is a cornerstone of many psychological theories and approaches and it is used widely in research and practice. That is why we cannot embrace all the problem fields in a single study. But the concept of motive is a problem by itself. There are several ambiguous interpretations of this concept, and there are even doubts about its psychological reality and its existence. One of the founders of cognitive psychology, G. Kelly, doubted the necessity to address the *motive-need* sphere, as well as the teleological determination of a person. According to Kelly, a person has the immanent feature of being the subject and source of his own activity, therefore we do not need to postulate some external causes for his actions. However, all knowledge already accumulated by psychology is stating that it is impossible to leave the problem of motive behind, to not take it into consideration.

Psychoanalysis was a revolutionary step in psychology. It convincingly showed that motive forces of human behaviour lie considerably in the field of the unconscious. S. Freud's discoveries in psychology are comparable to Galileo's, who was standing at the beginnings of a scientific method and science as a form of public consciousness. Science examines the phenomenon but keeps its essence distinct from the social world which gives it meaning. K. Marx once said that if phenomenon and essence coincided, we would not need any science. Galileo, by using physics, also tried to convince contemporaries not to trust life experience and common sense. In the same way Freud also argued for the inauthenticity of our consciousness as a form of data. He believed that we are convinced that we act reasonably and intentionally, but actually our behaviour is caused by impulses from the depths of the unconscious. Freud has shown that a person's ordinary image of himself/herself does not pass scientific criticism. A person's thoughts of self and his/her behaviour are based on the data of consciousness and self-consciousness – phenomena, not the essence of the psychic.

Undoubtedly the merit of psychoanalysis is the discovery of the fact that motive forces of our behaviour are hidden from ourselves. In Freud's teaching, these motive forces are innate, instinctive-like inclinations of biological nature. And here is a problem, because a person is not only a biological being. Numerous critics of the Freudian doctrine thereupon underlined the sociality of the person. However the sociality alone cannot be the sole characteristic of the person. The convergence of these two theories is also not helpful. For instance, the study of the person as a biosocial being is not satisfactory because this perspective is a compromise between two erroneous approaches – a study of the *natural* and a study of the *social* being do not lead to the problem's solution.

NATURAL APPROACHES – SOCIAL APPROACHES

Natural approaches to psychology cannot be a simple statement of the person belonging to the world of nature. No one would argue so. We have a body submitted to biological and physiological laws. We have sensations, determined by the states of our organism. The *needs* of our body present themselves in psychic, emotional experience and consciousness states. We feel pain, hunger, thirst, heat or chill, lack of fresh air, among many other things. But even these, which at the first sight appear as natural needs, are actually not purely natural. They are complex psychological mechanisms, formed in ontogenesis, which provide their presentation in our consciousness as organismic states and needs. Organismic states may not have connection to the corresponding psychological realities. For example, under hypnosis, a person does not feel pain. People who suffer from anorexia may die from a lack of nutrients but don't feel hunger because impulses from what physiologists call 'hungry blood' are blocked. But even the organismic states, which are adequately presented in the psyche, are abstract and uncertain. The 'need states' have certain 'emotional-sense colour' but at the same time they are aimless psychic reflections of organismic stress. They are not carrying a subject's characteristics and a way for gaining satisfaction. The same can be said for a person's innate reflexes. It is common knowledge that some reflexes disappear during infancy, whereas others remain throughout a person's life. However, neither reflexive cough, nor sneezing, nor pupil reflex can be called actions. These are physiological reactions which provide normal functioning of our body. Thus we can contend that a person, unlike an animal, does not have instincts as biologically determined behavioural patterns; neither do humans have genetically conditioned predispositions to particular types of activity. The biological basis of our life is just the material for a person's self-construction. From this position, all pathos of the Freudian doctrine is lost.

Social approaches to the study of psychology are no better than the natural biological approaches. It is the same dead end of scientific thought. Here however, we need to make one clarification about the necessity to distinguish the concepts of 'social' and 'public' or community. This distinction has been pointed out by A. Arsenjev (2001). *Community* is an aggregate of individuals who are united by a certain features, whereas *society* is all of humanity – all people who had lived before us, live now, and will live later. Community, no matter how large it is, is always terminal and limited, and the word 'social' correspond to the requirements of a given community. These requirements may be conventional and transient, like the directions of a particular community's morals. But the concept of a society's morals is not temporal and do not correlate with communities values. The particular individual is at the same time social and a public being, living in certain social-historical conditions. The person has a personality, has conflicts and contradictions with the community in which one lives. But the definition of personality covers a person's public, not social, essence. It means that personality and society cannot have contradictions because personality is the unity of individuality and humanity, the unity of humans and their genus. Here we can quote K. Marx, who said, 'We must not oppose an individual and an abstractly understood society. The individual is a complete public being'. Abstractly understood, society is a community. By claiming and underlining a person's sociality, we only insist on psychic adaptive possibilities. By defining a personality in the context of the 'social we', in the end we only receive social functions and do not determine real personality. Social approaches to the study of humans in psychology are limited and lose the essential core of personality.

HOLISTIC APPROACH

The problem of motivation in psychology has been studied in gestalt psychology, for instance, K. Lewin's ingenious experiments. Through his work he helped us to conceptualise a person's motive forces quite differently to that of Freudian psychology. Lewin's research showed that items may have a magnetic force and that we can soundly state their special status. That means that items in a child's environment are stimuli for behaviour – that is, motives and needs, and not some deep instinctive impulses. The object-ive character of needs gave Lewin the basis to create his concept of 'Field Theory'. Experimental study of field behaviour phenomenon allowed Lewin to extend the 'objective character of needs' as a principle of children's behav-iour as well as of adults' behaviour. Lewin introduced to psychology the concept of 'quasi-need'. These psychological formations are not conditioned by the body's vital needs. Lewin argued that most of a person's needs are quasi-needs. Quasi-needs are artificial psychological formations imposed on us by civilisation and the present community. The advertisement indus-try confirms Levin's thought that needs can be created artificially and pur-posefully, at least to ensure customer demand. Advertised items may have the same magnetic force as an attractive toy for a child.

MOTIVE AS OBJECT

The idea of the objective character of needs gained its place in Russian psychology through the particular works of A. N. Leontiev's theory in rela-tion to the concept of activity. According to this theory, motive acts as a dir-ect basis and criteria for a distinction between person's different activities. Motive is the object of an activity's achievement. Every particular activity has its own unique motive. Behaviour and actions may be and very often are polymotivated. But the activity, by definition, has only one object which is its motive. Behind motives lies an even deeper layer of psychological reality – needs. From this point of view, motive presents itself as the need which has found its object of satisfaction – in other words, motive can be defined as an 'objective need'. Motives and needs according to this theory are the core of personality. Motives and needs are usually not conscious, but become apparent in person's emotional reactions. Motive, as conceptual-ised by Leontiev, has two main functions – activity inducement and sense formation. Therefore, to reveal the motive means to understand what guides a person in his or her activity or to reveal the sense of a person's activity.

The logical symmetry of Leontiev's theory and elaboration of its con-cepts was one of the reasons for its popularity. Throughout the past decades, the activity approach has dominated Soviet psychology and even now it has a lot of followers. However in the 1960 and the 1970s, this approach was criticised, and often 'from within'. For instance, L. Bozhovich, a prominent representative of the activity approach, doubted the motive's objectiveness. Although sharing Leontiev's view on motive-need sphere as a core of personality, she disagreed with the view that the motive is the object of activity and, in general, that motive is an object. Really, the object in its general definition is the one which opposes the subject. The object is self-identical and unalterable. Otherwise it will be another object. Object may act as a real thing and as an abstract thing, that is, the notion of the object. In any case, the object occupies the pole opposite to the subject. Because of this we have difficulties with the theoretical understanding of Leontiev's personality concept as well as the process of psychic development. Neither the object nor the system of objects can develop. In Leontiev's theory of activity the core of personality is the hierarchically collaterally subordinated system of objects – i.e. motives of activity. But the personality is developing. More than that, the development is the way of the personality's existence and, as stated by L. S. Vygotsky, there is always self-development, which is characterised by the origination of a new quality at a higher level. The core of personality is the internal formation, whereas the objective sphere will be external to the subject.

THE DIFFERENCE BETWEEN BUILDING OBJECT MOTIVE AND WILL AS THE ESSENCE OF HUMAN ACTIVITY

Although Bozhovich agreed with the principles of the activity approach, she nevertheless developed an autonomous theory of will, whereas Leontiev created a typical heteronomous theory. According to Vygotsky, in autonomous theories, a will is recognised as the psyche's special function whereas in heteronomous theories, the will is reduced to one process among other psychic processes. In Leontiev's theory, a will is a purely subjective reflexion in consciousness of the motives' struggle and the process of their collateral subordination. In other words, there is no will, only the struggle of motives and its representation in individual's self-consciousness. This is reductionism, which is reducing will to an affective-requiremental sphere. The other variant of the same reductionist approach will be to reduce will to the intellectual, cognitive psychic sphere. Often in such theories the will is understood as a choice of alternatives and as making a decision. While criticizing the heteronomous theories of will, Vygotsky is saying: 'The difficulties of mentioned theories lay in the fact that they could not explain the essence of will, notably the voluntary nature of acts, volition per se and inner freedom, experienced by person in the process of making a decision, as well as external structural diversity of action, which distinguishes volitional action from non-volitional' (Vygotsky, 1982, p. 457). However, existing autonomous theories were also criticised by Vygotsky because of their voluntarism, with a tendency towards either spiritualism or agnosticism. At the same time, however, according to Vygotsky, 'voluntaristic theories had the positive moment, because they constantly attracted psychologists' attention to the unique phenomena of will, they constantly opposed the doctrines which tried to put paid to voluntary processes' (Vygotsky, 1982, p. 461). The problem of will and volition, the problem of free action, its conditions, and psychological mechanisms, is very daunting and pressing even nowadays. In other words, the problem of experiencing the free volitional process – the one, which defines voluntary action – is a fundamental mystery that many researchers from different areas have tried to solve.

Without an autonomous will theory it is impossible to correctly state the problem of personality and the problem of motivation. The question of psychological nature and the essence of that reality defined by the word 'motive' has paramount meaning for general psychology too. The initial point that must be addressed in the analysis of this question must be the general idea of what is a human. Natural and social interpretations as well as a nature-social relations are inaccurate because they are based on a partial and one-sided definition of a human. An extremely abstract but universal definition will be the conception of a human as a spiritual-corporeal being. Human's spirituality here is not a call to spiritualism but the statement of the fact that a human has consciousness and free will. Spirituality cannot be derived from the corporeal and cannot be reduced to one, but in a human these two origins are seamlessly merged with each other, forming, along with the mediating structural formations, the complex unity of the human. The mediating link between spiritual and corporeal is the motive-need psychic sphere.

PSYCHOLOGICAL TOOLS

The idea of mediation is the central methodological hypothesis in Vygotsky's cultural-historical theory. The development in this approach is understood as the transformation of the natural psychic functions into higher psychic functions, and this transformation is connected with the use of psychological tools. Just as implements help a person to master outer space, the psychological tools make it possible to master a person's own behaviour and psychic processes. According to Vygotsky, the fundamental psychological tool is a sign, and a word has a special place among all signs. Each sign has a meaning and this meaning is a generalisation. Only a human is living in a world of the general. Our consciousness and perception of reality are mediated by general 'apperceptional schemes', 'sensory models', 'personal constructs' and so on – in other words, meanings. During the process of forming the conception of mediation, Vygotsky opposed the tool-to-sign connection. But Leontiev rightly enough draws our attention to the fact that 'an axe is a generalizing too', meaning that an axe may be at the same time a tool and a sign. Leontiev stresses that when a tool as well as a sign are used as tools, they are only partially conscious. He describes the 'probe effect' where we consider the consciousness of a surgeon who is exploring the gunshot wound by being taken out on the very tip of the probe that he/she is using. We can catch this effect in every step of our life. For example, when a person is writing with a pen, the person is conscious of the pen's tip and what is being written but is not conscious of the pen itself or even the complex movements of his/her own fingers and hand. In the same way psychological tools are not conscious for a person or only partially conscious of the tool. Leontiev specifies as the fundamental psychological fact that we immediately and directly are seeing things in their objective meanings but we are not conscious of meanings themselves, which are making such perception possible. In other words, implements as well as psychological tools are growing in the psyche. According to Vygotsky, they become intra-subjective structural formations and thus they cannot be conscious. So even if the very first words of a little child are used as tools, he or she is only conscious of their direct meaning. Besides meaning, however, these words have subjective-sense content which is experienced by the child. However, the child is not conscious of this. Every implement has a working part, which is influencing the object, where the handle is merged with the master's hand which is providing a necessary movement characteristics – as a word, as a tool, they have objective meaning, addressed to the one this word is spoken to, and they have inner subjective sense, merged with the speaker him- or herself.

SENSE-MEANING AND ITS ROLE IN MOTIVES

The problem of sense and meaning as stated by Vygotsky is interpreted differently by Leontiev. Leontiev strongly disagreed with Vygotsky's point of view on this matter. Leontiev called it the greatest misunderstanding originating in philology. Meanings are initially objective and are simply assimilated by a person, but senses are deeply personal and, according to Leontiev, originate through motives. In other words, in Leontiev's doctrine, sense and meaning are heterogeneous realities with different origin. From Vygotsky's point of view, meaning and sense are two aspects of the same reality, and word is used as psychological tool. Meaning according to Vygotsky is generally accepted as a part of a multidimensional personal sense. The problem of sense and meaning is extremely important for understanding the inner structure of consciousness. From our point of view, the solution offered by Leontiev leads to naturalism in psychology. So if the sense of activity is originated by the motive of activity, then motives are conditioned by needs rather than as being seen as the basis of a need within a body's requirement. The ultimate explanatory principle for a body's requirements is the concept of nature. So in the end we are getting into naturalism. This is the problem that an activity approach is struggling with.

In the theory of activity, the function of sense formation is about getting this concept into the centre of the definition of personality. Leontiev strongly criticised 'role' theories of personality, calling them monstrous. These theories state that the concept of personality is something that is directly opposite to social functions. But activity theories are no better than role theories. D. B. Elkonin was right on the mark when, in the famous article on periodisation of the child's psychic development, he warned against improper reduction of personality to the motive-need sphere (Elkonin, 1971). In activity theory, the approach taken to understanding a personality's core suggests that the more needs a person has, the more complicated their hierarchy and collaborative subordination, resulting in a more developed personality for the particular person. Hence, we see the theoretical legitimation of a view that a person is a slave of one's own needs.

The idea of mediation and psychic's division of elementary and higher functions was for Vygotsky something like the idea of the lever and a place to stand for Archimedes. While considering the problem of psychological tools, it is important to keep in mind that every tool has a service nature and is a component part of a modus operandi. Means are what is leading to goal achievement. Leontiev reduced means to an operation code but simultaneously he underlined the role of tools – implements or signs in the structure of the act. There is reasons to believe that means are the organic unity of tools and operations. It is means that are interiorisated and 'grown' into the structure of operations, and tools are submerging into the depths of subjectivity, transforming into the unconscious program of possible acts. Sometimes these programs can be found in themselves segregated from the goals of act. For example, a person enters the room, then stops in bewilderment and begins to ask oneself and the people around: 'Why have I come here? There was a reason for it ...'. Or the teacher interrupts oneself: 'Why have I started to talk about this?' The goal and the sense of a particular act are lost, but the earlier created program goes on.

From this position, the nature of the unconscious is seen differently than in Freud's teaching. The unconscious in psychic is undoubtedly present and has extreme importance, but it is not the mythologised 'id'; rather it is an interiorised means of a person's actions. The unconsciousness of an interiorised means is the condition and the mechanism of conscious expansion, allowing us to ascend to a new level of consciousness of objective content. That which was initially the object of consciousness is 'growing in' and helps to relieve this consciousness for new objective content and voluntary acts. This idea can be explained by the example of learning complex locomotive skills. To learn how to ride a bicycle, drive a car, or skate, we first need to apply considerable concentration. In truth, we need to make nearly fifteen complex and highly coordinated operations just to start driving a car. An experienced driver just starts the engine and immediately move the car out into the road, joining moving cars. Whilst driving, the driver can easily chat with passengers and simultaneously check the dynamic road situation. The driver's hands and legs, as if by themselves, perform the complex operational system of driving a car. But all drivers remember the time when they were learning how to drive – when each operation was a subject of conscious action. Freedom and easiness of driving came not at once. These complex skills and abilities cannot be learned in one day. To consolidate skills, to submerge them into the inner layers of consciousness, mysterious psychic work needs to be done. And this work is going on in one's a sleep. According to P. J. Galperin, *you need to sleep with a skill*. Whilst asleep, conscious objective actions are transformed into inner tools and programs which improve one's skill level.

The laws of 'growing in' focused not only on movement skills, but on the whole behaviour of a person, on his or her acts and way of life. In daily life, we are doing many things almost automatically. In childhood, however, every person was proud that he or she could lace their shoes or fasten buttons on a shirt by themselves. Law-abiding, well-brought up people will never steal. It is against their 'nature'. They will warn an absentminded person that their handbag is open and everyone can see their purse inside. But at the same time, I. Ilf and E. Petrov described a very lifelike incident where a character was caught for stealing a purse even though he was sufficiently wealthy. It is well known in criminology that criminals who have completed their sentence and swear to never steal again are very often sentenced again for the same crimes. As the saying goes – the habit becomes second nature. It can be said that motives and needs do not differ from habits greatly. That is, inner programs set conscious guidelines and behavioural trends. At the same time motives and needs are not the core and essence of personality but service formations which make conscious acts possible. They are the psychological basis and the program of possible actions and acts, but they do not have self-sufficient force. However, there can be a situation where a servant occupies his or her master's place and begins to substitute for him or her. Materialist Marx mentioned that if a person is driven by a need, that person is a slave to the need. This is the very case when the tail begins to wag the dog.

THE PSYCHOLOGICAL TOOL OF PERSONAL ACTION – WILL AND NEED AS MEDIATING LINKS

From the position of the cultural-historical approach, we can suggest the difference between needs and motives. First of all, it is worth mentioning that they are one and the same by origin. Initially needs as well as motives are the means of conscious and purposeful action or communication. Second, they are substantially different by their place in the structure of personality and the structure of consciousness. Motives are the psychological basis of actions, the subjective component of activity and communication. Motives occupy the level at which activity, communication, abilities and the needs strike root in personality. A person who is accomplished as a personality acts holistically. The person is completely drawn into this action. The psychological tools of personal action are the will, and needs act as a mediating link. The will delegates to motives and needs the function of impulse and sense formation. Initially, however, both of these functions are the prerogative of will. Will can be defined as a conscious initiative and an instrument of free action, as a conductor of consciousness and initially as a higher psychic function. Without will, all development will be impossible.

Life shows that will's delegated functions and privileges can be usurped by needs. Even artificial needs can find nourishment in a body's physiology. A person addicted to alcohol, tobacco or drugs feels physical torments if the corresponding addiction is not satisfied. The same thing can be said about more innocent non-chemical addictions. Parents who are worried about their child's computer addiction forbid the child to play computer games beyond a strictly limited time period. But practice and studies (Maximov, 2009) show that teenagers with this addiction will spend all day long thinking of what he or she will do when they come to the computer again. The teenager experiences almost physical suffering because of this need.

THE ROLE AND PLACE OF MOTIVES IN THE STRUCTURE OF PERSONALITY

When we discuss the role and place of motives in the structure of personality, there are two perspectives to consider. On the one hand, we can show that the motive's role and place in the structure of personality; on the other hand, we must allow for an understanding of the result of the situation where motives begin to play a central part in a person's development. Two examples follow.

The first example is about play. The widespread acceptance of A. N. Leontiev's activity approach in the Soviet Union led to attempts to find the motive of play. To date, these attempts have not proven to be successful. The only conclusion which was made by researchers (e.g. S. L. Novoselova, O. S. Gazman & D. B. Elkonin) was that the motive of play lies in the play itself. In other words, the desire for playing is connected to the play.

The means of explaining this conclusion, offered by D.B. Elkonin, are well known. A child looks at the carriage and wants to drive it but cannot realise this desire in real life, which is why the child begins to play coachman. We will return to this explanation of play's motive later. For now, we only note that this is D. B. Elkonin cardinal contradiction. We also note another important conclusion made by D. B. Elkonin about play. He wrote that there is no motive which precedes play. This conclusion, on the one hand, nullifies the whole of Leontiev's theory and prejudices the concept of motive in relation to play. On the other hand, the absence of motive which precedes play contradicts the conclusion that the desire to ride the carriage leads to the appearance of coachman play.

A thorough study of different aspects of play allows us to make several important conclusions about its motives. Firstly, as shown by the study of play's prerequisites and genesis, motives form the basis of imagination. Imagination itself is the central psychological new formation of the developmental period of pre-school children. The basic function of imagination, as independent psychic function, is connected with the construction of a special field – the field of meanings, which is different from the optical (real) field. For instance, take a child who is lying on the floor, but whose parents wish the child to move. We could, of course, tell the child that this is wrong, or we could just get the child up on his or her feet, but there is another way. We could say: 'What a great snake we have here'. And after a while, a child (assuming that he knows what is snake and how it moves) will begin not just lying on the floor but crawling and emitting specific sounds. It is important to note that this is as a result of the realisation of the child's imagination, and is yet not play. A child is crawling like a snake, not by his or her own intentions – which, according to Vygotsky, is the essential characteristic of play – but by the adult's intention.

After several attempts, however, the child will not simply lie down on the floor but will consciously (by his or her own intention) imitate a snake, and if, for example, the mother will not mention it or will react differently than the child expected, then the child will stand up and say: 'Mother, look who has come crawling' or something along these lines.

In this example of the child being a snake on the floor, there are two important events to consider. Firstly, the child has begun to act on his or her own intent and secondly, the child 'has been divided in two' – the child is a snake and the child is oneself. The child can use his or her own individual ways of drawing the mother's attention to oneself. For example through directly addressing mother, with a call 'Mother'. Alternatively, the child can become the snake. Through these actions, the child begins to realise his or her ability of acting as one thing whilst at the same time being oneself. In other words, in the first case, the child was only realising his or her imagination; in the second case, he or she begins to play.

Now, if we analyse this given situation from the point of view of the concept of motives, than it appears that in the first case, the child was driven by the relations with an adult. The child could turn into a snake or could pay no attention to an adult's words or say that he or she is not a snake but simply a child. However, another situation is possible, where the child becomes the snake. In the second case, we see initially on the one hand, that the situation is the same. A child is oriented to his or her relationships with an adult. But now the child chooses his or her own way of communicating with the mother. In this context, the child playing snake is a way of communicating and interacting with the mother. On the other hand, a child can play snake long after the interaction with the mother is over. In addition, given the mother's positive reaction, the child can enact this image with other adults, children, or even toys. It is very unlikely, that a child actually wants to be a snake. Rather the child is pretending to be one, because such a transformation is impossible in reality.

These two cases are showing us the inner nature of the child's incitement to action. If, at first, the child, by using the mother's hint of transforming into a snake, is in need of her attention (we could even say demonstrative attention), later, when true play appears, the mother's reactions will be unimportant to the child.

If we try to answer what makes a child wish to transform into a snake and play, we can say that the reason lies in the child's own inner impulses, which, in the first place, help the child to assert oneself. In spite of the adult's importance for the child, when a child is imagining being a train whilst playing, the adult's words about a snake will not lead to a similar play. Instead they may cause serious personal conflict.

Children decide themselves what play they will be enacting and whether they will be playing or not. It is well known that a child can refuse to play in one or another game and can demonstrate the general 'non-playing' mood: 'I'm not playing right now. I'm speaking seriously', 'I'm tired of playing', 'I won't be playing in this game anymore' and so forth. Yet, in play, a child is constantly demonstrating his or her subjectivising: 'I don't want to play this way', 'I want you not to go to sleep but to ride in a train' and so on.

These features of play – the inner nature of its incitements and realisation of player's own subjectivity – appear in the very first plays and can be seen in all later types and forms of children's and adult's plays. A teenager playing an adult, a young woman playing family relationships, an old man playing the role of an all-knowing and many-skilled person – in all this plays, the inner incitements of play activity and its subjective nature can be clearly seen (if they all are 'plays' in psychological sense) – 'I want to be that adult and act that way', 'I see and understand family life that way', 'My experience allows me to understand everything about everyone' – all of this and similar incitements of children and adults, on the one hand, determine the person's play, but on the other hand, they are not the play's genuine motives. The genuine motive of play is more likely connected with the realisation of one's subjectivity, no matter if this subjectivity is also realised in other types of activity. And the main thing that incites people to play is related to their desire or, as it is usely said in psychology (especially in that part of it which is closely connected with philosophy), their freedom of will.

The second example, that demonstrates the role and place of motives and the structure of personality, is related to a learning activity. The motive of learning activity as well as the motive of play have been the subject of many studies (e.g. Elkonin, 1978). The results of these studies were similar. They found that the motive of learning activity, as well as the motive of play, are inner-conditioned. Elkonin stated that the learning activity is aimed at the transformation of oneself from unlearned to learned, from unskilled to skilled, but these findings are not helping in revealing the psychological content of the 'motive of the learning activity'.

Surely, the self-change, the transformation of oneself from one to another, from one who is unable to solve the task or get over the problem to the one who is solving tasks and overcomes problems, is present in genuine learning activity. We believe, however, that this feature of learning activity cannot be called its motive. A person is realising learning activity or accepting help in organisation of his or her own learning activity (and thereby transforming into learned and/or skilled) only if he or she has the corresponding desire.

V. V. Davydov (1986), the creator of the theory of learning activity, in one of his latest studies with V. I. Slobodchikov and G. A. Zukerman mentioned that they have learned to form the learning activity of primary-school children in experimental conditions, but this learning activity became unclaimed when children began secondary school. In other words, children can realise learning activity in special conditions and under the adult's guidance, but in secondary school, where learning activity should be the mean, the way of education, it was not realised. The reason, from our point of view, is that in primary school the learning activity is most motivated by relationships with the teacher, whereas in secondary school children *can, but don't want* to realise this relationship. Thereby, we are again speaking about the desire, the freedom of will in using and realisation of already formed activity in real life.

The concepts of 'spontaneous' and 'reactive' learning, created by Vygotsky, will help us to understand the specific of the psychological content of the motives of learning activity. The differentiation of these concepts is related mostly to the incitement for learning. In spontaneous learning, a subject is using one's own program and in reactive learning, a subject is able to use the programs of others. In other words, in spontaneous learning, a person has his or her own inner motive of transformation of him- or herself from unlearned to learned.

The study of different types of education allowed us to arrive at a conclusion that a person is always studying according to one's own program. The famous educator E. D. Dneprov stresses that a person cannot be taught. A person is always learning by oneself. In this context, if we have genuine education, then this education has a spontaneous nature. In other words, a person learns without the creation of any special conditions. In other cases, the teacher specially demonstrates and creates the conditions for such education, an environment in which the learner feels its spontaneous nature. Finally, in a third case, the learner is able to take the 'foreign educational program' and make this his or her own spontaneous activity.

In the conversation on the motive of the learning activity, we are mostly interested in cases in which the educator is helping the learner to make education a spontaneous activity. A further example taken from the Golden Key Schools in Russia illustrates this point for pre-school-aged children. One of the important features of teaching children of pre-school age in the

Golden Key programs is teaching them to orient themselves in space. For instance, in the kindergarten group, suddenly a toy bear appears. Children are playing with this bear, they take the bear and make it walk, they use the bear to help them learn and so forth. In the evening, children and adults are planning joint work with this bear. In the morning, however, the bear disappears and leaves a note that the bear went to the North.

Children are disappointed and want to bring back the bear. Besides, they are worried – the bear is little and maybe it will not make it to the North and back, or someone will harm the bear and so on. To bring back the bear, the children study maps, calculate the time they will need to go to the North, are deciding which type of transport they should use and so on. Through this they learn about the nature and the weather of the North, about people and animals who live there and the like.

On the one hand, we have clear education here. More than that, it is education created by the adult's program. On the other hand, however, it is the *children* who want to bring back the bear. It is them who decide to travel to the North after him. Thereby, an adult is creating conditions where their own program becomes the children's program.

It looks like we have the motive of learning activity here – children should solve the task of bringing back the bear. But the solving of this task is based on children's desire to bring back the bear. If for some reason they do not want to bring back the bear (e.g. they were not playing with him the previous day, they have other more interesting toy, they are afraid of bears), the children will not solve this task and thereby will not learn through the adult's program. So the motives of learning activity, as well as the motives of play, are based on the children's desire/absence of desire, on their free will.

The last, third example brought forward to illustrate the motive's place in the structure of a person's activity explains the situations where motives begin to play a central role in personality development.

As mentioned previously, in play, a child is realising a desire that cannot be realised in real life: A child is playing a coachman because the child cannot drive a carriage in real life. Maximov's (2009) study of people with computer games addiction has shown that computer games allow people to compensate for their real-world problems – if a person cannot communicate well enough in reality, the person can try to communicate virtually; if a person is not having the social status that they want, then the person can imagine a completely new biography and use it in relationships with other players; if a person cannot realise a particular type of activity, the person can realise it 'as if' in play and so forth. In other words, if a person is using the motive aimed at the compensation in play of the person's problems in real life, it leads not to play but to addiction. According to Maximov's research, this activity only outwardly resembles play, but it is not play in a psychological sense of this word.

The same situation can be applied to education. There is a concept in Russian literature – 'eternal student', that may be used in relation to any person of any psychological/real age. These persons usually can study and love to study, but they do not want and do not know how to use what they have learned in real life. They can have different types of education and frequently change professions and jobs, moving from one field to another. But the main thing that they like in this mosaic is that they start any activity from the perspective of education. In Russian language, there is a proverb which can be translated as 'it is caviar to the general', which means that persons who are studying eternally are characterised by education, which does not lead to development. In a cultural-historical perspective of 'education,' it can be said that it is not education in the psychological sense of this word.

CONCLUSION

The study of the motive concept in terms of Vygotsky's cultural-historical theory allows us to state that the content and functions of motive in Vygotsky's approach differ greatly from content and functions in other modern psychological theories. We could mark out two essential features of cultural-historical understanding of motive. According to the first one, the motive is tightly connected with a person's will. The desire to do something (or not to do it) is not about a person's motive, but rather that person's freedom of will. It is well known that a person's desire (motive) is not to carry out hard, uninteresting activity instead of participating in some interesting event. In any case, in the context of cultural-historical psychology, a motive is connected with the features of a subject's volitional development.

The second essential feature of motive understanding in cultural-historical approach is that motives, guide a person's acts and activity, are not helping person's development and even sometimes lead to various problems. Striking examples of this can be found in different playing addictions, as well as in people who are able and love to learn but cannot realise the content of education in daily life.

REFERENCES

Arseniev, A. S. (2001). *Philosophical basis for the understanding of personality. The cycle of popular lectures: The tutorial for institutions of higher education.* Moscow: Akademya publishing.

Bozhovich, L. I. (1968). *Personality and its formation in childhood*. Moscow: Prosveshcheniye Publishers.

(1972). *The problem of development of child's motivational sphere. The study of behavior's motivation of children and teenagers*. Moscow. Prosveshcheniye Publishers.

Davydov, V. V. (1986). *The problems of developmental education*. Moscow: Pedagogika.

Dneprov, E. D. (1994). *4th school reform in Russia*. Moscow: Interpraks, Dunstan.

Elkonin, D. B. (1971). To the question of child's psychic development periodization. *The Questions of Psychology Journal, 4*, 6–20.

(1978). *The psychology of play*. Moscow: Pedagogika.

Ilf, I. and Petrov, E. (1959). *12 stul'ev. Zolotoy telenok*. Odessa: Odessa book publishing.

Kelly, G. (1958). Man's construction of his alter alternatives. In G. Lindzey (Ed.), *Assessment of human motives* (pp. 33–64). Orlando, FL: Harcourt Bract Jovanovich.

Leontiev, A. N. (1975). *Activity. Consciousness. Personality*. Moscow: Politizdat publishing.

Maximov, A. A. (2009). *The personal features of computer games addicts*. Moscow: Pedagogika.

Marx, K. and Engels, F. (1956). *From early works*. Moscow: Gospolitizdat 566.

Slobodchikov, V. I. (2000). *The psychology of development*. Moscow: Pedagogika.

Sokolov, M. V. (1963). *Sketches about history of psychological views in Russia in 11th–18th centuries*. Moscow: APN RSFSR publishing.

Vygotsky, L. S. (1982). Collected works. Vol. 2. In V. V. Davydov (Ed.), *The problems of general psychology*. Moscow: Pedagogika publishing.

3

Advancing on the Concept of Sense: Subjective Sense and Subjective Configurations in Human Development

FERNANDO GONZÁLEZ REY

INTRODUCTION

The interpretations of Vygotsky's work in both Russian and Western psychology have predominantly focused on his work between 1928 and 1931 (González Rey, 2001, 2008a, 2008b; Leontiev, 1992, 2001), known as cultural-historical theory. In this dominant approach, his contributions concerning emotions and fantasy and his attempt to understand the mind as a complex system have been overlooked. The attempts to identify Vygotsky with American pragmatists have avoided those of Vygotsky's ideas which do not correspond to the interpreters' theoretical positions. This fact does not imply any deliberate intention; interpretations always represent new constructions based on the interpreters' views. But of course, some interpretations are always better supported and more convincing than others.

Until very recent times, those of Vygotsky's ideas that have been highlighted by most of his Western and Russian interpreters have been taken as an expression of Vygotsky's mature work. In Western psychology, this one-sided interpretation of Vygotsky's work has found its most extensive application in the Cultural Historical Activity Theory (CHAT), that has been put forth as a theoretical fusion between Vygotsky and Leontiev, omitting the great differences between them.

In this chapter I start from Vygotsky's contributions related to emotions and motives, including on this matter his short but interesting reflections on the concepts of sense and 'perezhivanie', concepts introduced by him in the last moment of his work. These two concepts are relevant to understanding Vygotsky's attempt to approach a new definition of human mind and development.

Emotions, in the more rationalistic and cognitive approaches, are considered as an effect of cognitive mediation. The importance of emotions

45

as intrinsic processes of higher human psychological functions has been overlooked by most modern psychological theories. In modern times, the relevance of emotions for the comprehension of psychical processes was ignored in favour of the prevailing rationalism and empirical approaches, whereas in postmodern times (Anderson, 1999; Gergen, 2006), the same rejection has taken place in favour of the reification of language, discourse and semiotic mediation. All of these approaches have in common a failure to acknowledge the complex nature of human emotions which are grounded in an individual's complex subjective organisation.

Finally it is the intention in this chapter to go further into the consequences of concepts of subjective sense and subjective configuration for advancing new theoretical questions regarding human development. In particular on the basis of those two concepts I will focus on the development of a more broad and complex definition of motivation.

VYGOTSKY'S LEGACY: ITS IMPLICATIONS FOR A NEW INTERPRETATION OF EMOTIONS AND MOTIVES IN HUMAN DEVELOPMENT

The weight given by Vygotsky to emotions and the psychological formations associated with them, such as personality and motivation, permitted the development of new alternatives for their theoretical constructions in psychology, by emphasising their cultural-historical nature. In this sense, a new ontological representation of the human psyche emerged in Vygotsky's works on emotions. The emotional emptiness of sign and word, as those mediators were used by Vygotsky in the second moment of his work, was recognised by Zinchenko (1993), who emphasised the need to understand symbol and myth as symbolic productions that embody emotions. Culture in psychology cannot be taken only as an expression observed in language and cognitive rational processes; it should be analysed through complex symbolic-emotional productions that cannot be directly grasped based on empirical human expressions or control by rational intentions.

The analysis of Vygotsky's works should begin from the original and too frequently overlooked *Psychology of Art*, where some of his foundational ideas concerning emotions and their generative character in the human psyche appear for the first time. Vygotsky's attention to art in a moment when art was banished from any relationship with science by positivism was not coincidental. Vygotsky himself was strongly influenced

by positivism as result of the mechanical materialistic viewpoint dominant in Soviet Marxist dogma. That positivistic influence was evident in
his emphasis on the definition of laws of psychological functioning as
well as in his recurrent claims oriented towards the construction of an
objective psychology. In his work, it is possible to identify two prevailing
tendencies: one oriented to an objective psychology and the other referring to the subjective side of human performance, emphasising the roles
of processes like fantasy, imagination, the emotional basis of thinking,
sense and *perezhivanie*.

The attention given by Vygotsky to the relationships between imagination, fantasy, emotions and sentiments in *Psychology of Art* revealed his
interest in psychological topics that cannot be reduced to cognition or
action. Even his critical dialogue with psychoanalysis in one chapter of
the book is evidence of his curiosity about these subjective aspects of the
human psyche.

He actively integrated affective processes as moments of perception.
As he explicitly expressed in *Psychology of Art*: '[W]e see that none of the
main theories of esthetic sentiments is in position to explain the internal
relation that exists between sentiments and representations in our perceptions of objects' (Vygotsky, 1965, p. 270). The idea of psychical unity was
implicit in this effort. The subject's psychological nature was represented
as inseparable from the image, distancing Vygotsky's theory on this topic
from Leontiev's position centred on object-based activity (Leontiev, 1972,
1981, 1994). This difference could explain the limited attention given to
Psychology of Art in Soviet psychology at the time when activity theory
was dominant. In *Psychology of Art*, Vygotsky defined perception as a
complex psychological process which possesses an emotional character.
With such a definition, he was closer to Merleau Ponty's approach to
perception than to the definition of perception prevailing in cognitive
psychology. Vygotsky attempted a new representation of psychological
functions as a dynamic system in which they appear in constant relationships with one another; the idea of psychological unity was drawn from
this representation.

Vygotsky's interest in the complex emotional processes of human life
is clearly expressed in his criticism of Freud's reification of unconscious
processes. However, in this criticism he pointed out the relevance of unconscious processes for the understanding of the human mind as a system
beyond the limits of consciousness, stating: 'There is a permanent living
dynamic relation, which does not stop for a minute, between the conscious

and unconscious spheres' (Vygotsky, 1965, p. 94). The relevance Vygotsky attributed to unconscious processes is made clear in the following remark: 'The two theories of art we examined above clearly demonstrated that if we restrict ourselves to the analysis of those processes that take place in consciousness, we cannot find answers to the most essential questions of the art' (Vygotsky, 1965, p. 93). (My translation.)

Vygotsky's ideas questioned the representation of the human psyche as being a result of direct external influences on a person. I use the term 'generative character of the psyche' to refer to the capacity Vygotsky attributed to emotions of creating new psychological states. Emotions are not the effects of external influences, but psychological productions based on an individual's psychological organisation. This was a recurrent idea throughout Vygotsky's work, to which he returned in the final phase of his work through his concept of 'social situation of development'.

Going in an opposite direction from the paradigm of reflection dominant in Soviet psychology, Vygotsky embraced the idea of the generative character of emotions as part of the blending of ideas which I consider relevant to the definition of the first moment of his work (González Rey, 2008a, 2008b). That position was very advanced in comparison to his concept of internalisation taken from Sechenov (Yaroshevsky, 1993) as the basis of higher psychological functions. The concept of internalisation was dominant in his writings only for a short period between 1928 and 1931.

As it has been stated by me in prior works (2009, 2010), Vygotsky attributed an ontological status to emotions, integrating them to the more important psychological functions. This fact was evident in *Psychology of Art*, as well as in some of his work related to defectology in a first moment of his work.

The importance given by Vygotsky to emotions and his emphasis on the close relationships between emotions, fantasy and imagination in *Psychology of Art*, as well as his focus on the inseparability of thinking and emotions in *Thinking and Speech*, created an important premise for approaching the topic of subjectivity in a new way, not as immanent to a person's psychological state, but as an emotional-cognitive complex system able to produce new realities. Although Vygotsky still referred to false representations as a distortion of reality – as Freud referred to 'defense mechanisms' – the fact is that he took into consideration the person's subjective capacity for producing realities. What Vygotsky did not understand at that moment was that every subjective state is a production which is different from any external, objective reality. This human characteristic is precisely the one which is present on the basis of culture.

FROM THE TOPIC OF EMOTION IN VYGOTSKY TO A NEW APPROACH TO SUBJECTIVITY FROM AN HISTORICAL-CULTURAL STANDPOINT: ITS IMPORTANCE FOR HUMAN DEVELOPMENT

One of the main characteristic of Soviet psychology was the effort it expended on creating a Marxist psychology. That attempt carried the dominant characteristics of the Soviet interpretation of Marxism, that was itself characterised by its mechanical and objectivistic character. As result of this dominant interpretation, Marxist psychology was identified with an objective and concrete psychology based rather on objective methods than on hermeneutical procedures, which may be one of the reasons why authors like Speth or Bakhtin never appeared as references in Soviet psychology. More recently, it has been possible to observe an active search in Russian psychology and philosophy oriented to the topic of consciousness as a subjective and complex human production (Akopov, 2009; Zinchenko, 2009).

Subjectivity differs from subjectivism because subjectivity is an active psychical person's production grounded in living experiences, that takes place based on historically situated cultural devices, whereas subjectivism refers to a mental production as an immanent, universal and a-historical one-sided expression of a given mind. I agree with Castoriadis's (1982) more general definition of subjective systems as those systems able to produce sense. Human subjectivity is a human-specific system which permits human individuals to produce multiple subjective alternatives when facing objective conditions from which those alternatives could not easily be explained or deducted. Subjective human production always represents a new kind of phenomenon in relation to those objective processes involved in its genesis.

The person is always within a network of symbolic processes and emotions, that characterises their social existence. Human activities and relations are configured to each other within a complex subjective system of the human existence. The person's subjective configuration results from the multiple collateral and interrelated effects of his or her relations into those networks of social life. Collateral effects represent a subjective production. Cultural, social and natural facts and their reciprocal relationships appear indissolubly organised in subjective terms within those subjective configurations which have resulted from lived experiences.

The argument being made in this chapter is that the generative character of emotion could be considered as the first step in the complex path towards a new alternative for the study of human development that integrates the topic of subjectivity from a cultural-historical starting point. The non-linear and direct correspondence between concrete external influences and their collateral effects on subjectivity is, I suggest, an important premise for understanding the creative character of human action.

The idea of collateral effects is an important theoretical device for under-standing the genesis of human subjective processes and configurations. The term 'collateral effect' always refers to an active generative character of the system on which external influences have acted. Any external influ-ence will be relevant for the development of complex subjective systems through the re-organisation of the system in development (Beck, 1995; Maturana & Varela, 1987). Collateral effects in the context of the human psyche result from a subjective configuration as an expression of subject-ivity as a whole in front of the network of social relations within which the subject is immersed. Subjectivity results from the complex human immer-sion into those symbolical networks organised as the social realities based on cultural productions. However, subjectivity is not a mimetic result of those symbolical configurations; it is a symbolical-emotional production which always pre-supposes the current subjective configurations of those interrelated subjects and social scenarios within which human experience is taking place. This definition carries neither a rationalistic nor a determin-istic representation of subjectivity.

VYGOTSKY'S CONTRIBUTIONS TO THE THEORETICAL CONSTRUCTION OF HUMAN DEVELOPMENT

Vygotsky's more consistent conceptualisations of human psychical devel-opment were organised in the last moment of his work. He posed the topic of development as a basic area of study for general psychology rather than a specific branch of applied psychology. Vygotsky revised many of his ori-ginal topics from his early work late in his life, between 1932 and 1934. His work 'On the questions of the psychology of the creative actor', written in 1932, is particularly relevant. In this work, Vygotsky discussed how emotion was emancipated from the biological organisation of the psyche, 'developing and breaking down their prior relationships; emotions come into new rela-tionships with the other elements of psychical life, new systems appear ... units of higher order emerge' (Vygotsky, 1984, p. 328). (My translation.)

In making such a statement, Vygotsky re-emphasised the generative character he attributed to emotions. By entering into new interactions with other elements of psychical life, emotions become a source of a new psych-ical system which is not exclusively cognitive.

In the third moment of his work, Vygotsky briefly employed two relevant concepts: sense, that is mentioned in a particular passage of *Thinking and Speech*, and *perezhivanie*. *Perezhivanie* was introduced by Vygotsky as a concept able to embody the integration of cognitive and affective processes central to the definition of the social situation of development. Using the concept of *perezhivanie*, Vygotsky overcame the social determinism of external facts over internal psychical functions. Of the social situation of development, he wrote:

> The child's experience represents that kind of simple unity from which it is impossible to say which is the influence of the environment on child or which are the child's psychological characteristics in themselves. The experience is the unit of the environment and personality as they exist in the process of development .... The experience should be understood as the child's internal relation as individual with some aspect of reality. (Vygotsky, 1984, p. 382)

Vygotsky understood the unity of personality and environment in *perezhivanie*. Personality is central to his definition of *perezhivanie*. The relevance of social influences on development would depend on *perezhivanie*, understood as a cognitive-emotional response based on the child's personality. *Perezhivanie* becomes, in Vygotsky's definition, the psychical unity of human development within which personality and certain environmental influences combine as a qualitatively new unity. *Perezhivanie* promised to lead to a radical change in the comprehension of human psychological development. As Bozhovich (1981, p. 123) stated: 'Vygotsky began to look at "unity" in his definition of the "social situation of development", and he defined that unity in "perechivanie". "Perechivanie", according to him, is the "unity" within which are represented, in an indivisible whole, the environment, or what the child experiences, as well as the psychological level the child has attained thus far in his life'. (My translation.) In this attempt, Vygotsky dialectically incorporated actual and historical moments of the child's life; in addition, he integrated external and internal elements into a new kind of psychological unity. Once again, as in many other instances in his work, Vygotsky seems to have created a new path for the explanation of the genesis of new psychical synthesis, orienting theoretical representations of human development to new and unexplored avenues of research.

In *Thinking and Speech*, Vygotsky explicitly advanced one step in the consideration of thinking as a complex psychological expression of the thinker, that opens an interesting path for the reconsideration of functions traditionally defined as cognitive to become integrated with senses as *perezhivanie*. Functions under this prism also become sources of emotions which actively engage in a subject's action; however, Vygotsky was not able to come to this conclusion. Concerning thinking, he stated:

> The first issue that emerges in the first chapter when we consider the relationship between thinking and speech and the other aspects of the life of consciousness concerns the connection between intellect and affect. Among the most basic defects of traditional approaches to the study of psychology has been the isolation of the intellectual from the volitional and affective aspects of consciousness. The inevitable consequence of the isolation of these functions has been the transformation of thinking into an autonomous stream. Thinking itself became the thinker of thoughts. Thinking was divorced from the full vitality of life, from the motives, interests and inclinations of the thinking individual. (Vygotsky, 1987, p. 50)

This approach to psychological functions could have had a strong impact in the form of a new definition of human motivation. Motives, in this case, would not have been only internal entities oriented to drive behaviour; they would have appeared as processes, as a quality of any psychical functions, that are not isolated elements, but expressions of a subject's subjective configuration of his or her performance. In promoting such a theoretical advance, Vygotsky paved the way so that the concepts of *perezhivanie* and sense could be integrated into a definition of psychological function, overcoming the affective emptiness of these functions as they had been defined by him as higher psychological functions.

When Vygotsky criticised the idea of thinking as 'divorced from the full vitality of life', he was attempting to turn thinking into a subject's active function. However, such an attempt requires psychological concepts which permit new representations of psychical processes, facilitating also new empirical access to the study of these complex representations. The absence of such concepts and representations in Vygotsky's repertoire at that point could have been the reason why he was unable to advance further with understandings of vitality in subject's active function.

Vygotsky, as the last given quotation suggests, could not go forward with his central idea of presenting thinking within the full vitality of life because he remained a prisoner of the old representations of thinking as motivated by external facts. Despite having introduced some very promising concepts, like sense and *perezhivanie*, Vygotsky could not use them as new psychical unities within which all psychological functions could be analysed.

Despite Vygotsky's failure to take forward the consequences of the concepts of sense and *perezhivanie*, both concepts brought into light different questions for the study of human development, permitting the visualisation of a new period in the development of a new representation of the human psyche, more centred on the idea of an integrative system based on cognitive-emotional unity. This representation differs essentially from the use of the concepts of reflection and internalisation, which were dominant in Vygotsky's cultural-historical approach (1928–1931). The lack of links between the concepts of sense and *perezhivanie* and the absence of references to sense in Vygotsky's other works from the same time period raises the question of whether the concept of sense was not mature enough to be used as the starting point of a new theoretical system.

The concept of *perezhivanie* opened a new avenue for advancing a new representation of human development in which the focus was psychological unities instead of activity. This emphasis revived interest in the concept of personality in this field. As Yaroshevsky (2007, p. 268) pointed out: 'In perezhivanie, the logic of ideas and the logic of sentiments combine, leading to the change of the "formations" of age periods. Perezhivanie should therefore be understood as a self-regulated psychological system of personality'. (My translation.)

I consider that *perezhivanie* represented a step forwards for understanding psychological development through singular psychological unities which become dominant under certain circumstances. Those unities necessarily are different in each person and are responsible for the psychological repertoire that permits opening new qualitative paths in human performances.

As Chudnovsky, one of Bozhovich's closest collaborators, stated: 'It is not activity itself, nor the interactions between different kind of activities, but the changes in the child's motivational sphere that define the change indicating a new level of psychical development' (Chudnovsky, 1976, p. 49). Chudnovsky's statement was in line with the definition of *perezhivanie* given by Vygotsky and which was banned from the theoretical principles on which the topic of human development was based in Soviet psychology, under the concept of leading activity.

THE SUBJECTIVE SENSE: A NEW STEP FORWARD
IN RELATION TO VYGOTSKY'S LEGACY

The relevance of sense for psychology lies in its ability to sustain a representation of the psyche which can be considered simultaneously as an individual and a social phenomenon. On the basis of the heuristic value of the category of sense described previously, I attempt to elaborate a concept which could be taken as a psychical unity on which a concept of subject-ivity, configured as an expression of the socio-cultural-historical character of human experience, can be based. The intention is to sustain the positive scope of sense in the way it was used by Vygotsky, and yet to overcome its limits. I will refer to such a unity as subjective sense.

Unlike sense, subjective sense is configured as a network of emotional and symbolic processes which emerge from the collateral effects of being human. These subjective senses flow as an interwoven movement of emo-tional and symbolic processes, where the emergence of one of them evokes the other without becoming its cause. This irregular and dynamic course unfolds into different and unexpected interrelated paths, configuring a truly recursive chain of subjective senses. Unlike subjective senses, subject-ive configurations represent relatively stable psychological systems, but they never have human expressions as external causes. Subjective configurations are very malleable, taking different forms according to the context and to a particular individual's psychological state at the moment of that concrete experience. Any action is configured as a subjective configuration; every relevant action is a subjective sense production.

Subjective configurations are dynamic systems which embody the individual's history through diverse subjective senses constantly emer-ging from different lived experiences in the person's ongoing development. Subjective configurations do not respect any formal categorisation external to the subject: There is no subjective configuration of studying, but there are subjective configurations related to a person who studies.

The real basis of human development is the actual subjective configura-tions as living and dynamic subjective productions. This concept is neces-sary in order to grasp the centrality of emotions and fantasy to human subjectivity. Those emotions and symbolic processes result from many dif-ferent lived experiences, but they join together in different ways, making up the network of subjective configurations, that defines human subjectivity. The expansion of subjective configurations in any domain of human life involves the emergence of multiple new psychological repertoires in such a process which can be understood as psychological development; new func-tions and subjective senses emerge, configuring new qualitative psycho-logical stages.

This account suggests that human development is a permanent ongoing process in which any new moment will appear as a result of the way in which a subject's experiences appear as an organised subjective configur-ation. At the same time, in this process, new subjective senses are emerging all the time, leading to changes in the dominant network of configurations from which they emerged. The definition of subjectivity in movement does not mean that development should be identified only with movement. New dominant systems of subjective configurations are appearing throughout this process, creating new subjective repertoires which are qualitatively different than those which characterised the preceeding moments. Each new moment of human development also implies new paths in subject's life, new alternatives concerning the system of activities and social relations in daily life.

Subjective configurations represent a kind of subjective bridge between a person's history and his or her multiple current social contexts. These interconnections take place within the subjective configurations. Subjective configurations continue to develop within a network of configurations in which personality is defined. Every subjective configuration takes multiple forms as a result of the complex inter-relationships of personality and new subjective senses resulting from the active subject's position within the network of facts of his or her social world.

Personality in this definition can be defined as the systems of subjective configurations concerning a person's more stable relations, activities and contexts, which are always culturally created; there is a subjective configuration related to our family, to each concrete member of our family, to one's profession, to the school and so forth, but those configurations do not extend themselves as a chain of separating unities; they are not static intra-psychical entities. Rather, they are configured in relation to each other within a recursive system in such a process in which one configuration turns into another as subjective senses which emerge as a result of an actual subject's living experience, in whose course a new subjective configuration emerges. Between subjective configurations of personality and the subjective configurations which permanently emerge on the ongoing action, there is a tension which is very important to human development. From this tension a new subjective sense appears, generating new psychological repertoires which lead to new psychological configurations in which the person as subject of this process takes new decisions and new paths in his or her ongoing living experience.

A concrete example of the theoretical process just outlined would be the case of an adolescent who falls in love with someone the family finds unacceptable. It may lead to a conflict between prior dominant subjective configurations in his or her personality and the new subjective senses organised around the new subjective configuration resulting from the conflict. As a result of this, the person who was felt by the adolescent before the conflict to be a good and honourable father may now be seen as an egotistical and authoritarian one, in a process within which the adolescent may take new decisions and positions around which arise new intellectual and emotional resources engaging him or her in a new process of development, with multiple and unpredictable paths of development. But the same process may lead the adolescent down a different avenue; he or she may lose the capacity to produce alternatives in the face of the conflict, and so remain in a paralysing emotional state which may evolve into negative psychological symptoms instead of development.

The concepts of subjective sense and subjective configurations permit overcoming the current fragmented taxonomy of concepts on which psychology as science is organised. (Danziger, 1990; Koch, 1992). These fragmentations are responsible for the fact that different areas of psychology, such as educational, clinical and social, are based on different concepts and are thus incompatible with each other. The psychological configurations and processes involved in those areas are in fact the same, as Vygotsky defended in his analysis of handicapped children and pathological cases.

Under this new approach, psychical processes should be analysed as subjective sense processes whose subjective nature impedes separating their symbolic side from their emotional character. Each subjective sense represents personality as a whole, because it exists in the movement of the complex network of subjective configurations that could be defined as personality.

The category of subjectivity is an attempt to make intelligible the nature of those psychical processes that support the generative character of the psyche. Mechanical determinism of the psyche is replaced by a recursive comprehension of the cultural, historical and social characters of human subjectivity. Subjectivity appears as a human production based on living experience, whereas experience gains a symbolic-emotional character which becomes intelligible in terms of an individual's subjective configurations.

This is the reason why Leontiev (1992, 2001) and I, in different times and following different theoretical approaches, have both attempted to use Vygotsky's definition of sense as a tool for advancing a broadening representation of the human psyche as a system.

SUBJECTIVE SENSES: A NEW APPROACH TO HUMAN MOTIVATION AND HUMAN DEVELOPMENT

In psychology, the motive has long been defined as a concrete element able to drive individual behaviour in one concrete field. Motives, once this definition is assumed, are treated as one more specific psychical function, like perceptions or thinking. This account is an expression of the classical positivistic foundation of psychology oriented by a behavioural and atomistic representation of the psyche.

Understanding subjective configuration as a psychical unity able to engage different subjective senses in its own course highlights a new definition of human motivation. Advantages of subjective configuration over the classic definition of motive can be summarised as follows:

- Subjective configuration does not correspond to any external object, content or activity. It does not have a reactive character. Unlike motive, subjective configuration always refers to multiple events whose convergence in terms of subjective sense reveals a new psychical unity. The concept of motive, within behavioural psychology, was defined by those behavioural expressions conceptualised as internal drives to an action, whereas subjective configurations are not defined by behavioural indicators but by symbolic-emotional expressions which can only be defined by hermeneutical procedures.
- Subjective configurations do not determine action as was implicitly attempted through the concept of motive. Subjective configurations are intrinsic to the action's course; they are, in fact, an arrangement of new subjective senses and psychological elements during the subject's action in any field.
- Unlike motives, subjective configurations are not the result of psychical elements in interaction; they are complex psychological systems with the capacity to lead to several different concrete expressions through the subject's action.

Emotions and symbolic processes interacting in functions like fantasy represent a qualitative moment of any psychological function. Every psychological function should be considered as a motive because it is subjectively configured. Starting from this new representation of psychological function, it would be possible to overcome the currently prevailing 'additive logic' in the study of psychical functions. In doing so, psychological functions become motives, involving in their psychological nature imagination, fantasy and a broad spectrum of emotional states which would qualify to function as subjective.

A psychological function gains subjective senses within the subject's network of subjective configurations organised on the basis of ongoing experience. The psychological functions as expressions of the subject always represent motives as they carry emotions produced by the thinker's personality. Productive thinking is always a subjective production; on

the other hand, assimilation involves thinking as a formal operation oriented towards a reproductive result. The emergence of subjective senses in
the ongoing course of any psychological function turns this process into
a moment of a given subjective configuration. Once cognitive function
becomes a moment of subjective configuration, that configuration rather
than cognitive function becomes a motive in itself and assumes a generative
character that leads to a truly subjective construction of reality. This process of construction integrates in itself fantasy, imagination and imaginaries
which are far beyond being simply cognition.

The concept of subjective configuration replaces the definition of a
motive as a specific content oriented to drive action. We can take the motive
to study as an example: It has been considered as equivalent to being an
active participant in classes, to studying in one's free time, to completing
one's school duties, and so forth. If a motive is defined in this way, everyone
would have the same motives if they behaved in a similar way concerning
their school duties. Each concrete behaviour carries a blending of subjective
configurations from which those subjective senses involved in the student's
current and contextual actions and relations arise.

Each student has his or her own dominant subjective configuration
regarding his or her school activities, that can change depending on the
different contexts and events of their school and personal lives. Whereas
one student may be curious about a concrete subject being taught in school
while actively seeking social recognition from parents and peers, another
may mainly be sensitive to the challenge of demonstrating to his or her
parents that he or she can achieve as well as an older sibling towards whom
he or she feels jealousy. These two situations are quite different, and the
motives involved have different psychological natures but similar behavioural expressions.

Every human performance represents an important context in which to
examine relevant subjective configurations of personality. Paraphrasing a very
popular expression of Vygotsky, we could state that the subjective configuration on which any concrete human action rests represents the 'microcosm
of a whole personality'. This way of analysing motivation sheds new light
on the importance of personality for the study of human development.
Motivation is not an element of personality; rather personality is the system
within which motivation is organised as subjective configurations.

The study of development has long been centred on the study of functions like cognitive processes and skills. A subjective system should be
understood as a whole on the basis of its psychical unities, not as a sum
of different and disconnected functions. I propose subjective configuration

as a new step in the path Vygotsky began when using categories like sense and *perezhivanie*.

It is not that there are different kinds of developments isolated from one another in different domains, such as moral, cognitive or sexual developments, at a given moment of personal life. The person grows up in such a subjective configuration which could be organised around, say, sporting practice, in which moral values among many other subjective senses emerge. Once some moral values emerge in that sporting performance, they will take other expressions in other fields of the experience of that person whereby those values may be expressed in different way from their embodiment in sporting practice. When they appear in other fields, they will be part of different subjective configurations.

Age is only one factor among many that can be critical in establishing particular moments in human development. Human development emerges not as a result of standardised moments or periods, but as a result of the occurrence of particular subjective personal engagements within which new subjective senses emerge configuring an endless process throughout which new psychical repertoires are created and new functions unfold into others, leading to a new step forwards in that person. Those moments through which human development organises may be quite different: a new loving relationship, the beginning of professional career, an unexpected illness, a school concert, a performance on a sports team may emerge characterising a new moment of human development for that person. Psychical development should not be understood as a regular sequence of stages, that remains stable as the basis for new moments.

The suggestion therefore is that human development takes place on the basis of different subjective knots configured in human action and activity. These configurations interweave with senses, making up an endless chain of subjective senses which are continuously unfolding into new senses, creating a truly subjective system. Emotional and symbolic processes from different personal experiences combine as inseparable subjective senses within the subjective configuration of a given concrete activity.

CONCLUSIONS

Human life is a a process of development as individuals create their courses of action arising from their experiences. As Chudnovsky indicated, it is the changes in the child's motivational sphere which capture the processes of child development. The arguments put forward in this chapter can thus be summarised as follows.

- Human development results from multivariate and complex processes that are impossible to standardise in regular and well-organised sequences of stages. Every individual's development is unique and results from different subjective configurations interwoven with different social networks within which human actions are expressed.
- Vygotsky's emphases on human development in the first and last phases of his work were centred on emotional processes such as fantasy and feelings. In those periods, Vygotsky seemed to be seeking the development of cognitive-emotional unities of human development. These attempts were not developed further in his work. The developments of those first and last moments of his legacy created alternatives for a new theoretical path along which the topic of subjectivity gains a cultural-historical connotation, becoming a specific and complex representation of the human psyche.
- Cultural-historical representation of human subjectivity permits a non-rational and dialectical approach to human development, which makes it possible to overcome the ideas of control, assimilation and internalisation as the processes involved in human development. New concepts such as dialogue, the generative character of subjectivity, social networks of activities and communication and collateral effects are gaining new relevance for the representation of human development. These concepts find their expression as psychological terms in subjective configurations and subjective senses.
- The concepts of subjective sense and subjective configurations cannot be reduced to a rational-intentional process or to merely instrumental-cognitive processes. The relevance of emotions for understanding human development implies that motivation should be considered as the cornerstone of this process. Motivation, as argued in this chapter, is not taken as a concrete content or as one more psychical process; motivation is the whole expression of subjectivity through an individual's particular subjective configurations of psychical processes, functions and living experiences. It represents a unity of the person and quality of the action.
- Human development takes place through certain core subjective configurations within an endless series of effects and consequences of different simultaneous social experiences within which individuals are constantly acting. In this subjective movement, new psychical functions and subjective configurations increasingly appear, that sustain new qualitative psychical expressions in different human domains.

REFERENCES

Anderson, H. (1999). *Conversaciones, lenguaje y posibilidad: un enfoque postmoderno de la psicoterapia*. Buenos Aires: Amorrortu.

Akopov, G. (2009). The problem of consciousness in Russian psychology. *Journal of Russian and Eastern Europena Psychology*, 47(5), 3–25.

Beck, U. (1995). A reinvençao da política: rumo a uma teoria da modernização reflexiva. Em A. Giddens, U. Beck, & S. Lash (Eds.), *Modernização reflexiva* (pp. 13–71). São Paulo: Editora UNESP.

Bozhovich, L. I. (1981). *La personalidad y su desarrollo en la edad infantil*. Habana: Pueblo y Educación.

Castoriadis, C. (1982). *A instituição imaginaria da sociedade*. São Paulo: Paz e Terra.

Chudnovsky, V. E. (1976). K vozrastnym etapam podxodu v izuchenii formirovaniya lichnosti shkolnikov (On age staging approach in the study of student's personality formation). *Voprosy Psikhologii (Cuestiones de Psicología)*, 4, 46–53.

Danziger, K. (1990). *Constructing the subject: Historical origins of psychological research*. New York: Cambridge University Press.

Gergen, K. (2006). *Construir la realidad: El futuro de la psicoterapia*. Barcelona: Paidos.

González Rey, F. (2001). La categoría sentido y su significación en la construcción del pensamiento psicológico. *Contrapontos*, 1(2), 13–28.

(2002). *Sujeto y subjetividad: Una aproximación histórico-cultural*. México: D.F. Editora Thomson.

(2008a). Different periods in Vygotsky's work: Their implications for arguments regarding his legacy. Personal presentation in the Annual meeting of the International Society for Cultural and Activity Research, San Diego, California.

(2008b). Subject, subjectivity and development in cultural – historical psychology. In B. Van Oers, R. Van der Veer, & W. Wardeckker (Eds.), *The transformation of learning* (pp. 137–156). Cambridge: Cambridge University Press.

Koch. S. (1992). The nature and limits of psychological knowledge: Lesson of a century of a 'science.' In S. Koch & D. A. Leary (Eds.), *Century of psychology as a qua 'Science'* (pp. 75–99). Washington DC: American Psychological Association.

Leontiev, A. A. (1992). Ecce homo methodological problems of the activity theoretical approach. *Multidisciplinary Newsletter for Activity Theory*, 11–12, 41–45

(2001). *Deyatelnyi um (deyatelnost', znak, lichnost') (The active mind [activity, sign, personality])*. Moscow: Smysl.

Leontiev, A. N. (1972). *Problemy razvitiya psikhiki (Problems in the development of psyche)*. Moscow: Izdatelstva MGU.

(1981). *Actividad, conciencia, personalidad. Editorial*. Habana: Pueblo y Educación.

(1994). *Filosofiya psikhologii (The philosophy of psychology)*. Moscow: Izdatelstva MGU.

Maturana, H., & Varela, F. (1987). *The tree of knowledge: The biological roots of human understanding*. Boston: New Science.

Vygotsky, L. S. (1965). *Psikhologiya iskustva (The psychology of art)*. Moscow: Izdatelstva Iskustva.

   (1984). K voprosu o psikhologii khudozhestvennogo tvorchestva aktera (On the question of the psychology of the creative artist). In M. G. Yaroshevsky (Ed.), *Sobranie sochinenii*, Vol. 6. Moscow: Pedagogika.

   (1987). Thinking and speech. In R. Rieber & A. Carton (Eds.), *The collected works of L. S. Vygotsky*, Vol. 1 (pp. 43–287). New York: Plenum Press.

Zinchenko, V. P (1993). Kulturno-istoricheskaya psikhologiya: Opyt amplifikatzii (Cultural-historical psychology: an experience of amplification). *Voprosy Psikhologii (Questions of Psychology)*, 3, 5–19.

Zinchenko, V. P. (2009). Consciousness as the subject matter and task of psychology. *Journal of Russian and Eastern European Psychology*, 47(5), 44–75.

Yaroshevsky, M. (1993). L. S. Vygotsky – zhertva 'opticheskogo obmana' (L. S. Vygotsky – victim of 'optical deceit'). *Voprosy Psikhologii (Questions of Psychology)*, 3, 55–60.

   (2007). *L. S. Vygotsky: V poiskakh novoi psikhologii (L. S. Vygotsky: In search of new psychology)*. Moscow: LKI.

4

Early Stages in Children's Cultural Development

VLADIMIR P. ZINCHENKO

Michel Foucault said, 'To approach the essence one must go backwards'. My own development as a psychologist can be seen as an inversion of the history of the Soviet psychology: First there was the cultural-historical approach; later – the psychological theory of activity. I started with the latter and am slowly approaching the former now. From my earlier research on sensory-motor skills and perceptual actions I had moved to studies of the development of visual image, visual thinking and visual memory; finally, through my fairly late interest in poetry and psychology of art, I have turned my attention to the word and culture – at last.

Naturally, I went back to re-reading Vygotsky. This time, I found myself puzzled by his description of a child as having natural 'lower' psychological functions that develop into higher mental functions only as a result of interiorisation and intellectualisation. I felt that this view contradicted his own theory of cultural-historical development and was rather similar to the gradual animation of a statue – a metaphor for human development proposed by the eighteenth-century French philosopher Etienne Bonnot de Condillac in his book *Traité des sensations*. Thus, I decided to take a closer look at child development in the light of my current understanding of the cultural-historical approach and the psychological theory of activity.

In a way, this text is an attempt to deal with certain confusion I experience every time I see the words 'culture' and 'activity' next to each other. It seems to me that the latter seems to engulf the former more and more; and along with culture, the human subjectivity too becomes superseded by activity. A similar thing happened once in the Soviet psychology when the theory of activity had supplanted consciousness and culture as major paradigms for understanding the human being. I see this tendency not only in psychology and other social disciplines, but also in the social reality as a whole.

Culture is alive as long as it can question itself, otherwise it becomes stagnant and dies. This is applicable to the cultural-historical psychology as well. I do not intend to dramatise this situation, to speak of the end of culture, or to question the cultural-historical approach. My goal is modest: I would merely like to discuss the intricate relationship between culture and activity and to pose some questions about it. I am planning to do so by concentrating on certain essential aspects of early child development – a topic that seems rather fitting for my advanced age.

Among the many important functions of culture is to cast incantation against chaos – chaos of human desires, emotions, wishes, motives, values. This is what the world's art deals with: consequences of this chaos and ways of overcoming it. One can even say that *emotion* and *affect* are the key words of culture and art. Regrettably, emotion and affect did not become a focus of psychology (with the exclusion of psychoanalysis). The fate of emotions in psychology has been often compared with Cinderella who received much less attention compared to her older sisters – thinking and volition. And this is in spite the fact that Aristotle and Spinoza paid so much attention to affects and emotions in their meditations about the soul. Psychology paid relatively little attention to emotional sphere. I think it happened not because it was deemed of little importance, but rather because of its resistance to rational conceptualization. In addition, psychologists, in spite of the history of their science, still are not tolerant of uncertainty. For emotions are more often than not viewed as a background accompaniment and not as a figure, the essential melody of human life. To be fair, I must say that many psychologists (and philosophers) pay enough attention to the role of emotions in human life. Below are some examples.

Reneé Descartes, who provided an epiphany of the cognitive vector of psychology, did not belittle the role of emotions. He said that action and passion is one and the same thing. Indeed, learning of a new action is always accompanied by overcoming external circumstances and oneself: Desire to master and the process of mastery bring satisfaction and, at last, the obtained freedom and ease in the process of execution of action brings happiness. Thus, for the individual, free action can serve as motive, goal or value.

Following Spinoza, Vygotsky spoke about unity of affect and intellect and about emotional and volitional components of thought. His student (and my teacher), Alexander V. Zaporozhets, considered emotions a nucleus of personality. Zaporozhets did not take the postulate of unity of affect and intellect as a given. He set out to study how it comes to be. He tried to investigate architectonics of the functional system of integrated emotional and cognitive acts that regulates behaviour and activity of an individual. He researched internal activity of 'affective-representational imagination' which, according to Vygotsky, is a 'second expression' of human emotions (besides the first, external one). As part of the unified system of behaviour regulation, emotions become 'intelligent' and anticipatory. Intellectual processes in this context assume qualities of affective-representational thinking which plays an important role in creation of meaning and goals (Zaporozhets, 2002, pp. 45–66).

Here, I shall get ahead of myself and say that mystery and magic of the word is that it presents rather than merely represents culture with all its qualities and functions; the word presents its affective, cognitive and practical aspects. The word presents not just culture, but the world itself. Boris Pasternak stated that image of the world was represented in word. The word presents our internal world too. Osip Mandelshtam said that *only our voice would let us understand what is there inside of us scratching and fighting.* 'Act of speech – even the most ordinary one – is a completion of internal maturation, the last stage of being subjective and the first stage of becoming objective' (Florensky, 1973, p. 367).

This rather brief excursus into meditations and research of emotions introduces an idea of heterogeneity of a psychic act, whether it is emotional, cognitive or manual. I develop this thought later in the chapter. At the same time, this excursus is an excuse for my contribution to this volume.

WORD AS THE ESSENTIAL CONSTITUENT OF CULTURE

Now I turn to the main subject of this work. The essential constituent of culture is word: an embodiment of the mind. According to Gustav Shpet, culture is a 'cult of cogitation' and word is the archetype of culture and the main principle of cognition. I can put it even stronger: Word is the foundation of human existence, not just *ratio cognoscenti*, but also *ratio essendi*. My argument is that this understanding of the word is true for all stages of child's development, starting with infancy.

This view seems to contradict what such prominent researchers as Lev Vygotsky, Jean Piaget and Jerome Bruner have said about childhood. Their theories postulate pre-verbal development of the mind and thinking. It looks as if the word is introduced into the psyche only at the age of two. Vygotsky agrees with Goethe: 'It was not the word that was in the beginning. In the beginning was the deed the word is the end rather than the beginning of development. The word comes at the end and crowns the act' (Vygotsky, 1982, Vol. II, p. 360). Piaget and then Bruner believed that the verbal stage of development comes after the stages of action and imagination. It goes without saying that these theories have made immense contributions to our understanding of child development; in many ways they underlie our current understanding of the child. I believe, however, that this view overly emphasises the gap between action, image and word, whilst not putting enough emphasis on their inherent unity. In my opinion, the resulting picture of developmental stages is overly simplified. When we postulate the existence of pre-verbal intellectual development and pre-verbal development of communication, the role and cognitive potential of the word on the earlier stages of development are ignored. On the later stages, the emotional and cognitive potential of the action and the image are underestimated (even at these later stages, action and image are still considered predominantly non-verbal).

Does the development begin with culture or activity? This artificial bifurcation brings to mind the old dichotomies of nativism and empirism and of nature and nurture. This 'dichotomania' feels nearly eternal. Even today such views as 'speech is the late phenomenon in ontogenesis' or 'most of psychological functions develop prior to speech development' are widespread (Sergienko, 2006, p. 302). There seems to be confusion between 'verbal' and 'verbalised', 'verbality' and 'verbalisation'. Comparative studies of thinking of anthropoids and of two-to-three-year-old children are based on these doubtful premises. Let me attempt an alternative view of the role of the word in child development.

The terms 'internalisation' and 'externalisation' have been used so often, they seem to have some magic to them, as if just saying these words offers an understanding of the relationship between the internal, psychic phenomenon and the external human activity. We all agree that internalisation and externalisation play a crucial role in child development; these processes are much studied empirical facts. Yet, they offer little help with understanding what is 'internal' (not that they say much about the nature of the external either).

Eminent scholars Wilhelm Humboldt and Gustav Shpet have suggested replacing the ill-defined notions of 'internal' and 'external' with the concept of 'internal and external forms'. This is not a mere name change. They believed these new terms would help us to overcome the dichotomy of internal and external and to relinquish the artificial opposition between them.

Russian philosopher Pavel Florensky said the word is a mediator between internal and external worlds. The word is like an amphibian which lives here and there and ties both worlds together. Florensky said that word is not an 'airy nothing', not merely an empty sound. The external form of the word

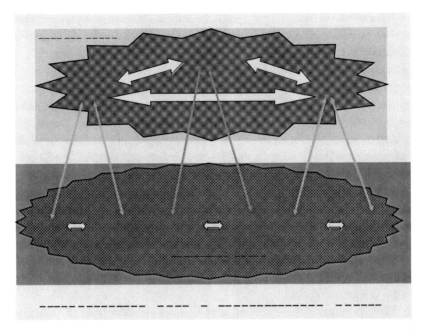

FIGURE 4.1. Schematical depiction of intricate relationships among internal and external forms of the word, image and action.

encompasses all richness of its internal contents. It is this complexity of the living word's architectonics that allows us to liken it to a functional organ, or even to an organism and an animate being (Florensky, 1973) .

THE UNITY OF WORD, IMAGE AND ACTION
IN CHILDREN'S DEVELOPMENT

The word in its external form includes action and image as its internal forms; the action in its external form includes word and image as its internal forms. Finally, the action and word are internal form of the image. This point of view is based upon the research of internal form of the word (Gustav Shpet); internal form of movements and actions (Nickolay Bernshtein, Natalya Gordeyeva) and internal form of the image (Alexander Zaporozhets) (Figure 4.1).

All these internal forms are of a dynamic nature. They are what ensures that we can find an adequate meaning of a word without uttering anything out loud or even to oneself, that we can manipulate images and generate new ones 'in our mind's eye', that we can execute actions in imagination before we actualise them in external reality and so forth.

It is a given that meaning is part of the internal form of word. In addition, however, object-oriented, perceptual and operational (motor) meanings (notions that 'hands know') are part of the internal forms of images and actions. Thus, we can talk of certain similarity in architectonics of the word, action and image. They all have their own external and internal forms which enrich and penetrate each other and, at times, are interchangeable. Each of the internal forms is contained within the other two, albeit in a transformed and reduced mode. The word, image and action taken in the full richness of their external and internal forms are complex 'centauroid' units. All these units are meta-forms (forms of forms) – condensed energy, meanings, emotions and affects. Yet, in this heterogenic unity of the word, image and action, the dominant role belongs to the word as the main bearer of meaning; it does not only crown the action and image, but also lies in their foundation. Richard Wagner said that his music begins with a word.

What are the origins of this inherent unity of meta-forms of the word, image and action? Let me turn to a discussion of the heterogenesis of the word, image and action.

My hypothesis is that the word accompanies a person from the moment of birth. Long before it manifests itself in all the beauty (or ugliness) of its external form, it penetrates (or, if you prefer, is internalised into) the internal forms of actions and images (as well as of motions and affects) of a child.

There have been many attempts to describe this primary 'word without words' – an example is Mandelshtam's poetic 'Wise silence'. The philosopher Mamardashvili called it the 'non-verbal inner word', whereas another philosopher, Bibikhin, referred to it as 'speaking silence'. This non-verbal inner word gradually matures within internal forms of action and image; only by having undergone this maturation process can the inner word find an adequate external verbal form. This is why philosophers of Ancient Greece spoke of 'logos spermatikos' (seed-bearing word); this is also Humboldt's 'live embryo of infinite formations'.

These metaphors of seed and embryo point precisely to the active, intentional and generative nature of the internal form of the word. Before it can find its immanent external form, the word lies hidden in the motor and perceptual languages, concealed in the baby's reactions to the world and to his caregivers, in its whimper and laughter, his coos and babble.

WORDS ARE CONNECTED WITH EMOTION FROM A CHILD'S FIRST MOMENTS

Penetration of the word into the child's soul is a mysterious process, as enigmatic as the soul itself. Michael Bakhtin said that soul is a gift his spirit gives to another person. From the excess of her love and generosity of spirit, mother gifts her soul to her baby. This gift is mediated by her voice, her nurturance and her words. Love is eloquent and articulate. Both the voice and the word become meaningful events in the baby's life.

According to the Catholic philosopher and theologist Claude Tresmontan, it was the biblical structure of the human thinking and language that prepared the Virgin of Israel to hear the words of Living God. This is what made her ready to receive and bear Logos Which Became Flesh and appeared before us. Thus, the Word (Logos) is a gift, a spiritual foetus (analogous to the 'logos spermatikos' of ancient philosophers) that is passed on through generations. In the New Testament, in the Parable of the Sower, the seed represents to us the Word (Tresmontan, 1996). This cultural interpretation of Immaculate Conception is more sensible in regard to the laws of nature than the literal understanding of the biblical story.

A gift of love is unique in that it is not really given away, quite the opposite – even though the giver does not expect anything in exchange, the gift gets replenished and even increased by the very act of giving. Russian psychologist Maya Lisina characterised infancy as 'the golden age of communication'. This is truly selfless communication, one that has no extrinsic goals and finds its infinite value in itself. This apparently pre-semiotic communication is full of felt meaning, even though it does not rely on meanings expressed with words. Rather it is filled with lived experiences, tactile and other sensations, mutual babbling. Later, they are mentalised into meaning-filled sensations and then into feelings, words and knowledge. From very early on, the word becomes an unalienable part of the child's developing picture of the world and his or her possible actions in the world.

When an external source of light reaches objects in the dark, it makes them visible by touching their surface; when the word makes its way into the soul, its contents are lit from within.

The child is not a passive recipient of this gift; on the contrary, he or she is rather active. This is how St. Augustine described his own early development and the latent process of gradual mastery of the word:

> I knew how to suck, to lie quiet when I was content, to cry when I was in pain: and that was all I knew. Later I added smiling to the things I could do, first in sleep, and then awake .... And gradually I began to notice where I was, and the will grew in me to make my wants known to those who might satisfy them; but I could not, for my wants were within me and those others were outside; nor had they any faculty enabling them to enter my mind .... Clearly then I had being and I had life: and toward the end of infancy I tried hard to find ways [and signs] of making my feelings known to others.

I have since discovered by observation how I learned to speak. I did not
learn by elders teaching me words in any systematic way, as I was soon
after taught to read and write. But of my own motion, using the mind
which You, my God, gave me, I strove with cries and various sounds and
much moving of my limbs to utter the feelings of my heart – all this in
order to get my own way. Now I did not always manage to express the
right meanings to the right people. So I began to reflect. [I observed] my
elders would make some particular sound, and as they made it would
point at or move towards some particular thing: and from this I came
to realize that the thing was called by the sound they made when they
wished to draw my attention to it. That they intended this was clear from
the motions of their body, by a kind of natural language common to all
races which consists in facial expressions, glances of the eye, gestures
and tones by which the voice expresses the mind's state – for example
whether things are to be sought, kept, thrown away, or avoided. So, as I
heard the same words again and again properly used in different phrases,
I came gradually to grasp what things they signified; and forcing my
mouth to the same sounds, I began to use them to express my wishes.
(Augustine, 2006, pp. 6–7)

This fourth-century, pre-theoretical description is free of biases of scientific psychology and psychoanalysis. Here, Augustine speaks about the
gifts he has received from God, but also about his own activity, feelings,
attention, reason and will which eventually lead to creation of words and
cultural signs. Many centuries later, this process of creation of signs by
infants became a focus of research and discussion of many psychologists
(Carl and Charlotte Buhler, Lev Vygotsky, Jim Wertsch, to name just a
few), as well as some psychoanalysts. Unfortunately, the space does not
allow me to do justice to this very rich field of research, except to point to
some empirical data that, in my view, proves the primacy of the word in
psychological development.

   It is well known that from the very first weeks, the infant's ear learns to
distinguish the phonemes of its native language and becomes 'deaf' to the
phonemes of other languages. What it means is that the infant is far from
being indifferent to the language atmosphere that surrounds it. This atmosphere is one of the most important conditions of child's existence and development. Hearing the sounds of human speech, newborns show signs of
activity. At three-to-four weeks, an infant shows signs of auditory concentration on the voice: a child quiets down and becomes still whilst adults are
talking. This is also the time when the first real human smile appears (the
twenty-first day of life, according to many authors). When mother's and
infant's smile co-occur, it leads to an 'amplification' of the facial expressions

of the two people, to a meeting of their dispositions for communication, trust and acceptance (Polivanova, 2004, p. 112). This live space is where the identification process begins and the seed of the future full communication is planted.

Language supports this identification and facilitates the meeting of the child and adults. Italian psychoanalyst Benvenuto says: 'When a child cries, his mother may interpret his whimpering not only by giving her breast or a milk bottle, but also by saying sweetly, "You are hungry ..."' (Benvenuto, 2006, p. 48). Thanks to mother's use of words, the infant will be initiated into and always remain within the realm of language: He or she would always interpret his or her own wishes in accordance with his or her mother's words (Benvenuto, 2006, pp. 110–111). And where are wishes there are emotions and feelings. Thus, word permeates not just internal form of images and actions, but also that of feelings. As a result of that, feelings could be signified and named.

The infant longs for the word. Already at two months of age, the infant focuses his or her gaze mainly on the eyes and lips of adults. This longing is the same as infant's longing for the physical contact with the mother and for the nurturance she provides. Trevarthen (1975) conducted a study comparing infants' behaviour in the presence of their mothers and in the presence of cuddly toys. This study showed a great many differences, both in infants' facial gestures and hand gestures. What perhaps is the most significant in the context of this discussion is that these pre-verbal infants (from one week to five months old) demonstrated specific positions of their lips and tongues when their mothers spoke.

Thus, the word is literally absorbed with mother's milk. This seed-bearing word (Plato's 'logos spermatikos') falls onto the fertile soil of child's lived experience (sensations and acts); it gets irrigated by affective states and begins to grow. This process is co-created by the child and the child's mother.

THE CHILD'S FIRST WORDS

Elena Chudinova (1986) studied mothers' understanding of their infants' vocalisations. According to her data, by three months of age, mothers distinguish from three to nine distinctly different types of crying. Thus, at such young age, the infant is already capable of making some distinction among its various internal states and even of communicating them to the caregivers. Upon hearing each type of cry, the mothers had some idea of what their infants needed and approached them with a set of specific expectations and a plan of action. The mother's accurate understanding of the infant's distress signal, her comforting actions and her words further facilitate development of a child's 'representational' and 'communicational' ability and so forth.

The child's own activity and ingenuity are even more evident in the uttering of the first words. Word becomes heterogeneous. It incorporates operational, emotional and object meanings. As Bakhtin (1975) pointed out, the word gathers depth rather than height or width. This still 'green' but maturing and growing word wants to be heard, understood and responded to.

The beginning of an active speech that usually dates by the end of the first year of life is very impressive: Maria Montessori called it 'an explosion of language'; Steven Pinker likened it to 'a volcano eruption'. It is very frustrating to the baby, who is erupting with words, when the adults do not understand him or her – as if the child is trying to satisfy a long-standing urgent need. Noam Chomsky describes the beginning of speech as 'instantaneous'. Indeed, to the outside observer, this is what it looks like: as if a baby – who has not been apparently learning to talk – simply starts talking. In reality, it takes nearly two years of preparation for this 'explosion' to come to life – this is a 'well prepared impromptu'.

A CHILD'S READINESS FOR CULTURE – THE BEGINNING

A couple of words about the zone of proximal development. When word is 'born' and takes an external form, a person becomes a complete voice and enters into an interminable dialogue. The person participates in it not only with one's thoughts, but also desires, destiny and all of one's individuality.

As we have discussed earlier, from the very beginning, the word becomes the most important event in the life of the newborn. It does take about two years for the word to find its external form, but I see this process as qualitatively different from an acculturation of 'natural', 'lower' psychological functions (in Vygotsky's terms). I am certain that the cultural realm is superfluous in relation to the child's nature. It is doubtful that an infant even has natural, lower or primitive mental functions. As I have attempted to demonstrate, child development starts with 'upper register' notes, from the child's congeniality to the highest manifestations of the human spirit: the mother's love for her child.

I have mentioned earlier that soul, love and word are gifts received from another. Augustine believed he had received his gifts from God. One would presume that this was possible only because humans have been created in God's image. Similarly, according to Tresmontan, the Virgin of Israel was prepared to hear and receive God by the biblical structure of human thinking and language. Lucky theologists! But what does psychology have to offer to explain how a child may be capable of accepting the gifts of culture and word? I believe here, too, there must be certain pre-experiential readiness and willingness to accept these gifts. I do not mean the so-called lower, natural functions. On the contrary, I maintain that from the very beginning, there has to be something in the child that has been created 'in the image of culture' to enable the child to take in the said culture. This readiness is not a result of child development, but rather a set of intrinsic conditions that allow development to occur.

There have been many attempts to describe such conditions. Noam Chomsky proposed the existence of inborn 'generative linguistic structures'; John Bowlby hypothesised infant's 'genetically programmed' readiness to develop attachment to the caregiver; a prominent Georgian psychologist Dimitry Uznadze spoke of 'pre-psychic mental sets that are not rooted in the experience'; Jerome Bruner talked about 'readiness for perception'; and Paul Fraise described child's inherent 'potential of activity'. Taken together, all these examples of pre-experiential readiness can be described as child's readiness to accept and understand the human world into which he or she is born.

The reader most likely noticed that all the aforementioned authors spoke about the *beginning*. If we believe Heidegger, the beginning, because it is a beginning, should be unmediated, spontaneous. The beginning cannot be primitive, because primitive (instincts, reflexes, natural functions) do not have future. Primitive cannot generate anything besides what it is imprisoned by. True beginning always contains formerly unknown enormous completeness; consequently it also contains an argument with everything that already happened. True beginning is always a leap forward; the end result is hidden within it (see Heidegger, 2008). Referring back to the beginning of the chapter, where I spoke about emotions, I want to quote Heidegger on mood, which he understood not as a subjective state, but as a primordial kind of being.

> The mood has already disclosed, in every case, Being-in-the-world as a whole, *and makes it possible first of all to direct one-self towards something*. Having a mood is not related to the psychical in the first instance .... We have seen that the world, Dasein-with, and existence are *equiprimordially disclosed*; and state-of-mind is a basic existential species of their disclosedness, because this disclosedness itself is essentially Being-in-the-world. (Heidegger, 1962, p. 176)

Even Heidegger notices parallels between his understanding of moods and Aristotle's understanding of affects.

Now when we named a few inalienable characteristics of the 'begin-ning,' let us think what can meet its requirements. Shpet (before Heidegger formulated his requirements) assumed that the 'beginning' might be an intelligible intuition. This is similar to an earlier quote from St. Augustine. I will not follow Plato and Kant, suggesting that such intelligible intuition is supersensory. Still, there is little doubt that it is unmediated and spontan-eous. Intelligible intuition precedes sensory and intellectual intuition.

Vladimir Bibikhin was thinking in the similar direction. He wrote a hymn to the first gaze – the gaze that understands without understand-ing, the gaze that sees meaning without apparent meaning. Pavel Florensky, although not claiming that his two-year-old son had consciousness, saw his 'superconscious' gaze. Bibikhin speaks about plurality of beginnings; he does not separate or divide them, like Condiliac does, on separate mental func-tions. Rather he links them in surpassing unity *may-think-understand*. This unmediated primary integrity makes possible understanding that is accept-ing and compassionate, understanding-being; love that understands; open to the world; I can. I can is a real and tangible possibility to make a choice which precedes meaning and volition (Bibikhin, 2007, pp. 222–226).

Naturally, emotions play an enormous role in this kind of 'beginning'. The primary intuition is as intelligible as it is emotional. Thus it makes its contribution into development of Ericksonian basic trust and then into development emotions. According to Bion, lived emotional experi-ence transforms into meaning, understanding and knowledge. Following Spinosa, Vygotsky's thesis of the unity of affect and intellect is applicable to all stages of human development. Thus this unmediated beginning, the unity of mental act, is a necessary condition of learning language and cul-ture. Later, language and arts take turn and claim their rights. The primary unity differentiates onto mediated acts. The latter might fragment and con-gest consciousness; a person then, if he or she is clever enough, should resort back to intuition. At this point, this intuition had become sensory or intellectual. The latter has traits of unmediated, intelligible intuition. It allows person to overcome blocks of mediated and to return to the real world. Unmediated and mediated, intuition and discourse, go hand in hand in the course of human development. However, this is already a genre of cultural-historical psychology.

CONCLUSION

Initially, the word manifests as some primary intuition of integral unity, a poorly differentiated mental action, which potentially contains such states as 'feel', 'understand', 'want', 'can' – in their embryonic forms. This may sound

like a teleological, reformist idea, but I am not talking about some inborn mental homunculus. As I said earlier, this is just a predisposition for development, which is ensured, as Shpet suggested, by the unity of birth and belonging to the human kind. At last, if God or nature gave instincts and reflexes to animals, why were the humans left out? Were it not we who left them out by depriving them of intelligible intuition and mind? This undifferentiated activity merely enables the infant to interact with the world – mediated by the caregiver – and to take word in, along with the caregiver's 'understanding' of the word. Through this process, the word puts roots in the child's soul and facilitates differentiation of the initial pre-experiential readiness into what we call our internal world.

The words of a Russian poet Maksimilian Voloshin describe well the primary spontaneity: *A child is an unrecognized genius among the dreary everyday people.*

I would like to recognise the patience of my readers and quote a beautiful poetic illustration to what I was trying to say in prose about the word taken in all the richness of its internal and external forms. This is a quote from T. S. Elliott's poem 'Ash Wednesday':

> If the lost word is lost, if the spent word is spent
> If the unheard, unspoken
> Word is unspoken, unheard;
> Still is the unspoken word, the Word unheard,
> The Word without a word, the Word within
> The world and for the world;
> And the light shone in darkness and
> Against the Word the unstilled world still whirled
> About the centre of the silent Word.

The poet said – *In my beginning is my end ... In my end is my beginning.* The word accepted by a newborn is the beginning of development. The word is the ultimate pinnacle of development because *What is left from man is part of speech* (Joseph Brodsky).

Only when the silent word will cease to sound, only when the wise silence will vanish and even the poet will not be able to gestate silence into verse, will the development of the word and the thought stop. Let us hope that this scenario will not become reality.

ACKNOWLEDGEMENTS

I want to thank my son, Dr. Alexander Zinchenko, and his wife, Dr. Alla Volovich, for translating this text into English. They are both psychologists; not only did they help me to translate the text, but they also came up with some good suggestions regarding its structure. I am very grateful to them – both for the translation and for their helpful comments. But what I am most happy about is that the translation process facilitated a series of long, lively and illuminating conversations about psychology between my son and me.

REFERENCES

Augustine, A. (1991). *Confession*. Moscow: Renaissance.
Bakhtin, M. M. (1975). *Questions of literature and aesthetics*. Moscow: Fiction.
Benvenuto, S. (2006). *Lacan's dream*. Saint Petersburg: Alteya.
Bibikin, V. V. (2007). *World*. Saint Petersburg: Nauka.
Chudinova, E. (1986). Development of a baby's crying. *Journal of Higher Nervous Activities*, 36(3), pp. 441–449.
Elkonin, D. B. (1960). *Child psychology*. Moscow: Uchpedgiz.
Florensky, P. A. (1973). The structure of word. In *Context – 1972* (pp. 348–375). Moscow: Agraf.
Gershenzon, M. O. (2001). *Key of faith. Gulf stream. Wisdom of Pushkin*. Moscow: Agraf.
Heidegger, M. (1962). *Being and time*. Oxford: Blackwell.
  (2008). *The source of art creation*. Moscow: Academichesky Proect.
Messinger, D. S., Fogel, A., and Dickson, K. L. (1997). A dynamic system approach to infant facial action. In J. A. Russell and J. M. Fernandes-Dols (Eds.), *The Psychology of facial expression* (pp. 205–226). Cambridge: Cambridge University Press.
Polivanova, K. N. (2004). Periodization of child development: The experience of comprehension. *Issues of Psychology*, 1, 110–119.
Sergienko, E. A. (2006). *Earlier cognitive development. New look*. Moscow: Institute of Psychology of the Russian Academy of Science.
Tresmontan, C. (1996). Mind. Pages. *Journal of Biblical-Theological St. Andrew's Institute*, 4, 49–67.
Trevarthen, C. (1975). Early attempts at speech. In R. Lewin (Ed.), *Child, alive. New insight into the development of children* (pp. 62–80). London: Temple Smith.
Vygotsky, L. S. (1982). *The collected works of L. S. Vygotsky*. Volumes 1–6. Moscow: Pedagogika.
Zaporozhets, A. V. (2002). Toward the question of the genesis, function, and structure of emotional processes in the child. *Journal of Russian and East European Psychology*, 40(2), 45–66.

PART TWO

CULTURAL PRACTICE MOTIVES AND DEVELOPMENT

5

The Development of Motives in Children's Play

MARILYN FLEER

INTRODUCTION

The relations between individual and collective activity become pronounced as children play. In these dynamic contexts, children make visible through their actions the rules and roles prevalent within a given society (Elkonin, 2005a, 2005b). The rules of everyday life and the child's experiences of everyday practice shape how play is enacted (Vygotsky, 1966), and it is argued in this chapter that this activity in turn leads to a motive for play. This perspective contrasts with developmental or maturational theories of play, that suggest that play is internally driven (e.g. Brock, 2009; Garvey, 1977; Smilansky, 1968). In these theories of play, what is foregrounded is the child's instinct or need for play.

Children's *natural need for play* is prevalent in most textbooks written for early childhood teachers and pedagogues (see Brock et al., 2009, Wood & Attfield, 2005), underpins most early childhood curricula (see OECD, 2006) and is central in many policy analyses devoted to early childhood care, education and development (e.g. OECD, 2006). Many researchers have also presumed a biological and naturalistic view of play where motives for play come from within the child (e.g. Ebbeck & Waniganayake, 2010). Elkonin (2005b) argues against this position, suggesting that 'the special sensitivity of play to the area of human activity and interactions among people shows that play not only takes its topics from the children's living conditions but also that it is social in its internal content and thus cannot be a biological phenomenon' (p. 46). He contends that because play arises out of the social conditions of life, that play is not driven by internal instincts or motives, but rather it is through the child's engagement with their social environment and their relationships to others and the material world that motives for play develop.

This chapter seeks to examine how motives develop in children's play and through this gain a deeper theoretical understanding of this concept. In the first part of this chapter, a cultural-historical discussion of play is given in relation to empirical data of children playing in a pre-school setting. Here the Vygotskian (1997a, 1997b, 1998) concept of imitation is used to better understand how roles and rules function in play. In the second part of the chapter, further empirical data is presented and discussed in relation to the concept of motives. It is argued that by understanding the concept of a play motive, we can better interpret the use of play materials in pre-schools and the role and function of play.

THE RELATION BETWEEN IMITATION AND RULES IN CHILDREN'S PLAY

Vygotsky (1997b) introduced the concept of *imitation* as an important theoretical term for helping to explain the cultural development of the child. This term was not used by Vygotsky in the everyday sense of the word. Imitation is not a 'mechanical, automatic thoughtless imitation' (Vygotsky, 1998, p. 202); rather, he saw it as 'connected with a certain understanding of the situation' (Vygotsky, 1997b, p. 95) 'based on understanding the imitative carrying out of some intellectual operation' (p. 202). What is foregrounded in this reading of imitation is a form of intellectual participation that is required by the child within the process of imitation.

Vygotsky (1997b) argued that '*the circle of available imitation coincides with the circle of the actual developmental possibilities*' (p. 95, emphasis in the original). As Chaiklin (2003) points out, when the child is in 'an interaction situation (collaboration), the child can only imitate that for which the maturing functions are present' (p. 53). In other words, if the child cannot imitate, then this would be an indication that the relevant mental functions had not yet formed. Vygotsky (1987) argues that '[t]o imitate, there must be some possibility of moving from what I can do to what I cannot' (p. 209). That is, cultural development of the child is supported not just through the tools and interactions found within a social situation, but through the relations between the child and the adult (where instruction moves ahead of development), as well as the child's own sense and meaning of the social situation.

It is through the imitation of everyday life experiences that children can investigate the rules that govern what they are expected to do or the social events they participate in or are surrounded by. For instance,

Vygotsky (1966) illustrates nicely, through an example taken from Sully, of how children investigate the rules governing the concept of 'sisterhood'. Vygotsky (1966) gives the example of two children who in real life are sisters and who pretend to be sisters in their play. To play at being sisters, they must follow the rules of how sisters interact together and through this they make conscious the concept of sisterhood. Through playing out the rules governing sisterhood they develop a deeper understanding of sisterhood. This conceptualisation can also be seen in the following play vignette taken from a study of play (see Fleer, 2009a, for methodological details), where two pre-school children are manipulating plastic dinosaurs that have been placed in a water trolley by their teacher. The trolley is half-filled with water, and the children have put into the water trolley a series of 30 cm square pieces of cellophane.

> *Jamie drapes a piece of wet cellophane onto the edge of the water trolley as he says: 'Now I make another home'. The other child asks: 'How many homes are you having?' The children take all of the cellophane pieces and drape them over the edge of the trolley, and discuss the number of homes in relation to the number of pieces of cellophane. Jamie announces: 'You're sleeping over'. This is accepted by the other child. Jamie asks, 'You want your blanket?' (referring to the cellophane pieces). This is accepted, and a dinosaur is placed on top of one of the pieces of cellophane. As Jamie looks at the dinosaur placed on the cellophane, he says: 'Now I am sleeping and you are sleeping'. 'You remember the stars?' The child responds: 'Yeah'. Jamie then announces, 'You going to bed'. This is rejected, as the child moves off saying 'I am going to take my dinosaur'. At this moment, the teacher walks past and asks: 'What's happening to the cellophane Jamie?' No response is made by Jamie, and the teacher moves on.* (Video observation of rural pre-school, August 1, morning)

In this play vignette we see Jamie and his play partner imitating the actions associated with having a 'sleep-over'. In the first instance, Jamie establishes the play where the idea of a home is created, and where blankets act as a placeholder for the game of 'sleeping over'. In this play, the idea of a bedtime, the use of blankets, and looking at the stars in the night sky collectively signal real-life experiences that both Jamie and the other child imitate in their game of a 'sleep-over'.

Vygotsky (1966) argued that '[w]hat passes unnoticed by the child in real life becomes a rule of behavior in play' (p. 9). This is a central idea in Vygotsky's writings on play and helps to explain the significance of his definition of imitation in children's play. For example, the imaginary situation created by Jamie of 'sleeping over' contains rules of behaviour, such as 'going to bed'. Jamie can imagine himself in the 'sleep-over' using the rules surrounding 'bed-time' in his play. Vygotsky (1966) suggests that only 'actions which fit these rules are acceptable to the play situation' (p. 9). Jamie and the other player must follow these rules if the game is to progress. The rules associated with a 'sleep-over' become important within the imaginary situation.

Vygotsky (1966) argues that 'whenever there is an imaginary situation in play there are rules. Not rules which are formulated in advance and which change during the course of the game, but rules stemming from the imaginary situation'. In the play, Jamie foregrounded the rules when he announced 'bed-time'. In this example of a 'sleep-over', Jamie and his play partner played out a 'sleep-over', making conscious the everyday practices and social rituals associated with this event. Vygotsky (1966) states that 'as soon as the game is regulated by certain rules, a number of actual possibilities for action are ruled out' (p. 10). In this play, Jamie's experience with a 'sleep-over' and the other child's experience of 'bed-time' were imitated, and the rules that underpin these real experiences were being examined through the dinosaurs acting out these rules of everyday life. Most research into children's play has not drawn upon these Vygotskian concepts. Imitation and the specific theory of play that was put forward by Vygotsky provide for quite a different kind of analysis of children's everyday play activity. In the next section, we examine imitation in play in relation to the concept of motives.

THE RELATION BETWEEN IMITATION AND MOTIVES IN CHILDREN'S PLAY

Elkonin (2005b) examined the origins, development and decline of play activities among children. In his historical research, Elkonin (2005b) has shown that 'as younger children become more and more cut off from joint work activities with adults, the developmental significance of the advanced role-playing forms of play increases' (p. 32). He suggested that in the anthropological studies of communities, the reported absence of children's role-playing could be attributed to the special position of children in society. That is, children did not find it necessary to play out scenes from everyday life, imitate the successful return of hunters, the ceremonies and dances valued within a community, simply because children actively participated in everyday life and did not have to imagine what adults were doing or pretend to experience these events through role-play only.

Elkonin (2005c) suggests that 'children are not exploited, rather their work is perceived as the satisfaction for a natural, social need' (p. 68).

Elkonin argues that historically a whole family unit performed the work of producing food, for example, as seen in agricultural food production. This kind of work originally only required simple tools and labour, such as digging with sticks and planting with hands. Children could participate in these kinds of agricultural activities in meaningful and productive ways, where their contributions helped to sustain the family unit or small collective community. Even the youngest mobile child within a community could contribute to food production.

However, in the transition to higher forms of production through the invention of new technologies, farming, hunting and fishing techniques and animal husbandry, Elkonin (2005c) argues that 'a new division of labor appeared in society … [and] … [c]hildren stopped taking direct part in complex forms of work' (p. 69). Children needed more strength and skill, and extended periods of training/practising in the use of tools and techniques. This resulted in an extended childhood period of development before they could meaningfully contribute to the sustainability of the community or family unit. In these communities children develop a motive for work. These ideas are represented in Figure 5.1.

Elkonin's findings have also been noted in more contemporary cross-cultural studies, such as mentioned by Rogoff (2003), where communities expect children to participate in meaningful ways in the life of the community in order to support the survival of the family unit. In Rogoff's (2003) research and extensive review of the literature, she found that children use real adult tools (e.g. toddlers use machetes to cut open coconuts, or use looms for weaving after a period of observation) in order to contribute productively to the family unit or community as a whole. Studies of children's play in these or similar communities have been undertaken by Gaskins (1999, 2007), Gaskins et al. (2007), Goncu (1999), and Goncu and Gaskins (2007), who have found that children are less likely to enter into role-play or fantasy play. Like Elkonin (2005b), they also noted the special place held by children within these communities, where children are positioned as active members of the community, contributing to the survival of the family unit. In these communities, researchers have noted that fantasy play is limited and role-play is infrequently observed or a rare occurrence amongst children. Here a motive for play is less prevalent.

In contemporary society, most Western communities have built institutional infrastructure where children of the same age are put together, such as pre-schools and classrooms. In the example of the two children playing

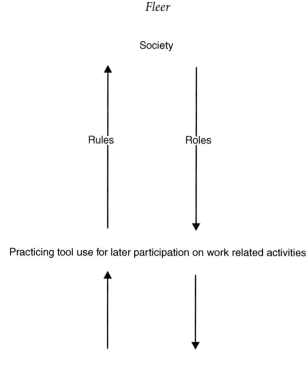

FIGURE 5.1. The development of a work motive.

the game of 'sleep-over' with their dinosaur figures, it is possible to see the implications of Elkonin's analysis in a contemporary context. The pre-school has been specifically designed to bring together groups of children who are aged four years, and the organisation of pre-schools in most countries foregrounds through the provision of play materials as well as through the teacher's beliefs about the purpose of pre-schools, opportunities for play. The pre-school centre has been organised to maximise opportunities for children to find and use materials for their play. Play materials are there for both role-play and for learning activity. In this particular example, the teacher has expressed her belief in the importance of not framing the play for the children, but rather allowing the materials to suggest possibilities for children's play (Fleer, 2009b).

In this particular community, there are many waterways, and fishing is an important source of employment for families, along with market gardening. If we are to accept Elkonin's position that everyday life provides the source of play for children, we would expect to see play with boats and market gardening to emerge in the children's play. As the pre-school children continued to manipulate the dinosaurs in the water trolley, they did not focus on the dinosaurs themselves, but rather began role-playing 'boating':

> *One child who is holding a magnifying glass that he had brought over to the water trolley says 'this can be an island'. He places the dinosaur on the magnifying glass. Jamie rejects this suggestion, stating that it is a boat game. Jamie continues to move the dinosaurs in and out of the water, singing, 'Sailing on a boat'. The first child says 'It fell out' as the dinosaur falls off the magnifying glass. The child picks up the magnifying glass and studies the dinosaurs. A third child joins the group and puts the cellophane into the water, announcing that it is an island. Jamie indicates he wishes to also have some cellophane. The first child passes him some wet cellophane (not the dry piece he has in his hand). Jamie says 'I want that one. I want a good one. Not that one'. The newcomer goes and finds more cellophane and drops in into the water. The children continue to move their dinosaurs in and out of the water, and onto cellophane and the magnifying glass, labelling these objects as islands, boats and beaches.*
>
> *As the third child continues to go inside to gather more cellophane for the boats in their play, the teacher intercepts his final trip by announcing that the quantity of cellophane cannot be used for just this activity, and she takes the bundle of clear cellophane and cuts off a small piece for the children to use.* (Video observation of rural pre-school, August 1, morning)

In examining this play vignette, it is clear that the everyday life experiences of the children had generated the theme for their play – boats and, as discussed earlier, the game of sleeping over. These play events are motivating because children can imitate what matters to them in everyday life. In both examples, the children were consciously examining the everyday rules for boating and having friends stay, displaying a strong motive for imitating everyday life. In most European heritage communities, it is unlikely that four-year-old children would have the opportunity to actually control a vessel on the waterways, or to make all the decisions surrounding when it is time to go to bed in a sleep-over. However, the children's 'boating' play could not progress because the children could not bring to the play an understanding or detailed observation of the sophisticated rules of boating prevalent within the community. Adult boating is simply outside of the children's experience. Because the teacher was excluded from the play, it was not possible to frame or extend the play with more meaning. The children's observations of boating in their community are peripheral, and imitation of boating is so crude that the rules of boating cannot be made conscious to the children in their play. That is, the circle of available imitation is so distant that it does not coincide with actual or proximal developmental possibilities. It is simply not possible in play for the children to fully explore the rules and roles associated with boating found in this particular rural and coastal community.

Observing everyday activities occurring in children's own lives generates action in relation to a powerful motive for participating in them, and in most European heritage communities, this translates into pretending to do these everyday events when at play (Bodrova, 2008). Karpov (2005), in citing Elkonin (1978), states that by the age of three years, children develop a strong interest in the world of social relations.

> The world of adults becomes very attractive for children, and they are looking forward to becoming a part of this world. In industrialised societies, however, children cannot fulfill their desire directly: They cannot be doctors or firefighters, that is why they 'penetrate' the world of adults by imitating and exploring social roles and relations in the course of sociodramatic play, Thus, *the motive of sociodramatic play is 'to act like an adult'*.
> (Elkonin, 1978, pp. 139–40; emphasis mine).

If children have limited experiences of what adults do during their working lives, it is difficult for them to imitate the roles and function of many aspects of what takes place within their community. Children in most European heritage communities attend childcare centres, pre-schools and schools, in which they have limited time to observe the adults around them. This contrasts with many children who are embedded within the full life of their communities (see Rogoff, 2003). With the exception of family-run businesses, employers usually do not encourage children to go to their parents' work sites. In addition to those institutions which have been specifically set up for children (e.g. pre-school and school), young children are often given child spaces at home, such as their own bedrooms, their own beds, their own play spaces, and so forth. The distance between the real world and the world of the child has stretched, and this means that children need to fill the void by imagining what the adult world is like, and their future role within it. Unlike traditional communities where children develop a motive for actual and active participation in the production of food (Elkonin, 2005b), children in contemporary Western communities display action in relation to a motive for play. The imagining of the adult world by the child has created different kinds of activity, and these activities suggest that these children have developed a play motive. This representation is shown in Figure 5.2.

With such a strong motive for participating in important life events noted by Rogoff (2003), it is not surprising that the children introduced in

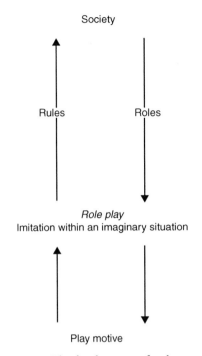

FIGURE 5.2. The development of a play motive.

an earlier episode of the dinosaurs-and-water play did not direct their play to focus on dinosaurs, as they had no experiences to bring to this kind of play. The plastic dinosaurs were irrelevant to the children's play. Vygotsky (1966) has shown that in play, children can and do give new meaning to objects they use in play. For instance, the cellophane became an island and the dinosaurs became boats. These imaginings allowed the children to move their crafts around the waterways inside the water trolley. Kravtsova (2008) posits that in this theorisation, the child in play is in the imaginary situation. In play, the child sees one thing (within their optical field) and can give the object a new meaning. For example, when a plastic dinosaur becomes a boat and a piece of cellophane becomes an island new meaning is given to the objects. The plastic dinosaurs were purchased by the pre-school teacher at great expense, yet their expression in the children's play was to act as a pivot for playing out meaningful everyday events observed in their local community, and not the world of dinosaurs.

Bodrova (2008) has argued that children in the communities she researches are frequently given replica toys of TV characters, or stylised dolls, such as Barbie and Ken, and intervention programs are needed to help children to move beyond using replica toys and towards being able to give new meaning to objects, so that the children's focus of attention centres on playing with the rules governing everyday life. Bodrova and Leong's (2001) research focuses specifically on developing children's play through the provision of rich experiences of everyday events or community life, such as taking the children to visit a hospital in order to learn about the roles and activities of a range of staff who work in these contexts. This experience is used as the basis for developing children's play (through adults and children co-constructing play plans). In essence, Bodrova and Leong's (2001) play development programs provide the adult support structures needed to help children to move from imagining 'hospital professionals at work' to gaining insights into the rules and activities adults engage in when working, so that children can meaningfully imitate community life in play and gain greater insights into the rules that govern community, work and everyday life.

In this section, it was shown that children have a strong motive for participating in important life events, but the leap between the competence of adults and the capacity of children has been stretched due to both the technological developments over time which have excluded their participation until adulthood and their isolation from the everyday life events as a result of the institutionalisation of children in childcare, pre-school and school – thus affording a *play motive*. In the following section, we examine the concept of motives in relation to the use of play materials in pre-school for supporting children's play, but also in relation to learning.

MOTIVES AS A CENTRAL CONCEPT IN PLAY

Sometimes some experiences set up by pre-school teachers do not easily connect with the children's everyday lives or allow them to act in relation to their motive. For example, in the same pre-school centre where the sleep-over play was occurring, the children were also introduced to a *mortar and pestle* for crushing fragrant leaves to create perfumed potion. The teacher intended for the children to learn science concepts in play by making fragrant potions (i.e. mixing substances), as well as to play with the materials and tools. Play was to drive the interaction situation. The objects were introduced to the children at the commencement of the pre-school session at group time, the materials were then put into trolleys in the outdoor area, and the teacher waited for the children to engage with the materials, as is shown in the following vignette:

> *All the pre-school children are seated on the floor facing their pre-school teacher who is perched on an adult chair. She has a bowl (to simulate*

a mortar) and a wooden pestle and a selection of fragrant leaves. She shows the children the tools and invites them to tell her what they could be used for. One boy suggests that the leaves could be put into the bowl. Another boy states that 'What you can do is put some soil in there (pointing to bowl), then you can put the leaf in there, and then you can put the stick (pestle) on and tie it up, and then you can make our very own little tree to tag on'. The teacher acknowledges this suggestion, inviting others to put forward their ideas. Eventually the teacher repeatedly hits the pestle into the bowl making a loud thumping sound, stating 'Oh look, I got some green out of it. You could probably make some more out of that'. As she says this, the children comment negatively about the smell that results.

The teacher then places the leaves, bowls and pestles into two trolleys into the outdoor areas for the children to use during their free playtime. A group of boys rush past the trolleys on their way to the shed. Individual girls wonder past on their way to the shed also. No interest is shown in the materials. Eventually, one boy looks into the trolley of leaves, picking one up and then dropping it. He then walks over to the second trolley and looks in. He then moves on.

Later, the teacher takes some of the material to an area close by the trolleys. She begins pounding the leaves into the bowl with the pestle. Two boys join her. One boy pours water over the leaves. He then watches on as another boy begins to pound the leaves using the same actions as the teacher. This boy asks, 'How does the water get that colour (green)?' The teacher replies, 'I don't know, how does it get that colour? Can you make some in it?' The child does not respond but continues to pound the leaves. The other child says, 'Yeah'. No other children join the group. Later a third boy joins the group (after the teacher has left) and he also stirs and pounds the leaves. In time, only one boy remains. No further interest is shown, and this child eventually moves on. (Video observation of rural pre-school, August 14, morning)

Even though the teacher introduced the materials to the children at group time, no participation in the activity was evident. The introduction of new materials into the pre-school environment as shown in the aforementioned example is not an uncommon approach in many European heritage communities. It is well understood that pre-schools actively support the play of children, and the introduction of new play materials usually does not involve a lot of teacher intervention or teacher control (see Fleer, 2010). However, many teachers also introduce new play materials with the view to setting up play opportunities which in themselves are thought to generate academic learning for children. In most pre-schools, teachers work with the assumption that play acts as the vehicle for framing learning. In the example of the leaf crushing, when the teacher sat and used the materials, some interest was generated and some children copied the activities of the teacher, but this involvement in the activity was not sustained. Soon after the teacher left, so too did the children. Even the teacher acknowledged this challenge:

> ... I'm thinking about what my issues are with science set ups is ... that we haven't really had enough time to actually sit and talk to the child or talk them through the activity ... children might explore it there and spend two seconds and then move on. (Interview with teacher G, August 18)

This example points to a major problem found throughout most Western literature on play, where play and learning are theoretically collapsed together, and teachers struggle to tease out their relations in practice and in education. This problem requires further thought. A deeper understanding of the concept of motives is important here and a further discussion of this concept is necessary if we are to understand the diversity of play activity found in this particular pre-school (but also many other pre-schools which support the idea of free play).

It is acknowledged that there are substantial definitions and usages of the concept of motives (Viliunas, 2007). We will begin with the work of Leontiev (1978). Leontiev (1978) suggested that in Vygotsky's general collective meaning of activity, researchers must consider specific activities, 'each of which answers a definite need of the subject, is directed toward an object of this need, is extinguished as a result of its satisfaction, and is produced again perhaps in other, altogether changed conditions' (p. 62). The central idea in Leontiev's theory is that every activity is aroused in relation to motive and these motives do not arise from within, but rather are the objects of the material world. Stetsenko and Arievitch (2004) argue that what Leontiev 'wanted to achieve by introducing the notion of object-motive was to convey the idea that human activities are always aroused in relation to something objectively existing in the world, rather than by some event and occurrence in the hidden realm of mental processes or human souls' (p. 482). As such, motives are socially produced within the human world and 'an individual activity bears the birthmarks of and reflects these collaborative practices, never becoming completely isolated from the social processes that give rise to it' (Stetsenko & Arievitch, 2004, p. 487). Stetsenko and Arievitch (2004) suggest that although the positioning of motives outside of individuals seems counterintuitive, it is nevertheless a central and important concept in cultural-historical theory. As children grow, they 'increasingly enter into connection with historically established human experience, and come to know objective reality with increasing breadth and depth' (Leontiev & Luria, 2005, p. 47).

Motive defined in this way – as something generated through observing or participating in an activity – rather than as something that comes solely from within is a powerful concept for understanding play. However, this theorisation does not take account of the child's perspective. For instance, Hedegaard (2002) in researching school-age children has stated that 'it is important to integrate consideration about children's development of a learning motive' (p. 21). In the mortar-and-pestle play, the tools and the making of perfume were outside of the children's everyday experiences. The teacher indicated that she did not have the time to discuss the materials further with the children or consider how they might *develop a learning motive* for the activity she was introducing at group time or a *play motive* for stimulating interaction during play time in the centre. The children's motive was not realised through the materials provided or through the way the teacher introduced the activity to the children.

Hedegaard (2002) recommends that school-age children should be given 'tasks that motivate them to research activity so that a relation between the pupils' own problems and the problems of the subject area is created' (p. 21). In the mortar-and-pestle activity, the teacher had set this up to generate play activity with the materials, thinking this might develop a motive for children's participation in making perfume. This example illustrates the confusion that arises in early childhood education between a motive for learning and a motive for playing out everyday life events, where the latter will result in some form of learning. Hedegaard (2002) makes this distinction clear within the school context when she states that '[t]he learning motive thereby can become connected to subject-matter concepts, and on the other hand subject-matter concepts become the basis for the child development of a reflected and theoretical orientation to the world. The learning motive develops from the child's participation in teaching activity, *but the interest the children bring* to this teaching has to be a starting point for their development of motivation' (p. 21, emphasis mine). The development of a learning motive is different from the development of a play motive.

If we move beyond a reading of motives as being predominantly focussed on the activity and accept the definition of Hedegaard and Chaiklin (2005) where motivation and motives are conceptualised 'as the dynamic relation between person and practice' (p. 64), then we can analyse motives in play in new ways.

Hedegaard and Chaiklin (2005) argue that children develop motives primarily through participation in institutional practices. That is, a child can be so engrossed in and motivated by an activity introduced by the pre-school teacher, that they may decline an offer of snacks despite being hungry. This view of motives foregrounds the institutional perspective, but also the child's perspective. If we examine the perfume-making activity from the child's perspective, we can see that the materials were introduced as new tools (mortar and pestle) at group time, with resources not usually associated with their use (fragrant leaves from flower garden). The children had difficulty with providing an explanation of what the tools might be used for, and they certainly could not work out what the teacher had in mind (making perfume). Even with the teacher's explicit modelling of tool use at group time, and later during free play, no child was observed engaged with the materials in relation to perfume making. The children simply copied the actions of the teacher. They had no social context to draw upon to make meaning of their actions. The children's activities did not move beyond copying the teacher's modelled actions. The teacher did not make a connection with the children's prior experiences of perfumes or fragrant leaves. There was also no framing of the materials around a purpose – to extract scented oil from the leaves – so that the reason for the tools could be understood. When the children's perspective is considered, it is possible to see that the materials provided by the teacher were disembedded from a social context and children's real-world experiences. The materials and the teacher's modelling did not provide a way for children to act in relation to their play motive or contribute to developing a motive for learning.

The teacher saw her role as providing the materials to afford play opportunities. If we accept Hedegaard and Chaiklin's (2005) conception of motives as the 'dynamic relation between person and practice' (p. 64), then we see that the relations *between* the child and the social environment is critical for generating actions in relation to a motive. Had the teacher introduced the idea of making perfume, this would have constituted a socially framed way of thinking about the objects the teacher introduced, and a real connection between the child and the social environment would have been established, developing a play motive for those who found this interesting. Capitalising upon children's motive for play is possible by teachers, but the selection and framing of materials must be motivating for children. This representation is shown in Figure 5.3, where a play motive is embedded within the processes for developing a learning motive.

There is no guarantee that children will actively seek out discipline knowledge within a play context. However, if the activity introduced by the pre-school teacher is to progress, and children are to learn academic discipline knowledge from their participation in the pre-school activities (if this is

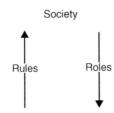

Society

Rules Roles

Motivation – Teaching practices connected with children's experiences/interests

Role play – Imitation within an imaginary situation

Play motive

Learning *school discipline knowledge with the purpose of expanding play*

Rules Roles

Learning motive
for later participation in work

FIGURE 5.3. The relations between play motives and learning motives in pre-school practice.

the societal goal for pre-school education), then the teacher must do more than simply provide materials for the children to use. When the activity is motivating and connected to the children's interests and experiences, children are likely to engage with the materials in play. When the materials are introduced with a sense of purpose (or problem formulation), it becomes possible for the children to know what to do with the materials and to be motivated to engage with discipline knowledge for expanding their play or for solving the problem. When a teacher draws upon a maturational theory of child development where play is viewed as naturally unfolding within the child, the teacher's role is minimised. No thought is given to how to develop a motive for play or give purpose for engaging with discipline knowledge. This view of play and child development does not position the teacher as taking an active role in relation to motivation and motives for play and for learning. We can now see through this kind of analysis of the mortar-and-pestle activity, and the previous boating play, that the cultural-historical concept of motives helps us to understand better why some activities are successful in pre-school programs and others are not. The relations between play motives and learning motives in pre-school practice must be actively contemplated by the pre-school teacher if the learning outcomes that are now valued within many European heritage communities are to be realised in early childhood education.

SUMMARY

The psychological concepts of 'motives' (Hedegaard, 2002; Hedegaard & Chaiklin, 2005), 'imitation' (Vygotsky, 1987) and 'rules' (Vygotsky, 1966) were discussed in this chapter in relation to young children's play activity. The play of children from one pre-school within Australia was examined, and it was shown that the concept of motives was useful for analysing the multiple ways children played at the centre. Understanding the concept of motives can help with interpreting the use of play materials in pre-school and their role and function in play. Through these kinds of analyses, a different theoretical reading of play emerges, and greater insights can be gained into those pedagogical practices which dominate early childhood education.

ACKNOWLEDGEMENTS

I acknowledge the important contribution that Professors Mariane Hedegaard, Elena Kravtsova and Gennady Kravtsov have made to my own work through sharing with me their research and generously discussing theoretical ideas which have informed my own thinking. Further, an important motive to improve the theoretical discussions within this work resulted from the challenging questions posed to me by Seth Chaiklin. I acknowledge the Australian Research Council (Discovery Grant) which funded the research cited in this chapter, and I thank Avis Ridgway for acting as a senior research assistant on this project.

REFERENCES

Bodrova, E. (2008). Make-believe play versus academic skills: A Vygotskian approach to today's dilemma of early childhood education. *European Early Childhood Education Research Journal, 16*(3), 357–369.

Bodrova, E., & Leong, D. J. (2001). *Tools of the mind: A case study of implementing the Vygotskian approach in American early childhood and primary classrooms.* Innodata Monographs – 7. Geneva: UNESCO, International Bureau of Education.

Brock, A. (2009). Curriculum and pedagogy of play: A multitude of perspectives? In A. Brock, S. Dodds, P. Jarvis, & Y. Ousoga (Eds.), *Perspectives on play. Learning for life* (pp. 67–93). Harlow: Pearson Longman.

Brock, A., Dodds, S., Jarvis, P., & Ousoga, Y. (Eds.) (2009). *Perspectives on play. Learning for life*. Harlow: Pearson Longman.

Chaiklin, S. (2003). The zone of proximal development in Vygotsky's analysis of learning and instruction. In A. Kozulin, B. Gindis, V. S. Ageyev, & S. M. Miller (Eds.), *Vygotsky's educational theory in cultural context* (pp. 39–64). Cambridge: Cambridge University Press.

Ebbeck, M., & Waniganayake, M. (Eds.) (2010). *Play in early childhood education. Learning in diverse contexts*. Melbourne: Oxford University Press.

Elkonin, D. B. (1978). *Psikhologiya igry (Psychology of play)*. Moscow: Pedagogika.

  (2005a). The psychology of play. *Journal of Russian and East European Psychology*, 43(1), 11–21.

  (2005b). The subject of our research: The developed form of play. *Journal of Russian and East European Psychology*, 43(1), 22–48.

  (2005c). On the historical origin of role play. *Journal of Russian and East European Psychology*, 43(1), 49–89.

Fleer, M. (2009a). Understanding the dialectical relations between everyday concepts and scientific concepts within play-based programs. *Research in Science Education*, 39(2), 281–306.

  (2009b). Supporting conceptual consciousness or learning in a roundabout way. *International Journal of Science Education*, 31(8), 1069–1090.

  (2010). *Early learning and development: Cultural-historical concepts in play*. Cambridge: Cambridge University Press.

Garvey, C. (1977). *Play*. Cambridge, MA: Harvard University Press.

Gaskins, S. (1999). Children's daily lives in a Mayan village: A case study of culturally constructed roles and activities. In A. Goncu (Ed.), *Children's engagement in the world: Sociocultural perspectives* (pp. 25–61). Cambridge: Cambridge University Press.

  (2007). The cultural relativity of Vygotsky's theory of play. Paper presented at the Invited Symposium on Play and Culture. Seville: International Society of Cultural Activity Research.

Gaskins, S., Haight, W., & Lancy, D. F. (2007). The cultural construction of play. In A. Goncu & S. Gaskins (Eds.), *Play and development. Evolutionary, sociocultural, and functional perspectives* (pp. 179–202). New York: Lawrence Erlbaum.

Goncu, A. (Ed.) (1999). *Children's engagement in the world. Sociocultural perspectives*. Cambridge: Cambridge University Press.

Goncu, A., & Gaskins, S. (Eds.) (2007). *Play and development. Evolutionary, sociocultural, and functional perspectives*. New York: Lawrence Erlbaum.

Hedegaard, M. (2002). *Learning and child development: A cultural-historical study*. Aarhus: Aarhus University Press.

Hedegaard, M., & Chaiklin, S. (2005). *Radical-local teaching and learning: A cultural-historical approach*. Aarhus: Aarhus University Press.

Karpov, Y. V. (2005). *The neo-Vygotskian approach to child development*. New York: Cambridge University Press.

Kravtsova, E. E. (2008). Zone of potential development and subject positioning. Paper presented at Vygotsky symposium, Monash University, Peninsula campus, December 17.

Leontiev, A. N. (1978). *Activity, consciousness and personality*. Englewood Cliffs, NJ: Prentice Hall.

Leontiev, A. N., & Luria, A. R. (2005). The problem of the development of the intellect and learning in human psychology. *Journal of Russian and East European Psychology*, 43(4), 34–47.

Organisation for Economic Co-operation and Development (OECD) (2006). *Starting strong II. Early childhood education and care*. Paris: Organisation for Economic Co-operation and Development.

Rogoff, B. (2003). *The cultural nature of human development*. Oxford: Oxford University Press.

Smilansky, S. (1968). *The effects of sociodramatic play on disadvantaged pre-school children*. New York: Wiley.

Stetsenko, A., & Arievitch, I. M. (2004). The self in cultural-historical activity theory. Reclaiming the unity of social and individual dimensions of human development. *Theory and Psychology*, 14(4), 475–503.

Viliunas, V. (2007). Promising problems and general characteristics of motivation. *Journal of Russian and East European Psychology*, 45(5), 36–83.

Vygotsky, L. S. (1966). Play and its role in the mental development of the child. *Voprosy Psikhologii*, 12(6), 62–76.

    (1987). Lecturers in psychology. In R. W. Rieber & A. S. Carton (Eds.), *The collected works of L. S. Vygotsky, vol. 1, Problems of general psychology*, trans. by N. Minick (pp. 289–358). New York: Plenum Press.

    (1997a). Problems of the theory and history of psychology. In R. W. Rieber & J. Wollock (Eds.), *The collected works of L. S. Vygotsky, vol. 3*, trans. by R. van der Veer. New York: Plenum Press.

    (1997b). The history of the development of higher mental functions. In Robert W. Rieber (Ed.), *The collected works of L. S. Vygotsky, vol. 4*, trans. by Marie J. Hall. New York: Plenum Press.

Vygotsky, L. S. (1998). Child psychology. In Robert W. Rieber (Ed.), *The collected works of L. S. Vygotsky, vol. 5*, trans. by M. J. Hall. New York: Kluwer Academic and Plenum Publishers).

Wood, E., & Attfield, J. (2005). *Play, learning and the early childhood curriculum* (2nd ed.). London: Paul Chapman.

6

Developing Motivation through Peer Interaction: A Cross-Cultural Analysis

JOSE SANCHEZ MEDINA AND VIRGINIA MARTINEZ

This chapter focuses on how peer interactions in play constitute a setting which contributes to the children's acquisition of motives. We also argue that the study of peer interactions can shed light on two gaps which persist in the explanation of psychological development within the cultural-historical theory (Vygotsky, 1978; Wertsch, 1985). The first is that, although this theoretical approach has placed great emphasis on the social and cultural construction of psychological development, in this construction the role of adults such as caregivers and teachers is highlighted and that of peers has been neglected. The adults are seen as holding the keys to the cultural adult world, organising the interactions and regulating children's behaviours in ways which give access to the cultural system of values and cultural norms. The second gap is, as Stetsenko and Arievitch (2004) point out, that although the cultural-historical theory recognises the active role of individuals in the appropriation of tools and systems of motives and cultural values, it has paid much less attention to the active role of individuals in creating and changing culture itself. Hedegaard (2005, 2008) has shown that the child is not a passive participant in these exchanges. The position, the way of behaving, and the degree of engagement of children in everyday practices can transform the practices substantially, playing a leading role in how these practices are developed. By focusing on peer interaction without adult direct supervision, we are able to analyse the active role of children acting in a setting in which they take over the values and norms of the adult world.

To illustrate this argumentation, we present a research on peer interaction in two different cultures. We will use the Corsaro's (1997) concept of *peer-cultures* to analyse how children create and recreate the adult cultures in their interactions. The distinction between individualistic and collectivist cultures will be the backbone on which we will build our argument.

Based on observational studies of pre-schoolers' behaviour during free playtime at school, we show that the way children play and resolve their conflicts reflects and recreates the society's motive system. We argue that peer interactions are a distinctive setting for socialisation and development in which children acquire the motives to act in relation to their adult world of reference.

CHILDREN'S SOCIALISATION

The process of children's socialisation has been studied in psychology from a number of different perspectives. Although various definitions of the concept can be found, most emphasise the acquisition of a set of mental skills, both communicative and cognitive, which include motives, values and social norms that allow children to establish social relationships with the rest of the members of their culture or social group.

The debates generated around the concept of socialisation reflect the main paradigmatic discussions over human development. In a general sense, there are two different approaches to this subject. On the one hand, individualistic perspectives propose that children acquire, through their development, a set of cognitive abilities which allow them to interact with other human beings. In this case, the possibilities of socialisation are limited by the child's mental development. Alternatively, more socially oriented approaches emphasise the role of the social processes as generators of consciousness and human mind. Proponents of this view argue that from birth, children participate in social activities which allow them to acquire motives and values systems which, over time, promote their psychological development.

A major contributor to this socially oriented account, influencing, among others, Bruner, Cole and Wertsch, was Lev S. Vygotsky. The core idea of his perspective is that individual psychological functioning has a social origin, and his social dimension can be analysed from two different planes: the institutional and the interpersonal plane. If we focus on the communicative processes and the skills required to achieve a successful exchange, we emphasise the interpersonal dimension of the interaction. However, this interaction does not take place *in vacuo*. It occurs within activities such as work, school, play and so forth. The two planes are linked because the general institutional framework will condition the way the interchange takes place and it always will be present (see Hedegaard, this volume). Our premise is that institutional settings provide children with sets of competences which influence interpersonal exchanges, and that these competences reflect the distinctive motives which arise in and give shape to the cultures in which the children are growing up.

Vygotsky referred to internalisation processes to explain how social interaction is transformed into psychological functioning: 'The transformation of an interpersonal process into an intrapersonal one is the result of a long series of developmental events. The process being transformed continues to exist and to change as an external form of activity for a long time before definitively turning inward' (Vygotsky, 1978, p. 57).

Following Wertsch (Wertsch, 1985; Wertsch & Stone, 1985), two elements characterise the Vygotskian concept of internalisation. The first is that the inner plane has its origin in the external plane or the plane of the social interactions. That genetic relation that Vygotsky establishes between the external-social plane and the internal-psychological plane is critical. As Zinchenko (1985) pointed out, the relationship between both planes is not a mere similarity or equality. If that were the case, the idea of internalisation would lack of all theoretical value, because it would be enough to study the plane of the social relations to know the structure and dynamics of the psychological functioning.

The second characterising element of the internalisation process is the role played by semiotic tools in the mediation of social and individual processes. Children learn to use instruments in interaction with other members of their cultural groups. As children become more expert in the use of these instruments, they take control on them, and as part of their ontogenetic development each child uses them in an individual and autonomous way.

In terms of socialisation processes, a Vygotskian analysis implies that children, from the moment they establish exchanges with other members of their cultures, are showing socialised behaviour (Fogel, 1993). The key question then is not the difference between socialised and not socialised behaviour, but the continuity between hetero-regulated, inter-psychological behaviour and independent, auto-regulated intra-psychological one. Along the developmental process, children participate in a higher number of cultural activities, gaining the ability to be more autonomous. At first, this participation is guided by experienced members, but as children grow they will take progressively more responsibility and their acts will become more individual in the sense of being more independent or auto-regulated (Rogoff, 1990, 2004). The processes of socialisation and individuation are, at some extent, comparable, as both consist of the mastering of culturally suitable forms of behaving.

Nonetheless, the idea of socialisation as a dimension of internalisation processes has certain limitations which can be highlighted. Firstly, the emphasis on the cognitive dimension of the process ignores some elements linked to emotional and motivational development. It seems that socialisation is mainly a matter of gaining cognitive skills which allow children to behave properly within the sphere of cultural activities. Secondly, social interaction and participation in practices are only taken into consideration as far as they promote individual development. This failure to recognise that socialisation processes possess a series of characteristics and peculiarities which warrant direct study is problematic. In Corsaro's words:

> Although these developments are clearly in the right direction, they still cling to what Harré (1986) referred as 'the doctrine of individualism'. For example, interpersonal alignments (e.g. adult-child versus peers) are contrasted to show how they affect individual development differentially. This work, however, does not consider seriously how interpersonal relations reflect cultural systems, or how children, through their participation in communicative events, become part of these interpersonal relations and cultural patterns and reproduce them collectively. (Corsaro, 1992, p. 161)

THE ROLE OF PEER INTERACTION IN THE SOCIALISATION PROCESS

Adults have usually been considered the main agents of children socialisation. They have been seen as better able to understand and adapt to children interests and needs, and to be more expert in managing cultural norms and demands. In that way, adults have been considered the perfect support for a child's socialisation process (Hartup, 1983; Ross & Rogers, 1990).

Nevertheless, in recent years, many authors have given more importance to the role of peers in the process of child development (see the review of Rubin, Bukowsky, & Parker, 1998). Nowadays peers are considered as another essential force in the socialisation process, with a great number of articles being published which highlight the enriching and specific effect of peer interactions in development of children (Asher & Coie, 1990; Coie & Dodge, 1998; Damon, 1994; Hartup, 1990).

Peer interactions are constituted by definition as symmetric relationships. That means that participants assume similar roles in the interactions. Skills, abilities and knowledge are similar. None of them is situated in a privileged position over the rest, and their interactions are based on the joint construction of activities. The role of guide disappears and children must take the responsibility for maintaining the relationship themselves. All these facts endow peer interactions with a set of features which give them a specific worth during child development. In peer interactions, children have the opportunity to negotiate rules and roles, to be engaging in conflicts as equals, and to exert control over their social world for themselves (Rubin, 1986). In peer interactions, children are allowed to act and express their preferences freely, away from the feeling of having to accept the proposals of others because they have greater life experience (Rogoff, 1995). In these interactions, children learn to move within a framework of mutual respect in which the principle of obedience is not the rule. They must generate solutions to their own problems, give opinions about the activities of others and share with less competent participants what they have learned previously. Children collaborate with others to regulate and model behaviours by reinforcing those which they consider appropriate and penalizing or ignoring those that fall short of the standards of the interactive setting (Rubin et al., 1998). In short, peer interaction settings offer children their solo confrontations with the social world, making these settings and children's interactions within them worthy of detailed study.

However, this autonomy of interaction and the absence of a regulatory adult presence do not turn peer interaction in a *culture-free* phenomenon. Numerous studies have shown that peer interactions have a strong cultural structure and content. As Corsaro pointed out (1986, 1988, 1997; Corsaro & Rizzo, 1988; Corsaro & Schwarz, 1991), during school age, especially during playtime on the playground, children are engaged in peer interaction with proper dynamics, creating authentic *peer cultures*. These *peer cultures* reflect the 'children's common and continuous attempts to grasp and control a social order, which is first presented to them by the adults, but that later becomes their own reproduction' (Corsaro, 1988, p. 1). To talk about *peer cultures* implies then considering children as social beings who, through their interaction with other children, are active builders of their own social world as a re-creation of the adult one.

In this sense, children's interaction is relevant, not only because peers are the main agents of socialisation and development of cognitive, motivational and emotional skills and abilities, but also because children play an active role in re-creating the cultural norms and values of the adult culture. Through peer interaction children gather these cultural values and norms and transform them into motives that guide their actions.

The contextual-developmental perspective, proposed by Chen and colleagues (Chen, French, & Schneider, 2006), considers that 'social interaction processes serve to mediate cultural influence on human development' (Chen & French, 2008, p. 593), focusing on how children's participation in interactions are guided by cultural norms and values which, at the same time, regulate individual behaviour and development. Peer interaction as a social process is then bi-directional in its influence, whilst at the same time it is transactional in its nature (Chen & French, 2008).

In the next section the aim is to show how children's behaviour differs according to the cultural values of their socio-cultural reference framework. These cultural values and norms are transformed by children in motives that are going to guide them to interact with peers in ways that are close to those cultural orientations.

PEER INTERACTION AS LINK BETWEEN
CULTURE AND MOTIVES

Some examples are presented here to illustrate how children's interactions with each other offer a research setting that can link culture and individual behaviour (Hinde, 1987), and how peer interactions play an important role as a cultural influence on individual motives to act.

Hold-Cavell, Attili and Schleidt (1986) studied pre-schoolers from Italy and Germany. The results showed that Italian pre-schoolers more frequently revealed behaviour relating to physical contact. German pre-schoolers displayed behaviour that implied more personal distance, with minimum physical contact. The authors established a distinction between *contact cultures* and *non-contact cultures*. Italian culture was considered a contact culture, where the collective functioning and the social cohesion were prioritised. German culture was included among non-contact cultures, conformed by individuals who preferred a more intimate personal space and displayed less permissiveness to the intrusions of others in their interactions. Farver and Howes (1988), in a similar study, analysed the social behaviour of North American and Indonesian children. The results showed that whereas in Indonesia, peers participated with a high frequency in mixed groups and with children of different ages, Americans did it in more homogeneous groups, both in terms of age and in sex. This behaviour reflected cultural priorities which, in the case of Indonesia, were linked to collective values related to, according to the authors, the predominance of a subsistence economy. In these settings parents had to spend almost all their time at work away from the family in order to get by, which forced children to become involved in behaviour including taking care of younger children. In contrast, North American child interaction was based on playful activities with peers of the same age, with individual preferences prevailing on the demands of social collaboration.

In another comparison, Corsaro (1992) and Corsaro and Rizzo (1988) studied the behaviour of Italian and North American pre-school children during playtime. In their analysis they identified common patterns, recurrent and predictable behaviour that they labelled *routines*. Some of these routines were shared by children of both cultures, whereas other appeared in only one of them. However, even if a routine appeared in both cultural settings, they were developed in a substantially different way. An example was the routine of protection of the interactive space, which was the behaviour that the children displayed when, once involved in a game with other peers, another child approached with the intention of joining the activity at hand. Children of both countries developed a series of behavioural patterns which were directed at protecting the interactive space from possible interferences, and they finished them by excluding or not admitting the child who tried to join in. In both scenes, this behaviour of exclusion appeared frequently, but the way in which it took place was substantially different. Among North American children, the control of interactive space occurred in an explicit way, denying inclusion in the activity to the child. Italian children sometimes did this but mostly accepted the incorporation of the new child in principle. However, at the same time, they imposed conditions of participation in the activity which were so restrictive that the child who wished to be integrated ended up rejecting the idea of entering the game.

These research programmes and others (see the article of Chen and French, 2008) show how children, through their interaction, create a social dynamic that suggests an active reproduction of the adult world. It seems that through participation in their play cultures, children learn motives and competences that allow them to act in specific settings full of rules, values and norms that limit their behaviour. Transcultural studies into peer interaction underline the special relevance that the collective setting of peer socialisation has in the acquisition of motives that impel children to act in a certain way when they interact with peers.

DEVELOPMENT OF MOTIVES IN PEER INTERACTION

A Study of Play and Conflicts in Pre-schoolers of Andalusia and The Netherlands

In order to analyse how the values relating to cultural setting of reference influence the way children play and how they manage the conflicts that arise during free-play activity, a study of free play of pre-schoolers from Andalusia (an autonomous region in southern Spain) and from The Netherlands was carried out. Our starting point was the differences between collective and individualistic cultures (Triandis, 1990; Triandis, Marin, Hui,

Lisansky, & Ottati, 1984). Here we were building on a well-established route to grasping the differences that appear when different children's developmental niches are analysed (Super & Harkness, 1986, 1997; see the review of Goudena and Vermande, 2002). The Netherlands is considered an individualist culture which belongs to the protestant Anglo-Saxon and Northern European cultural contexts, whereas Hispanic cultures, such as Andalusia, are mainly regarded as collective cultures (DeRosier & Kupersmidt, 1991; Triandis, 1990). In individualistic cultures, there is a prioritisation of individual objectives; individual rights are very important; the self is understood as a unique, autonomous and separated entity; personal initiative and competitiveness are highly valued; and their members are independent and with a marked emotional distance amongst each other. Collective cultures are more oriented to give priority to collective aims instead of particular ones; group duties and obligations prevail; the self is understood as a part of the whole; harmony and consensus prevail over individual opinion or position; and their members tend to act as interdependent individuals with high emotional closeness (Gudykunst & Bond, 1997; Kagitçibasi, 1997; Triandis, 1995).

Our objective was to obtain information about the motives which guide the children's acts in these different cultural settings when they are interacting with peers without the direct supervision of an adult. Taking the differences between individualism-collectivism into consideration, we expected that Andalusian children would be more motivated to act as a part of the social group than Dutch pre-schoolers, who we anticipated would defend their own interests and position rather than the group ones.

To examine this hypothesis, we carried out an observational study of the peer interactions of children attending to their first year in four schools in Andalusia and The Netherlands. Behaviour patterns were observed during the free time in the playground at school when they were free to act on their own without adults' directives. Adults were taking care of children but without direct participation in children's interactions, except if an unusual or threatening event took place.

First, play behaviour during playtime at school was analysed (Goudena & Sánchez, 1996). Then, the analysis was complemented through the observation of conflict behaviours (Martínez, Sánchez, & Goudena, 2010).

It is important to note that the playgrounds in each country had different physical organisations. In The Netherlands, some objects could be found in the playgrounds, such as wheels, construction blocks, some toys. In contrast, the Andalusian playgrounds did not have any objects, only some sport structures, such as goalposts or basketball hoops, that usually were not used by pre-schoolers.

Play Behaviour and Social Interaction during Playtime

The research into play behaviour studied forty-three Andalusian and thirty-seven Dutch pre-schoolers. Children were between four and five years old. The Rubin Observational Scale was adapted (Sánchez & Martínez, 1997) and used to analyse the behaviour during *play* and *not play* that preschoolers developed in the playtime. Play behaviour was classified according to its social and cognitive level. Behavioural patterns were observed by two trained observers.

Observations indicated that Dutch children showed preferences for functional or constructional play, games based essentially on the individual acting and manipulating the physical context, and tended to develop activities with a high individualistic component. Andalusian pre-schoolers were more frequently engaged in dramatic games and rule-based games, behaviour which involved more social contact and in many cases negotiation with other children. The size of the play group led to similar conclusions. Andalusian children tended to form groups comprised of four or more children, whereas Dutch children interacted mainly in dyads and, on a very few occasions, in groups of more than four children. There is no doubt that a pre-schooler needs to use different abilities to participate effectively in a large social group than to play with a particular partner. Certain individualism can be found in pair interaction: It is easier to negotiate and decide what to do and how to do it, with a minimum of disagreement. In contrast, in large groups, the collective sense of the activity and togetherness must be prioritised.

A general view of the data showed *socially oriented behaviours* in Andalusian pre-schoolers, not only because there was a greater social contact among them, but also because this contact was produced in a qualitatively different way. In the Dutch sample, the predominant behaviour was centred more on individual activities.

Conflict Management during Playtime

In a later study we employed conflict analysis as a tool to explore more deeply the internal dynamics of peer interaction in Dutch and Andalusian pre-school cultures. In this study the participants were sixty-four preschoolers – thirty-two Andalusian, and thirty-two Dutch – between the ages of four and five years. Behaviour patterns were on video-recorded, and the audio recording were made using remote microphones. Later, conflicts were coded by two observers trained in the category system.

Following Sheldon (1990), conflict was defined as 'an interaction which grows out of an opposition to a request for action, an assertion, or an action (…) and ends with a resolution or dissipation of conflict' (p. 8). To analyse conflict episodes in more detail, a coding system based on studies of Kinoshita, Saito and Matsunaga (1993) and Shantz and Shantz (1985) was elaborated. Using this category system, we distinguished three main phases of a conflict: issue, strategy and outcome. Issue refers to the origin of the conflict, and it could be caused by instrumental control (i.e. control of objects or space), by control of play behaviour or by control of non-play behaviour. Strategies refer mainly to the use of language in the conflict, that is, the use of verbal negotiation, disengagement, or coercion. Outcomes showed if agreement was reached (compromise and submission) or not (physical or social rupture).

Results showed significant differences between Andalusian and Dutch samples in the three categories. Relating to the issues or causes of conflicts, data showed that Andalusian pre-schoolers tended to confront their partners when trying to control the social space or the play behaviour organisation. Dutch children started a conflict more frequently over the possession of objects or for the control of a physical space. The strategies were different as well. Even though the use of directive strategies was relatively frequent in both settings, possibly due to the age of the children (Kolominskii & Zhiznevskii, 1992; Phinney, 1986), the use of non-directive strategies marked important differences between them. The use of non-directive strategies, that involved argumentation and negotiation with partners, was more frequent among children from Andalusia than among those from The Netherlands. Dutch children more often used a combination of directive and non-directive strategies – that is, they combined the use of argumentation with orders and impositions, habitually directed towards maintaining or imposing their own perspective. This differential use of strategies was found by Eisenberg and Garvey (1981) to be responsible for the outcome of the conflict. When the strategy employed was pure opposition and rejection, disruption of the interaction was almost inevitable. In contrast, when the children displayed arguments and tried not to impose their point of view, the conflict was resolved more frequently without disruption. In Andalusia, pre-schoolers solved their conflicts by reaching an agreement, either as a compromise or submission of one of the partners. Among Dutch pre-schoolers, most of their conflicts resulted in the rupture of the relationship. This rupture was usually evidenced by the physical removal of one of the children, or by a change of activity.

Of course we do not assume that both cultural contexts are homogeneous. In our study we analysed the ways to resolve conflicts on the basis of gender and school context (rural and urban). Although significant differences in terms of these variables were founded, the country showed a greater explanatory power of differences in the ways pre-schoolers managed the observed conflicts.

In general, these analyses tell us how children, in their conflicts, reflected the values that organised their respective cultures. We suggest that children interiorised these and thus those became transformed into motives that organised and guided their disagreements and negotiations.

We now move to a more detailed conflict analysis in order to discuss the role of *being together* as an action motive in the Andalusian sample, versus *to keeping one's own position* as the main motive in Dutch pre-schoolers.

A Micro-Analysis of the Conflict

These examples of conflicts aim to illustrate how children act as they follow the motives that reflect the cultures in which they were raised. Pre-schoolers from The Netherlands managed their conflicts by looking for the goal of assuring individual independence, whereas Andalusian children looked for the goal of keeping the interaction running.

The following episodes illustrate conflicts, strategies and outcomes that were characteristic of each cultural setting.

Episode 1.

Child: Wietse, Dutch boy. Issue: object control; Outcome: physical rupture

1. A boy (Thijs; (T)) is playing with other children. They are playing with some blocks. Wietse (W) approaches the group and takes one of the blocks.
2. T: *No, you must not take that* (tries to take away the block that W has just taken)
3. W: *Why not?* (he holds the block out of reach from T)
4. T: *That's for* (me).... (now T takes the block and grabs it from the hands of W)
5. T continues playing and W turns his back to the group and walks away.

Episode 2.

Child: Arjan, Dutch boy. Issue: object control; Outcome: physical rupture

1. Arjan (A) and Martijn (M) are making a road in the sand. With the aid of a container, M marks the limits of the road.

2. (A. walks to M.) A: *May I use it? (referring to the container)*
3. M: *What?*
4. A: *May I use it?*
5. M: *No!!!*
6. A walks away from M.

These episodes illustrate types of conflicts, strategies and outcomes which are commonplace among children from The Netherlands. The control of objects was the cause which initiated both conflicts. Conflict 1 arose because a child, who was not integrated into the activity at hand, tried to take part in it by sharing the objects of play (taking a block). The new peer altered the activity and therefore required an adjustment in the behaviour of the other children. The reaction of the rest of the children was to continue their activity without any changes, rejecting the possibility of the other child joining in with them. The physical rupture was then the solution to the conflict. A similar situation was illustrated in episode 2. In this case, the conflict arose as a dispute between two children who were cooperating in the same activity (drawing a roadway on the sand) about the control of an object. Although the children were engaged in the same activity, and the activity was at that moment underway, the dispute over the object provoked a very similar resolution: The children's negative reaction occasioned the rupture of the interaction. There was no negotiation; it seemed as if each child respected the other child's opinion and left the discussion. In this example, children showed that maintaining the game already underway was less relevant to them than to respect the other's decision. The motive to act is to keep one's own position. This corresponds to prevailing values from individual cultures which demand certain competences of children, that finally emerge as motives to act.

Episode 3.

Child: Ana Cecilia. Andalusian girl. Issue: object/place control; Outcome: agreement

1. Isabel and Ana Cecilia are playing with a doll that Isabel has. Ana Cecilia attempts to grab the doll.
2. Ana Cecilia: *Give it to me now.*
3. Isabel doesn't give it to her, but takes it, lifting it.
4. Ana Cecilia (leaves, feeling upset): *Well, I won't play.*
5. Isabel: *Well, then I will play by myself then.*
   –
6. (… They both go into a flower bed)
7. Isabel: *Eh, here I am. Ana, I am not going to move.*
8. Ana Cecilia: *Even though I have given you a pile of peanuts before… And even though you have been there for ages…*

9. Isabel: *I haven't been here for ages. I have just been here a minute...*
10. Isabel: *Well ... I'm taking it.* (Gives Ana Cecilia the doll and they begin to talk and play with the doll ...)

Episode 4.

Child: Maria. Andalusian girl. Issue: behaviour control; Outcome: agreement

1. Maria (M) and Ana Cecilia (AC) are deciding whether to play a game of Sleeping Beauty or Snow White.
2. AC: *I want to play Snow White.*
3. M: *Well ... you play, not me.*
4. M. (Lets go of AC and leaves upset).
   –
5. AC: (Goes after her). *Well ... al right Maria* (again takes her by the hand).
6. M: *Do you want to play a game of Clowns?*
7. AC: *No, I don't feel like it.*
8. M. Begins to act silly, imitating a clown and they both end up laughing together.

Episodes 3 and 4 illustrated typical conflicts that occurred between children in Andalusia. Episode 3 showed a conflict brought about by the control of an object (a doll) between two girls. Episode 4 was initiated because of the behaviour control regarding which game to play. In both cases, the conflict started, and after a while there was a temporary rupture, as if they were done, but really the conflict did not finish. The negotiation continued and the interaction kept running. Although there was a brief attempt at rupture, the children remained in the same physical space, very close to one another. They continued their verbal interaction almost without any temporary delay, and a new negotiation started. These situations allowed children to maintain the interaction and guided the girls towards solving the problem. In episode 3, girls resolved the conflict by a way of a compromise, sharing the object and play space. In episode 4, the retreat seemed more like a strategy adopted to put pressure on the opponent rather than an attempt to disrupt the relationship. The girl who began the retreat succeeded in making the other girls react in a way which allowed them to continue the interaction.

Considering only the first part of the conflicts, there are not many differences between the Dutch children's conflicts. The conflicts finished quite fast because of a difference in the individual point of view, and the end of the conflict was real. Children separated and started a new activity with other children. In the Andalusian conflicts, although everything suggests initially that rupture was the outcome of the episode, there was not a real end. The girls explicitly showed their annoyance with each other because of the difference in their opinions; nonetheless, that did not end the interaction. The annoyance was not an outcome, but another strategy of negotiation used by both participants to convince the other. The girls introduced emotional components as strategies, and in none of the cases did the conflict end. They did not relinquish their position even if it meant capitulating from their own point of view. The motives which caused their acts are addressed at maintaining the group cohesiveness. Togetherness is a motive which moves them to initiate a negotiation where both parties are going to cede some of their interest. To maintain the interaction over the individual viewpoint corresponds with a value which is highlighted in collective cultures. To be together is a social demand for children and this demand is appropriated by them and transformed into children's own motives.

CONCLUSIONS

The data presented in this chapter show that peer interactions, even in early childhood, exhibit a marked cultural component. The way in which peer groups were organised, the type of activity they developed, and even the conflicts issues and the way of negotiating and resolving them reflected values and norms of the adult cultures in children's motives for interacting in play. Children re-built, in their acts, this world of reference. They re-created these values and norms conforming to a *peer culture* where those cultural issues play an important role as motives which guide and organise their own acts.

The participation of children in a cultural setting or activity is the key to understanding this process. We need to recognise the important role of peer interactions in child development. Adult participation is not a direct guide in this kind of interactions; instead, they participate in the organisation of *peer culture* in an indirect way. They organise the physical space where children interact. This organisation is an important key to guide the acts of children. In our studies, the playgrounds were physically different. Whereas in the Dutch playgrounds there were many objects for children to interact with, in the Andalusian ones there were no objects. In Andalusian culture, interpersonal relationships are prioritised and to learn to be together is an important aim of school. In contrast, in The Netherlands, objects are considered an important instrument for cognitive development. Their manipulation and the individual interaction with them is an objective in these schools. Different competences are demanded of children in relation to this physical organisation. Children learn to act prioritising specific values demanded by the adult culture of reference. These demands are interiorised by children, forming their own system of motives which organise and shape a particular way of acting.

In line with what many authors see as the prevailing social dynamics in collectivistic cultures (Kagitçibasi, 1997; Triandis, 1995), in Andalusia, the value of seeing themselves integrated into a group was more important than their individual interests and was the motive for children to organise their acts. The value of being together and maintaining the social relationship reflected the collective nature of many of the activities of adults in Andalusia. In contrast, The Netherlands pre-schoolers prioritised maintaining their own point of view and their own autonomy; their acts were guided by these aims and were seen as a motive for their activities. The children from The Netherlands demonstrated considerable independence and personal autonomy, in line with the characteristics of the adult world, that can be seen as a representative of an individualistic culture.

In sum, in this chapter it has been shown how peers can be considered as relevant agents in children development, with their interactions providing a relevant setting where they acquire motives to act in relation to the values and demands of the society. In peer interactions, children not only learn how to act, but also recreate a cultural order which will be part of the maintenance of the culture in the future.

REFERENCES

Asher, S. R., & Coie, J. D. (1990). *Peer rejection in childhood.* New York: Cambridge University Press.

Chen, X., & French, D. C. (2008). Children's social competence in cultural context. *Annual Review of Psychology, 59*, 591–616.

Chen, X., French, D. C., & Schneider, B. (2006). Culture and peer relations. In X. Chen, D. C. French, & B. Schneider (Eds.), *Peer relationships in cultural context* (pp. 3–20). New York: Cambridge University Press.

Coie, J. D., & Dodge, K. A. (1998). Aggression and antisocial behavior. In W. Damon (Series Ed.) & N. Eisenberg (Volume Ed.), *Handbook of child psychology. Social, emotional and personality development* (pp. 779–862). New York: Wiley.

Corsaro, W. A. (1986). Discourse processes within peer culture: From a constructivist to an interpretive approach to childhood socialization. In P. A. Adler & P. Adler (Eds.), *Sociological studies of child development* (pp. 81–101). Greenwich, CT: JAI Press.

(1988): Routines in the peer culture of American and Italian nursery school children. *Sociology of Education, 61*, 1–14.

(1992). Interpretive reproduction in children's peer cultures. *Social Psychological Quarterly, 55*(2), 160–177.

(1997). *The sociology of childhood.* Thousand Oaks, CA: Sage.

Corsaro, W. A., & Rizzo, T. A. (1988). Discussione and friendship: Socialization processes in the peer culture of Italian nursery school children. *American Sociological Review*, 53, 879–894.

Corsaro, W. A., & Schwarz, K. (1991). Peer play and socialization in two cultures. In B. Scales, M. Almy, A. Nicolopoulou, & S. Erwing-Tripp (Eds.), *Play and the social context of development in early care and education.* Early Childhood Series (pp. 234–254). New York: Teachers College Press.

Damon, W. (1994). Commentary to the paper of M. Verba. *Human Development*, 37, 140–142.

DeRosier, M. E., & Kupersmidt, J. B. (1991). Costa Rican children's perceptions of their social networks. *Developmental Psychology*, 27(4), 203–215.

Eisenberg, A. R., & Garvey, C. (1981). Children's use of verbal strategies in resolving conflicts. *Discourse Processes*, 4, 149–170.

Farver, J. A., & Howes, C. (1988). Cross-cultural differences in social interaction. a comparison of American and Indonesian children. *Journal of Cross-Cultural Psychology*, 19(2), 203–215.

Fogel, A. (1993). *Developing through relationships. Origins of communication, self, and culture.* Hertfordshire: Harvester Wheatsheaf.

Goudena, P. P., & Sánchez, J. A. (1996). Peer interaction in Andalucia and Holland: A comparative study. *Infancia y Aprendizaje*, 75, 49–58.

Goudena, P. P., & Vermande, M. M. (2002). A review of cross-cultural studies of observed peer interaction. *Early Child Development and Care*, 172(2), 141–151.

Gudykunst, W. B., & Bond, M. H. (1997). Intergroup relations across cultures. In J. W. Berry, M. H. Segall, & Ç. Kagitçibasi (Eds.). *Handbook of cross-cultural psychology. Vol. 3. Behavior and Applications* (pp. 119–161). Needham Heights, MA: Allyn & Bacon.

Hartup, W. W. (1983). Peer interaction and the behavioral development of the individual child. In W. Damon (Ed.), *Social personality development: Essays on the growth of the child* (pp. 103–196). New York: W.W. Norton & Company

(1990). Peer relationships and social skills in childhood: An international perspective. *Human Development*, 33(4–5), 221–224.

Hedegaard, M. (2005). Strategies for dealing with conflicts in value positions between home and school: Influences on ethnic minority students' development of motives and identity. *Culture Psychology*, 11(2), 187–205.

(2008). Children's learning through participation in institutional practice: A model from the perspective of cultural-historical psychology. In B. van Oers, W. Wardekker, E. Elbers, & R. Van der Weer (Eds.), *The transformation of learning. Advances in cultural-historical activity theory* (pp. 294–318). Cambridge: Cambridge University Press.

Hinde, R. A. (1987). *Individuals, relationships and culture.* Cambridge: Cambridge University Press.

Hold-Cavell, B. C. L., Attili, G., & Schleidt, M. (1986). A cross-cultural comparison of children's behavior during their first year in a preschool. *International Journal of Behavioral Development*, 9, 471–483.

Kagitçibasi, Ç. (1997). Individualism and collectivism. In J. W. Berry, M. H. Segall, & Ç. Kagitçibasi (Eds.), *Handbook of cross-cultural psychology.*

Vol. 3. Behavior and Applications (pp. 1–49). Needham Heights, MA: Allyn & Bacon.

Kinoshita, Y., Saito, K., & Matsunaga, A. (1993). Developmental changes in antecedents and outcomes of peer conflict among preschool children: A longitudinal study. *Japanese Psychology Research, 35*(2), 57–69.

Kolominskii, I. L., & Zhiznevskii, B. P. (1992). A sociopsychological analysis of conflict among children during play. *Journal of Russian and East European Psychology, 30*(5), 72–86.

Martínez-Lozano, V., Sánchez-Medina, J. A., & Goudena, P. P. (2010). A cross-cultural study of observed conflicts between young children. *Journal of Cross-Cultural Psychology*, first published on September 9, 2010 as doi:10.1177/0022022110381361.

Phinney, J. S. (1986). The structure of 5 years-olds' verbal quarrels with peers and siblings. *Journal of Genetic Psychology, 147*(1), 47–60.

Rogoff, B. (1990). *Apprenticeship in thinking: Cognitive development in social context.* New York: Oxford University Press.

   (1995). Observing sociocultural activity on three planes: Participatory appropriation, guided participation, and apprenticeship. In J. Wertsch, P. del Río, & A. Alvarez (Eds.), *Sociocultural studies of mind* (pp. 139–165). Cambridge: Cambridge University Press.

   (2004). *The cultural nature of human development.* New York: Oxford University Press.

Ross, D. D., & Rogers, D. L. (1990). Social competence in kindergarten: Analyses of social negotiations during peer play. *Early Child Development and Care, 64*, 15–26.

Rubin, K. H. (1986). Play, peer interaction, and social development. In A. W. Gottfried & C. C. Brown (Eds.), *Play interactions* (pp. 163–174). Lexington, MA: Lexington Books.

Rubin, K. H., Bukowsky, W., & Parker, J. G. (1998). Peer interactions, relationships, and groups. In W. Damon (Series Ed.) & N. Eisenberg (Volume Ed.), *Handbook of child psychology. Social, emotional and personality development* (pp. 617–700). New York: Wiley.

Sánchez, J. A., & Martínez, V. (1997). Interacción social durante el recreo en preescolares. Un estudio observacional en un centro de acogida y una escuela ordinaria. *Infancia y Aprendizaje, 77*, 113–124.

Shantz, C. U., & Shantz, D. W. (1985). Conflict between children: Social-cognitive and sociometric correlates. In M. W. Berkowitz (Ed.), *Peer conflict and psychological growth: New directions for child development* (pp. 3–21). San Francisco: Jossey-Bass.

Sheldon, A. (1990). Pickle fights: Gendered talk in preschool disputes. *Discourse Processes, 13*, 5–31.

Stetsenko, A., & Arievitch, I. M. (2004). The self in cultural-historical activity theory. Reclaiming the unity of social and individual dimensions of human development. *Theory & Psychology, 14*(4), 475–503.

Super, C. M., & Harkness, S. (1986). The developmental niche: A conceptualization at the interface of child and culture. *International Journal of Behavioral Development, 9*, 545–569.

(1997). The cultural structuring of child development. In J. W. Berry, P. R. Dasen, & T. S. Saraswathi (Eds.), *Handbook of cross-cultural psychology. Vol. 2. Basic processes and human development* (pp. 1–39). Needham Heights, MA: Allyn & Bacon.

Triandis, H. C. (1990). Cross-cultural studies of individualism and collectivism. In J. J. Berman (Ed.), *Nebraska symposium on motivation. Cross-cultural perspectives. 1989* (pp. 41–133). Lincoln: University of Nebraska Press.

(1995). *Individualism and collectivism.* Boulder, CO: Westview Press.

Triandis, H. C., Marín, G., Hui, C., Lisansky, J., & Ottati, V. (1984). Role perceptions of hispanic young adults. *Journal of Cross-Cultural Psychology, 15,* 297–320.

Vygotsky, L. S. (1978). *Mind in society: The development of higher psychological processes.* Cambridge, MA: Harvard University Press.

Wertsch, J. V. (1985). *Vygotsky and the social formation of mind.* Cambridge, MA: Harvard University Press.

Wertsch, J. V., & Stone, C. A. (1985). The concept of internalization in vygotsky's account of the genesis of higher mental functions. In J. V. Wertsch (Ed.), *Culture, communication, and cognition: Vygotskian perspectives* (pp. 162–179). New York: Cambridge University Press.

Zinchenko, V. P. (1985). Vygotsky's ideas about units for the analysis of mind. In J. W. Wertsch (Ed.), *Culture, communication and cognition: Vygotskian perspectives* (pp. 94–118). New York: Cambridge University Press.

7

Developing Social Identities and Motives
in School Transitions

DITTE WINTHER-LINDQVIST

INTRODUCTION

One of the major achievements in the cultural-historical and activity approach to human development is the attempt to describe the child in his or her wholeness by approaching the child within its relations to the environment, as a totality, involving always, and at the same time, social, emotional, cognitive and motivational aspects (Leontiev, 1978; Vygotsky, 1982). This wholeness approach involves specifying the transactions between the child and others, and their participation in societal institutional practices in dialogue with the activities, traditions and values within these (Bozhovich, 2009; Hedegaard, this volume; Stetsenko, 2009; Valsiner, 1997).

With a point of departure in the European tradition of social representations theory (Moscovici, 1988, 2001) and the work on the development of social identities that it informed (Duveen, 1997, 2001), the aim in this chapter is to bring this tradition together with a cultural-historical approach in order to enhance our understanding of the development of children's social identities and motives during school transitions. The cultural-historical approach suggests an explicit account of the role of motives in development, whereas social representations theory offers a conceptualisation of social identities. I argue that these academic traditions can fruitfully complement each other to enhance an understanding of children's development during institutional transitions. The thesis in this chapter is that different ways of belonging to a peer group directly influence the child's development of a motive towards learning in school. I show how motive development is connected to social identity processes in a dynamic relationship with institutional demands expressed by adults such as parents and professionals, as well as by peers.

The transition into school is recognised as a highly emotional journey for children, involving adjustment to a new social identity as a pupil and conversion of motives via changes in affiliation with the new leading activity of learning in school. In this chapter, the attempt to understand the developmental interplay between social identities and motives is exemplified with reference to two five-year-old boys, Benjamin and James, during their transitions between day-care and school. With illustrative examples, it is shown how the emergence of new social identities colour the children's conversion of motives that is influential for integration into school life.

WHY ADOPT A CONCEPT OF SOCIAL IDENTITIES WHEN TAKING A CULTURAL-HISTORICAL APPROACH?

Around their first birthday, children, at least in Scandinavian countries, start participating in institutional arrangements of care in the form of nursery or a family day-care, and thus start leading lives with and among peers on a daily basis. Through participation in these institutions the children come to share a history together, and thus form relationships of a potentially strong emotional kind. This societal condition actualises the questions related to social identity: Who am I in this group? Who shall I become? As children mature, they come to express and inhabit an individual relationship to the world which they know and act within, in ways which situate them within this world (Duveen, 1997, p. 71) This means that representations shape ways for the subject to become a particular person within a group, in her or his community, and shape the outlines of possible ways of being and participating. Duveen summarises these enterprises in the term 'social identities' (Duveen, 2001).

Social identity has been defined differently in various disciplines, but within social psychology, Tajfel defines the phenomenon as 'that part of an individual's self-concept which derives from his knowledge of his membership of a social group (or groups) together with the value and emotional significance attached to that membership' (Tajfel, 1978, p. 63). Tajfel does not describe the developmental process of social identities; rather, he calls attention to its origins – that is, the social group and its subjective significance. Duveen's account supplements this view by describing the process. He explains that the person's knowledge of how he or she belongs to the group is created through dialogues between its members when making and receiving identifications in everyday life (Duveen, 2001).

What we need to add to this conception of social identities from a cultural-historical approach is that it is the person's participation in the central activities within the particular institutional practice that establishes a person's membership in the group, and that the values and emotional significance attached to that membership do not just depend on social representations of possible and desirable ways of belonging, but also are reflected in the motives the child develops. Institutional activities like that of play in pre-school and learning activities in school carry values embedded in the historical traditions of the institutional practices which translate into social expectations which persons orient themselves towards and are evaluated up against by others (peers, teachers and parents) as part of social practice.

'The influence of the collective on an individual personality depends not only on features of that collective but also on the place the school-child occupies within the activity of the collective' (Bozhovich, citing Shnirman, 2009, p. 80). The child's experience of this 'place' I interpret as social identity, and as this 'place' varies with the different institutional settings, groups and relationships children are part of they are likely to inhabit, explore and experience a plurality of social identities. The concept of social identity allows for this plurality in experiences with self in activities, in various roles and relative positions towards others in different institutional practises.

Inspired by Leontiev's (1981) concept of the child's (objective) position, discussed in his book *Problems in the Development of Mind*, Bozhovich (2009) suggests a concept of internal position to account for the integrative wholeness of the person's experience with herself or himself as participant in life. The internal position is described as a developmental product built on experience from action and participation, conditioning the structure of the attitude towards reality; in every moment, the effects from the environment are refracted through this position (Bozhovich, 2009, p. 81). I argue that the concept of social identity is useful when trying to specify the particularities related to the positions the child occupies within its social world, that are, in turn, connected to institutional practices like those of a day-care unit, or a classroom.

Negotiating Social Identities as Part of Peer-Group Life among Children

Pre-school children in Scandinavian countries are developing motives for participating in activities with peers and are creating social identities in the communities of which they are part. Most children show a longing for belonging to particular groups and seem to strive to achieve a sense of social security within friendship groups among their peers. This striving reflects the immense power of the Other in relation to self and identity, and the fundamental condition behind social life and interaction, which is that we never truly know what the Other thinks of us (Boesch, 2007). The exist-ence of a private world creates a sense of insecurity and ultimately a fear of exclusion which is easily awakened as part of social interaction, not least in peer groups. Trying to overcome the strangeness of the Other through communication is a fundamental motive guiding social life in peer groups.

The motives behind the construction and negotiation of social identities lie in the desire to belong to a particular group and also protect and enhance self-esteem. We approximate ourselves towards desired others, to become like them, and become identified by others as like them. Identification as the act of approximation is in its very process emotionally rewarding. Identification, identities and motives are produced in the realm of sub-junctive anticipation of what might be, who and what one might become and the simultaneous personal evaluation of these anticipated representa-tions. This process is sometimes tangible, visible, even verbal, but often it is only imaginary and part of people's private worlds of longing and dreaming. How motives are developed and how they are hierarchically organised is the central factor in personality development in the cultural-historical trad-ition (Chaiklin, 2001; Hedegaard, 2002). The cultural-historical approach regards motives as always produced and formed by social interaction and cultural-institutional traditions and values (Hedegaard, this volume). Needs are only partly innate and their higher formation is a process which is 'a part of the general growth of the child into the life of the social whole to which he belongs' (Vygotsky, 1998, p. 11). When concerned with the whole-ness of a developmental system, it makes sense to operationalise concepts in their inter-relatedness, and so is the case for the relation with identities and motives. When identifying others, making sense of who they are and who we ourselves are, we make judgements about our own and others' motives for participating. It is essentially these judgements which establish whether communications are interpreted as criticism, praise, recognition, invitations or exclusions.

Developing New Identities and New Motives at Times of School Transitions

A child's development takes place through participation in societal institu-tions and can be thought of as qualitative changes in his or her motives and appropriation of competences and tools connected to particular institu-tional practices and goals (Hedegaard, 2009). The transition between day-care and school implies a change in identity, as the child prepares for and becomes a pupil and is recognised anew in the new classroom. Transitions are taken to be those periods of time where persons enter new socio-cultural arrangements involving culturally expected and personally anticipated changes in status and/or institutional setting. Day-care and school provide different goals, tasks and demands on the children, who also experience changes in the peer-group constellation so that social positions, leading activities, tools and personal orientations are in a state of rupture (Zittoun, 2006). Times of transit are therefore often times for conversion of motives for the developing person (Hedegaard, 2008, p. 11). Leontiev proposed the notion of different leading activities for different age groups, where leading activity was a concept encompassing the child's motives (Leontiev, 1981). Hedegaard has built on this starting point and has developed it further by analysing how the relations between the child's motives and participation in particular societal institutional settings can constrain the child's participation (Hedegaard, this volume). The argument is that as children engage with the societal expectations of their development, they appropriate a motive towards learning around the time they are starting school. The process of acquiring a new motive is not automatic, but relies on a dynamic interplay between the traditional practices of the institutions and the activities and possibilities children generate for themselves in these institutions (Hedegaard, 2008, p. 15).

METHODOLOGY

Generating Theory on the Basis of Studying Children's Perspectives

Taking children's everyday-life concerns and experiences seriously and researching them systematically is a tradition sometimes referred to under the term 'the child perspective' (Hedegaard, 2008; Hviid, 2008). This approach is mainly methodological and inspired by anthropological and sociological accounts to studying children's lives, cultures and activities; but it is highly compatible with Vygotsky's wholeness approach to accounting for children's development. With the aim of getting closer to the child's 'point of view', it tries to understand the meaning children make and ascribe to different aspects of their lives, activities and development (Hedegaard, 2008; Hviid, 2008). Vygotsky's concept of the child's social situation of development in many ways describes the points of orientation and relevant unit of analysis when conducting research from the 'child's perspective' within developmental psychology.

Choice of Setting and Background Information

Following children during the transition into school is an optimal time for studying social identity processes and the appropriation of new motives, as many of the children are developing motives towards formal learning and school activities (Karpov, 2005).

In the study reported here I worked in a village where I was able to follow the same children from day-care into the local school. The village, 'Heatherfield', 30 km from Copenhagen, has two day-care centres which provide pupils almost exclusively to the local school. The area is inhabited primarily by ethnic Danish families of lower-middle-class and middle-class income. With no formal curriculum in the Danish pre-school system, the five-to-six-year-olds are mostly engaged in and occupied with playing with peers. Playing is recognised as a leading activity for this age group at an institutional level; however, the last year in pre-school is typically organised around some pedagogically guided preparation for school life, and I focused on children during this preparation.

METHOD

The Empirical Study

In order to understand the practice and process of children's social identity formation during transitions, I undertook a motivated-ethnographic field study (Duveen & Lloyd, 1993) and followed the children during their everyday activities: playing, eating, discussing, quarrelling, drawing, bicycling, playing soccer, being bored and unoccupied. I observed the children's relationships, friendships and who they played with, conflicts and status hierarchies, in order to come to understand how the question *who am I?* in relation to peers and activities was answered. When children are interacting with peers, friends and teachers, they 'tell each other' and 'are being told' who they are by making and receiving invitations, greetings, criticism, praise, recognition, exclusion and rejection. The data consisted mainly of written protocols produced on the scene; on many occasions I also audio-recorded conversations where it was difficult to write things down.

I observed the same group of 12 five-to-six-year-old children in the last four months of their time in day-care for 20 full days (approximately 120 h), and I was able to follow 8 of them into their first 3 months of primary school for 21 full days (approximately 126 h).

ANALYSIS OF MOTIVE DEVELOPMENT
DURING TRANSITIONS

Identifying Motives as Part of Children's Activities

Motives distributed through various activities require the researcher's inter-pretations to be identified. I recognised a child's motive(s) in the ways the child approached, participated in and ended participation in activities. Therefore, for example, I looked for a child's attitude towards an activity (enthusiasm, thrill, disengagement, resentment). These attitudes might be displayed consistently over time or might reveal a changing orientation as children adjusted their orientation within activities.

Vygotsky employed Buhler's concepts of *Vorlust, Funktionslust* and *Endlust* to account for different emotional processes and shifts (Vygotsky, 1987, p. 334). The shifts in emotional life are, I suggest, also a function of the mixed motives inducing participation in activities. For instance, in soc-cer playing, the desire to play with one's friends is added to the desire to be recognised by a particular co-player (a best friend), which then again reinforce the initial desire (*Vorlust*) for playing soccer. In this case, the rele-vant motives all pull in the same direction, but often the motives are con-flicting, or one motive is denied where the others are realised, in particular activities. If there is a consistent pattern in the motives the child seeks to stimulate across situations, these are recognised as the dominant motives.

Activities and Projects

When analysing the empirical material, I made a distinction between activities and projects which referred to the status of the child's motives in the activity. An activity becomes a project if the child realises his or her motive(s) through it. Projects are often shared with friends and peers in the group. A group of children may meet around an activity which is only a project to one, or a few of them: 'Come on let's play soccer. It'll be fun! (*Vorlust*). During the activity and with the group as catalyst of new contents, the children produce motives as they are playing the game and creating a story around it they find exciting (*Funktionslust*). The group which is play-ing have produced motives in one another and turned the activity into a shared project between them. Across time, the motive for soccer playing and participation in the games become central to social identities for these boys in day-care' (Winther-Lindqvist, 2009a). Vorlust is not a pre-condition for *Funktionslust* to appear, although this is a likely connection. Motives can be realised as a consequence of participation in an activity which suddenly proves engaging and promising for the child's interests and orientation. For instance, an unoccupied child in search of an activity may start doing something carelessly, like moving the bikes around the shed, and realise through this action that they all need to be re-arranged according to size and find it rewarding and exciting (enjoying the challenge of the task and the aesthetics of a logical system in the making [*Funktionslust*], as well as imagining the rewards from others as they see the result [*Endlust*]). In this way a motive is realised, as this is an occupation to which the child gives personal meaning across a range of situation. What started out as an ad hoc activity is turned into a project.

On the Transition into School

The transition from day-care to primary school has received considerable attention because a positive transition into reception class is important for how children adjust to school life generally, both scholastically and socially (Doucet & Tudge, 2007; Entwisle & Alexander, 1993; Ladd & Price, 1987; Mangione & Speth, 1998). It is a common finding that the possibilities for continuation of friendships across the transition is important to the children's positive integration into school life, and that relations with friends and peers is a major concern among the children (Corsaro & Molinari, 2000; Corsaro et al., 2003; Hartup, 1996; Hay, Payne, & Chadwick, 2004; Ladd, 1990). The day-care children await and prepare for schooling with curiosity and positive anticipation as well as anxiety. In the following sections, I draw on evidence from two five-year-olds, James and Benjamin, in the village day-care setting and again in primary school, to illustrate the development of motives for school life and learning activities. Their cases show clearly that realising motives is a social process which can be supported and denied by peers and institutional practices, and that social identities play an important role in appropriating a motive for learning.

James's Motives and Social Identity in Day-Care

James was welcome in any friendship group among the boys in day-care, but the one he preferred was the group around the game of soccer. James was regarded as the best player by his friends and co-players. He took his time eating lunch, and when he turned up at the playground, his friends were waiting for him to start making the teams for another game. Positioned at the top of children's hierarchy, James pursued his main interest and project of playing soccer – he made the rules and decided if a goal counts or not, and all the children wanted to be on his team. I asked James's best friend,

Ollie, who decides on things in day-care. 'The adults', he replied. 'Are there any children who decide things?' I ask. 'Yes, James, he is like King of the playground', was the reply. Alongside his motive for playing soccer follows a motive for social dominance within the group of boys. During the last three months of day-care, he also showed a growing interest in school life.

> *James is sitting in the couch with a book when Ollie asks him if he is coming outside to play soccer. 'Yes, when I have finished reading this book', he says. It is a spelling-pointing book. He pronounces every word carefully as he points at it. Sometimes he asks me to read a word aloud if he is not certain. 'I know my dad's telephone number', he says and recites it for me, and 'I am attending school next Friday', James says. 'Only after the holidays', I correct him. 'No, we are to visit them next Friday and they will show us around and everything', he says with excitement. 'That is why I practice reading', he says.*

James rehearsed reading and thus showed a motive for learning which is relevant for school life, as he identified with his future social identity as a pupil. Underlying this identification and motive to learn was the desire to perform appropriately according to the social representations of what it entails to be a school-boy. He thus also expressed a fundamental motive to achieve a sense of belonging to the institutional setting he awaits.

James in School

'The soccer boys' were split into two different classrooms, and Jamie and Ollie were in the same classroom. After the first weeks of being thrilled, nervous and excited about school, the major new condition and difference for James was that they stopped playing soccer. The football ground is the furthest away from their play area and always full of older children. Consequently he lost the opportunity to realise his leading motive for playing with his friends. Also, his social identity as a soccer-boy and as a proper sports-boy was questioned in the new constellation of adults and peers. After six weeks, his parents complained that he cries in the morning and does not want to go to school. Eight weeks into the school year, every child was interviewed by the class teacher about how they like school.

> *James draws an unhappy face to the general question: How do you like school? And the class teacher asks him what it is about school he does not like. He shrugs and cannot tell her. 'Is there something you miss from day-care?' she asks him. 'I miss my friends', he says. 'But you have nice friends also in school, don't you?' He shrugs. Regarding the questions about scholastic activities, James also says that lessons are boring and learning rhymes and singing is dull.* (Protocol notes from the school interview)

James still took his time eating lunch, which was not a problem in day-care but a practice that was problematical in school. When he joined the others outside, for the break, they were already engaged in different games and groups, and he was unsuccessful finding his way into these. The game the boys play in school is Dungeons & Dragons, and when invited in, James was offered the unattractive role as Magic-man. After eight weeks, the teacher asks them to suggest peers they would like to sit next to. James answered that he wants to stay sitting next to Ollie, but Ollie names Mickey (a new classmate) instead of James. The contours of a new social identity as more marginal and peripheral were taking form, and James was unable to realise his motives, which were oriented towards playing soccer with his friends and being in a dominant social position. Even though he was fully capable of meeting the teacher's demands for participating in subject matter, his social crisis overshadowed his general evaluation of school life and inhibited his motive for learning.

Benjamin's Development of Motives and Social Identity in Day-Care

Benjamin belonged to a friendship group with three girls, but this group failed in pursuing shared projects and only rarely managed symbolic group-playing together. As a result, they often participated in adult-guided activities – like baking cakes or decorating items for Easter Holidays. When they were on their own, they were often unable to decide on what to do, and it is not unusual for one of them to ask, 'What are we doing? Are we playing?' One of them will then try and define what it is that they are doing, which then leads to a disagreement and often a quarrel. Benjamin's preferred alternative to the girls' company is playing soccer with James and the other boys. When I first met him, he sometimes played soccer, often in the role of referee (which is a commentator in this local peer-group culture), but generally his time on the soccer squad is difficult for him. Benjamin is not willing to submit to a low social position in the soccer-playing boys' hierarchy and as a consequence he withdraws from this activity:

> DITTE: Weren't you just playing soccer?
> BENJAMIN: Yes, but then Fred says I am bad at it. So now I don't anymore. I just hate Fred.
> DITTE: So what now?
> BENJAMIN: I'll just wait. What time is it? My mum picks me up at 14:30.

Benjamin is experiencing a conflict in different motives when confronted with the soccer game. His motive towards performing well puts high

demands on his own achievements, and he is dependent on positive recognition from others. This he is consistently denied by his peers, but he is
interested in being part of the boys' shared project of playing soccer, so there
is a conflict in his motives. As it turns out, his motive towards recognition is
stronger than his motive to be part of the group of soccer-boys, so he withdraws from them as he is not willing to put up with criticism of his playing
abilities. Withdrawing from this activity excludes him from being part of the
boys' strong community around soccer and places him in a marginal social
identity where he plays with different peers but is also often unoccupied and
alone. He then seeks adult company or manages to decide on a project for
himself, in which he challenges his competencies and rehearses his skills,
like deciding to colour all the pictures in a paint book or rearrange the bikes
in the shed. He often talks about his older brother and how he does homework with him at evenings. He also is looking forwards to joining his older
brother when starting school. I recognise these activities and this identification as producing a motive for school life and learning.

Benjamin in School

When school started, Benjamin chose a seat close to the teacher's desk
and pursued the project of learning. He was recognised by all teachers and
peers for his hard work with drawing, counting, writing letters, remember-
ing rhymes and lyrics, putting his hands up when wanting to speak and so
forth. Benjamin was occupied with his new tools for school, among other
things his pencil-box containing a magnifying glass, which he uses to refine
his writing and drawing. In one episode, he turns to the teacher to show her
his work. 'You are really working hard, Benjamin. I can tell, only perfect is
good enough!' the teacher says.

However, Benjamin remained isolated in school, only rarely playing
Dungeons & Dragons, sometimes joining his older brother or just not
being with anyone in particular during breaks. His parents and the teacher
were worried about his lack of good friends, but Benjamin seemed to be
less bothered. He enthusiastically participated in performing the tasks the
teacher told them to work on, facing trouble only when he was corrected
or answered wrongly. During a game by the blackboard, Benjamin failed to
answer correctly, so the teacher asked another child; Benjamin was devastated and his eyes filled with tears. When performing well, which is most
of the time, he seemed to enjoy school life, often acting as an instructor to
his peers, discussing solutions to tasks and competing with those around
his table or correcting them. When asked who he wants to sit next to, he
had no one in particular in mind. But he stated: 'I would like to keep this
chair, this seat'.

DISCUSSION

The examples of James and Benjamin serve as illustrations of how social identities are connected to motives through the leading activities and values held by both adults and peers in institutional settings. Both boys were regarded school-ready and motivated to learn, but they managed the transition differently due to both coincidental circumstances and to how their personal motives matched the institutional demands and possibilities differently. In the cultural-historical approach to understanding development, the driving forces of transformation from one leading activity and motive to the next is adult guidance and institutional settings which act as mediators enabling the child's conversion of goals into motives and actions into (new) activities (Karpov, 2005; Leontiev, 1978). By analysing children's social identities as they are created in the social life with peers, I suggest that peers and friends and the social position among them are a crucial factor for developing motives for learning when entering school. Both boys start developing a motive for learning already in day-care, but not in a way were it necessarily subordinates the motive for play. In James's case, the motive for learning and school life appears as a supplementary motive leading to activities with learning content in day-care, but it does not gain a privileged position, because his motive to play and be with friends is strongly supported by the rich and rewarding social life he has with the soccer-boys. Playing with friends remains the leading motive four months into the school year, and his lack of success with it appears to be blocking the development of a learning motive. Benjamin, who is in a marginalised social position among his peers in day-care, experiences conflicting motives (his longing for belonging to the soccer-playing boys conflicts with his desire to achieve recognition and defend himself). In this environment he develops a leading motive towards learning before entering school and identifies with his big brother at home instead of his peers. In Benjamin's case, his social identity does not support a playing motive in day-care, nor does it directly support a learning motive. Left to himself, he draws on motives and relations from his home environment where he takes part in and imitates his older brother's learning activities through homework. He brings this experience into the day-care environment as an occupation (correcting other's mistakes) and occasionally a project (instructing others in how to draw within the lines etc.). When a motive transgresses institutional settings, it works under different conditions, and in this case his learning motive is less rewarded in day-care than at home (his friends are annoyed that he corrects them, and the professionals thinks he is weird because he does not play properly). These vignettes suggest that motives are not individually given but produced in the social-personal transaction process related to the models we identify with the institutional value traditions and the social identities allowing or denying recognition from others.

Adjusting Motives and Expectations to the Reality of School

The social representations of school circulating in the community of day-care children for a large part misinform the children about what to expect from their first school class. They expect more subject-matter teaching and to get homework from the start. Jamie and Benjamin are both a little disappointed with, for example, drawing and singing rhymes instead. James shows his boredom by yawning and bending over the table, which upsets his teacher. His disappointment with his friends, in combination with the lack of challenges related to learning tasks in school, inhibits his initial enthusiasm and his motive towards learning. Benjamin also complains that the tasks are too easily and quickly solved, but he states this with a kind of satisfaction, as he also thereby self-presents as someone appropriate to the leading activity and goal of school. Even though he is sometimes impatient, he is happy with solving tasks and receiving adult recognition; thus he strengthens his motive for learning and performing well during this transition.

Vulnerability Accompanies the Conversion of Goals into Motives

James finds himself early in a confused and disappointed state in school, with no projects and certainty about his friendships and status among the new group of boys. This crisis in social identity arouses a sense of insecurity and vulnerability to negative identifications. Benjamin contrarily finds himself in a situation where his learning-like activities in day-care are turned into formal learning activities when starting school where this motive for learning is supported and encouraged by his surroundings. The goal of the action is turned into a leading motive in the dialogue between his readiness and the adult mediation, support and supervision in the institutional practice of school. This conversion of a goal into motives is also followed by a greater emotional commitment to performing well. This commitment represents a strong sense of belonging to what is appropriate, and thus he achieves a positive social identity; however, it is accompanied by a new vulnerability as well. Benjamin is devastated when failing and corrected by the teacher, which is a new vulnerability developed alongside his motive to learn and perform well.

Longing for Belonging

When participating in institutional arrangements like day-care and school, a major task is finding one's place in the social environment, or achieving a sense of belonging to the particular setting (see also Wardekker & Boersma, this volume). Experiencing belonging is important at all ages and at all levels, from pre-school through high school (Osterman, 2000, p. 343), and connects to the social motive to interact and belong to a social group. I have argued that children move from different points of orientation when evaluating their own belonging, and I have shown that some children rely more on their belonging to peer groups than do others. Benjamin belongs in school because he is absorbed by the task of learning. Being recognised and identified in ways which are appropriate to school goals is more important to him than his peers' approval. James does not feel that he belongs in school because he cannot recognise himself positively in the school practice without high social standing among his friends. He seems disoriented when it comes to forming direction and creating new motives in school. There is a collectively constituted peer culture carrying values and ideas about appropriateness regarding leading activities – to which one belongs or not as part of institutional practices. In the peer-group culture, particular children are more popular and influential than others and recognised as being so by the other children in the group. These popular children are more active and influential in making identifications of themselves and others, and identify themselves as personifying appropriateness.

In day-care, these values and ideas concern soccer playing and symbolic group-play, supported and expected also by the adults in day-care. Within these parameters, James enjoyed a positive and popular social identity and Benjamin experienced a rejected, marginal one. In the reception-class environment, playing Dungeon & Dragons with the boys and conforming to appropriate classroom behaviour, by meeting teacher demands of engagement, self-regulation and compliance, replaces the virtues of playing soccer.

How one's social identity is negotiated and evaluated by the self in the new situation depends on expectations formed with relation to one's prior social identity and one's motives regarding who one shall become. James is not deemed inappropriate altogether in school, but he loses out compared to his prior situation, with which he obviously compares it. Benjamin integrates more positively, and his sincere engagement, combined with good school performance, makes his adjustment to school and sense of belonging easier to achieve.

CONCLUDING REMARKS

In this chapter I argue that the concept of social identity as understood within the tradition of social representations theory is relevant to a cultural-historical approach when addressing children's development of motives during transitions into school life. Different ways of belonging to the peer group directly influence the child's development of a motive towards learning in school. The examples have shown how motive development is connected to social identity processes in dynamic relations to institutional demands expressed by both adults and peers. When children identify each other in peer groups, they also identify each others' motives as more or less appropriate compared to circulating social representations of how to perform properly as a boy, girl, pupil, friend and classmate (Winther-Lindqvist, 2009b, 2009c). I suggest that modern life conditions in day-care create a fundamental motive for belonging to and relating to particular others in the peer-group life, but whether this is realised or denied relies on a complex interplay between the particular group of children, their local values and how the social hierarchy creates access to valued activities such as playing soccer in day-care and learning and playing Dungeon & Dragons in school.

According to the cultural-historical approach, motives are developed in the course of the person's interaction in social institutional practices. In this chapter I have suggested that social identities as the child's experience of the special place a child occupies in the social landscape are consequential to which motives are inhibited or promoted during the transition into school life. A successful transition into school involves adjustment to a new social identity as a pupil and the conversion of motives aligned to the new leading activity of learning in school. The development of a motive towards learning in the first months of schooling is influenced by the child's possibilities for creating or sustaining a positive social identity among peers, friends and teachers.

Institutional activities and projects carry values embedded in the historical traditions of the institutional practices which translate into social expectations that persons orient themselves towards and are evaluated against by others. In some children, the social motive is so dominant that if it is not satisfied, the outcome can be the restricted development of a motive for learning in school. In others, the lack of a positive social identity in day-care and the longing for belonging takes forward the process of achieving a motive for learning before starting school. Through these examples, I have argued that the conceptualisation of social identities inspired by social representations theory helps to account for children's development of motives within the tradition of a cultural-historical approach.

REFERENCES

Boesch, E. E. (2007). The enigmatic other. In Simäo L. M., & Valsiner, J. (Eds.), *Otherness in Question – labyrinths of the self, A volume in Advances in Cultural Psychology* (pp. 3–10). Charlotte, NC: Information Age Publishing.

Bozhovich, L. I. (2009). The social situation of child development. *Journal of Russian East European Psychology, 47*(4), 59–89.

Chaiklin, S. (2001). The category of 'personality' in cultural-historical psychology. In S. Chaiklin (Ed.), *The theory and practice of cultural historical psychology* (pp. 238–259). Aarhus: Aarhus University Press.

Corsaro, W., & Molinari, L. (2000). Priming events and Italian children's transition from preschool to elementary school: Representations and action. *Social Psychology Quarterly, 63*(1), 16–33.

Corsaro, W., Molinari, L., Hadley, K., & Sugioka, H. (2003). Keeping and making friends: Italian children's transition from pre-school to elementary school. *Social Psychology Quarterly, 66*(3), 272–292.

Doucet, F., & Tudge, J. (2007). Co-constructing the transition to school – reframing the novice versus expert roles of children, parents, and teachers from a cultural perspective. In R. C. Pianta, M. J. Cox, & K. L. Snow (Eds.), *School readiness and the transition to kindergarden in the era of accountability* (pp. 307–328). Baltimore: Brookes.

Duveen, G. (1997). Psychological development as a social process. In L. Smith, P. Tomlinson, & J. Dockerell (Eds.), *Piaget, Vygotsky and beyond* (pp. 67–90). London: Routledge.

(2001). Representations, identities, resistance. In K. Deaux & G. Philogène (Eds.), *Representations of the social – bridging theoretical traditions* (pp. 257–270). Oxford: Blackwell.

Duveen, G., & Lloyd, B. (1993). An ethnographic approach to social representations. In G. Breakwell & D. Canter (Eds.), *Empirical approaches to social representations* (pp. 90–110). Oxford: Oxford University Press.

Entwisle, D. R., & Alexander, K. L. (1993). Entry into school. The beginning school transition and educational stratification in the United States. *Annual Review of Sociology, 19*, 401–423.

Hartup, W. (1996). The company they keep: Friendships and their developmental significance. *Child Development, 67*, 1–13.

Hay, D., Payne, A., & Chadwick, A. (2004). Peer relations in childhood. *Journal of Child Psychology and Psychiatry, 45*(1), 84–108.

Hedegaard, M. (2002). *Learning and child development – A cultural historical study.* Aarhus: Aarhus University Press.

(2008). A cultural-historical theory of children's development. In M. Hedegaard & M. Fleer (Eds.), *Studying children – a cultural-historical approach* (pp. 10–30). New York: McGraw Hill/Open University Press.

(2009). Children's development from a cultural-historical approach: Children's activity in everyday local settings as foundations for their development. *Mind, Culture and Activity, 16,* 64–81.

Hviid, P. (2008). 'Next year we are small, right?' Different times in children's development. *European Journal of Psychology of Education, 23*(2), 183–198.

Karpov, Y. V. (2005). *The neo-Vygotskian approach to child development.* Cambridge: Cambridge University Press.

Ladd, G., & Price, J. (1987). Predicting children's social and school adjustment following the transition from preschool to kindergarten. *Child Development, 58,* 1168–1189.

Ladd, G. W. (1990). Having friends, keeping friends, making friends, and being liked by peers in the classroom: Predictors of children's early school adjustment. *Child Development, 61,* 1081–1100.

Leontiev, A. (1978). *Activity, consciousness, personality.* Englewood Cliffs, NJ: Prentice-Hall.

Leontiev, A. N. (1981 [1959]). Problems of the development of mind. Moscow, Progress. Available at http://marxists.org/archive/leontev/works/development-mind.pdf

Mangione, P. L., & Speth, T. (1998). The transition to elementary school: A framework for creating early childhood continuity through home, school, and community partnerships. *The Elementary School Journal, 98*(4), 381–398.

Moscovici, S. (1988). Notes towards a description of social representations. *Journal of European Social Psychology, 18,* 211–250.

(2001). *Social representations – explorations in social psychology.* New York: New York University Press.

Moscovici, S., & Marková, I. (2001). Ideas and their development: A dialogue between Serge Moscovici and Ivana Marková. In G. Duveen (Ed.), *Social representations: Explorations in social psychology* (pp. 224–286). New York: New York University Press.

Osterman, K. (2000). Student's need for belonging in the school community. *Review of Educational Research, 70*(3), 323–367.

Stetsenko, A. (2009). Vygotsky and the conceptual revolution in developmental science – towards a unified (non-additive) account of human development. In M. Fleer, M. Hedegaard, & J. Tudge (Eds.), *World yearbook of education 2009: Childhood studies and the impact of globalization: Policies and practices at global and local levels* (pp. 125–141). London: Routledge.

Tajfel, H. (1978). Social categorization, social identity and social comparison. In H. Tajfel (Ed.), *Differentiation between social groups: Studies in the social psychology of intergroup relations* (pp. 101–140). London: Academic Press.

Valsiner, J. (1997). *Culture and the development of children's action.* Oxford: John Wiley & Sons.

Vygotsky, L. S. (1982). *Om barnets psykiske udvikling.* Nordisk Forlag, Arnold Busck A/S, KBH.

(1987). Emotions and their development in childhood. In R. W. Rieber & A. S. Carton (Eds.), *The Collective Works of L. S., Vygotsky, Problems of a General Psychology, vol. 1. lecture 4* (pp. 325–339). New York: Plenum Press.

(1998). Development of interests at the transitional age. In R. W. Rieber (Ed.), *The Collective Works of L. S., Vygotsky, Problems of a General Psychology, vol. 5, chapter 1* (pp. 3–29). New York: Plenum Press.

Winther-Lindqvist, D. (2009a). Symbolic group-play and social identity. In B. Wagoner (Ed.), *Symbolic transformation: The mind in movement through culture and society* (pp. 249–269). Cultural Dynamics of Social Representation Series. London: Routledge.

(2009b). Children's development of social identity in transitions. PhD dissertation, Department of Psychology, Copenhagen University.

(2009c). Game-playing. Negotiating rules and social identities. *American Journal of Play, vol. 2, no. 1* (pp. 60–85). Rochester, NY: Strong National Museum of Play.

Zittoun, T. (2006). *Transitions – development through symbolic resources* (Advances in Cultural Psychology Series). Charlotte, NC: Information Age Publishing.

8

Motives Matter: A Cultural-Historical Approach to IT-Mediated Subject-Matter Teaching

KÅRE STENILD AND OLE SEJER IVERSEN

INTRODUCTION

The aim of this chapter is to analyse and discuss how information technology (IT) and especially mobile technology can be successfully integrated in teaching practices to support and motivate students for subject-matter teaching. IT-supported learning does not solely depend on how the IT is designed, but also on how the students are motivated to use IT in a pedagogical practice. In this chapter, we argue that IT can help to mediate between teaching practice and learning activity when children's everyday IT competences are taken into account in the practice of school teaching. Furthermore, we suggest, that provided as part of a coherent and interconnected teaching practice and IT usage; IT can potentially motivate the 'the double move approach'[1] in which subject-matter knowledge is naturally integrated into the children's everyday life (Hedegaard 2002; Hedegaard & Chaiklin, 2005).

In the first part of the chapter, we develop a theoretical model for understanding children's development of motives as a result of both teaching practice and learning activity. The model draws on Vygotsky's distinction between scientific concepts and everyday concepts (Vygotsky, 1982, 1987). Following Hedegaard and Chaiklin's line of argument that it is essential for children's development to combine the subject matter taught in schools with their everyday life, we position IT as a tool for bridging both knowledge and motives to connect the distinct but intertwining practices of school and everyday life.

---

[1] The main point in 'the double move approach' (Hedegaard 2002) is to create learning tasks that can integrate local knowledge with core conceptual relations of a subject-matter area so that the person can acquire theoretical knowledge that can be used in the person's local practice.

We exemplify our interest in using IT and mobile technologies to mediate between subject-matter knowledge in school environments and everyday knowledge with an IT application, the eBag, which was implemented and evaluated in four primary schools as part of a research project in Denmark. The overall finding was that the eBag did motivate the children to engage more actively in the subject-matter teaching. Here we discuss the data derived from the eBag research project in terms of motives and conclude the chapter by stating how IT and mobile technology supports engagement as a dynamic process of using everyday knowledge and motives in pedagogic practice.

THE DISTINCTION BETWEEN SUBJECT-MATTER KNOWLEDGE AND EVERYDAY KNOWLEDGE

The main argument in this chapter is that mobile technology is a resource than can support connections between the institutionalised teaching practice in schools and the informal learning practice in children's everyday life. In what follows, we use Vygotsky's theoretical distinctions between subject-matter knowledge (scientific concepts) and everyday knowledge (everyday concepts) to characterise the two practices. We will use Hedegaard's terms 'subject-matter knowledge' and 'everyday knowledge' as they incorporate the meaning of the concepts to societal practice and children's social situation of development.

Children's unstructured spontaneous acquisition of everyday knowledge takes place long before school age, while the structured acquisition of subject-matter knowledge only begins when the child starts in school. This implies that both the acquisition and the developmental paths of the two forms of knowledge are quite different. The acquisition of everyday knowledge is mainly upwards in the sense that everyday knowledge is learned and assimilated into immediate collision with various objects and in different situations. By trial and error or imitation, the child can learn how to ride a bike or how to play an online computer game without understanding the underlying concepts of balance or computing.

However, the acquisition of everyday knowledge is also to some extent from the top down, because children surround themselves with adults and peers who can answer questions and explain how different actions are performed (Vygotsky, 1982, p. 131). Children can learn the login procedure to play an online computer game by asking or by simply imitating peers. By imitating or reproducing the activity of peers, children can access computer games even if they are unfamiliar with the concepts of the letters and numbers.

The acquisition of subject-matter knowledge is, according to Vygotsky, mostly opposite – that is, downwards – where the child starts to understand a general meaning of a concept and learn how to connect this concept with other concepts and form logical relations (Vygotsky, 1982, pp. 133–134). The downward directionality does not imply that subject-matter knowledge is always introduced to children in areas where they have no prior knowledge or experience. Vygotsky uses the example, that a child can learn in school, that water becomes ice at zero degrees Celcius, and even though the child is previously acquainted with water in the frozen state, it is here that the child acquires subject-matter knowledge about the regularities of physics behind the relationship between ice and water. This difference between being able to talk about something and being able to define a concept behind every-day experience of something is the significant difference between everyday knowledge and subject-matter knowledge (Vygotsky, 1982, p. 145). The sub-ject-matter knowledge begins with linguistic formulation of a concept and is then connected to the everyday knowledge that relates this knowledge to the conceptual area. By learning to express themselves about an aca-demic topic and to obtain systematic knowledge of the subject, children's subject-matter knowledge becomes more stable than everyday knowledge. Connecting children's everyday knowledge with subject-matter knowledge can substantiate and even qualify everyday knowledge. This means that subject-matter knowledge is not a direct replacement for everyday know-ledge, but can cause children to change their naive views and reflect on their experienced everyday knowledge.

In the next section we describe the goals of Danish primary education, that regulate the teaching of subject-matter knowledge and the use of IT resources within subject-matter teaching as it unfolds in Danish primary schools.

Goals Set for Danish Primary Schools

The goals for Danish primary schools are formulated by the Ministry of Education but implemented by school principals, teachers and parents, each with different motives, individual goals and objectives. We acknowledge that the goals are practiced within a tradition, in this case the tradition of the Danish educational system. However, to establish and emphasise a gen-eral model for the dynamics of IT-mediated engagement, we depart from the goals as the societal expectations and demands enacted in the teaching practice. The goals of Danish primary schools are based on political and societal values. They frame how subject-matter knowledge is taught and in what context teaching takes place. Here we present how these goals are related to subject-matter knowledge, everyday knowledge and IT usage.

The legislation that regulates primary schools, is divided into *general* goals for schools and *specific* goals for each subject-matter area, that focus on what the students should learn in the individual subjects.

The general goals for the Danish primary schools are:

> The Primary school, in cooperation with the parents, must give students knowledge and skills to: prepare them for further education and give them the desire to learn more, make them familiar with Danish culture and history, give them an understanding of other countries and cultures, contribute to their understanding of human interaction with nature and promote the individual student's all-round development. (Ministry of Education, 2006, Act No. 572 Section 1 of the Danish Education Act)[2]

In this first paragraph, the emphasis is on creating engagement among children. According to the goals, 'the desire to learn' is pursued both within the formal schooling system and within the children's everyday life supported by the parents. The goals emphasise children's ability to gain trust in their own possibilities and provide a basis to decide and act.

The goals also imply that children should be able to use the knowledge acquired in school in their everyday life, so that the children can be a part of the community and develop self-awareness. In this respect, the goals resonate with the 'Radical-Local' learning theory as they both emphasise the child's ability to appropriate subject-matter knowledge into the realm of everyday life, as is discussed later in this chapter.

Goals for IT in Schools

One of the goals of the Danish Education legislation is to ensure that IT plays a crucial part in the education system, and that IT should be integrated into subject-matter teaching at all stages and all levels of education. IT in education is seen as the way to meet the increasing demand for professionalism and quality in a globalised economy.

The Danish government has the following goals for IT in education – to ensure:

- IT is used in teaching to effectively supports the individual student's potential for high academic achievement;

---

[2] The primary school's goals translated from the Danish Ministry of Education homepage http://pub.uvm.dk/2006/faellesmaal/folkeskolens_formaal.html (our translation).

- The use of IT becomes a natural part of students' everyday lives as early as possible;
- That children and teenagers have the best conditions for interacting in a society where IT occupies an increasingly important role in an increasing amount of areas.[3]

Our earlier outline of the goals set for the Danish primary school draws a line from the overall goals from the Ministry of Education down to the subject-matter teaching practiced by the teachers. There is a clear goal to ensure that the students can use the subject-matter knowledge in everyday life as well as an emphasis on creating motives for engagement among children. The goal of IT in schools is generally to assist the subject-matter teaching and to support the overall goals of preparing the students to become valuable citizens in society.

We will take a closer look at learning and how development of motives is taking place in order to connect engagement and motives with the goals of the educational system. We describe Hedegaard's theoretical conceptions of a cultural-historical approach to learning and creation of motives to clarify how everyday knowledge is linked to engagement.

MOTIVATION AND MOTIVES

In her theoretical account of engagement, Hedegaard (2002) distinguishes between motivation and motives. According to Hedegaard, motivation is the dynamic that characterizes a person's actions and relationship to the surroundings in a particular situation. For the person, motivation characterizes the dynamic of her situated activities.

When a school child is allowed to retrieve information on the Internet as information gathering for a school assignment, the computer usage will almost inevitably motivate the child to proceed with schoolwork. The motivation derives from that fact that computers are still a meagre, and thus restricted, resource in most primary schools, and accordingly, the children are excited when computers are available. Moreover, the children will acknowledge the legitimacy of surfing the Internet as a part of a school assignment as a rewarding activity that resembles their leisure-time activities and thus be motivated. The motivation will to some extend have a positive effect on the teaching practice. Some children will be encouraged to go deeper into subject matter provided by computer resources. However,

---

[3] The Danish primary school's IT goals taken from the Ministry of Education homepage (our translation).

the motivation caused by the computer usage itself will almost inevitably decline unless the children are re-engaged with other engaging activities such that the computer becomes a tool for these activities.

Motives, as opposed to motivation, have cross-situational goals which characterize the actions of a person in different activities over an extended period of time (Hedegaard, 2002). As the use of computer-supported teaching most often will cause motivation, the connection between the child's motives and the computer usage are more complex and highly dependent on how the computer usage is supported pedagogically and how it relates to the child's personal development within the institutional practice.

Hedegaard builds upon Leontiev's (1978) activity theory in her interpretation of children's motive formation in formal school education. The main assumption is that human motives are culturally and socially created and simultaneously linked to the individual. Motives are developed and acquired throughout the child's life through the activities the child is a part of in the various social institutions (family, day-care centres, schools, sports).

A person's various motives are related to each other and can be seen as a hierarchical structure (Hedegaard, 2002, pp. 63–64). This hierarchy is not very stable in children. Children's primary (dominant/leading) motives may be quickly changed when a child is confronted with new activities. Development can occur by qualitative changes in the practices that a child participates in. Whether there is development of a child's motives and knowledge entering a new practice or a change in the practice depends on whether the child is given the opportunity to become aware of his or her intentions and to create his or her personal goals in the new activities. An activity or task can be motivating if it relates to a person's motives.

It is important for teachers, therefore, to make clear what motives they have, as well as what motives the students have for using IT in the practices of the classroom. If a teacher's motive for using IT is to comply with demands from the head teacher, who follows the education system's overall goals, it will not be a motive for using IT in the teaching that the students can acquire.

Hedegaard uses Leontiev's (1978) distinction between three kinds of motives: The *dominant*, the *meaningful*, and the *stimulating* motive. The dominant motives are the motives which are most important and which are linked to the type of activities that are central and meaningful to the person's life. For the pre-school child, the play motive is dominant. For school children, learning should become the dominant motive. When the child enters puberty, acceptability by friends and self-realisation become the dominant motives (Hedegaard, 2002). A dominant motive is always a meaningful motive, otherwise it cannot be the dominant motive. It is important to note that several meaningful motives can co-exist.

A stimulating motive is a motive, which in another context is meaningful, but placed into a new activity, it can possibly motivate new activity in the way the old and new activities are combined (Hedegaard, 2002, pp. 63–64). An example of such a motivation is the use of students' own mobile phones in school education. All students see the mobile phone as the main communication tool and they are motivated to use, and experts in using, their own mobile phone.

Motivating children to engage in new learning practices is essential for developing new motives and acquiring new knowledge. It is not a novel idea to include everyday knowledge into pedagogic practices, and we acknowledge that many teachers successfully make use of teaching practices that draw on children's everyday experiences and everyday knowledge to be combined with subject-matter knowledge in their teaching.

INFORMATION TECHNOLOGY AS A BRIDGE BETWEEN TEACHING PRACTICE AND LEARNING PRACTICE

One of the Danish primary schools goals is that IT must be included in all subjects. However, it is not specified how or why IT must be utilised in the teaching practice.

For a successful integration of IT into teaching practice, IT must support the goals of the school system. From the teachers' perspective, the question is whether they can and how they can help children with their learning in specific subjects.

Teachers will first become engaged in using IT if it makes it easier for them to achieve their professional goals because teachers' practices always have motives which are usually based on the goals set for the subjects they teach. The introduction and use of IT must relate to the relevant motive.

Our claim is that IT as a teaching tool needs to be built up to support existing teaching practices, while also opening up possibilities for new teaching practices that use technology in more productive ways. The introduction of IT to support teaching practices cannot avoid affecting these practices and the organisation of practices within a school as a whole. It is therefore essential to review the specific practices when introducing IT in schools, to ensure that the schools are able to benefit from the full potential of IT and from students' already existing experience in IT.

From the student perspective, it is important to link the subject-matter teaching that they encounter at school to their everyday knowledge, both because the school's subject-matter knowledge must be used and applied outside the school and because students' everyday knowledge helps to give meaning to the teaching and helps to connect motives to the teaching. From the teacher's perspective, it is important to achieve the goals set for school subjects through the dissemination of the content of the specific subjects. The task is then to link the school's goals and subject-matter knowledge with the children's involvement and everyday knowledge. It is in this context that IT can be a support and form a bridge.

It is necessary to achieve children's involvement to realise the goals we have for education in school; and children's involvement in education is reflected in the degree to which they can connect learning to their lives and their everyday knowledge. Such a bridging can be illustrated in the following model in which the school's subject-matter knowledge can be seen as part of a teaching practice, and how everyday knowledge can be seen as part of children's learning activities. IT and mobile technologies may be seen as a possible mediator between the children's everyday knowledge and the school's subject-matter knowledge.

We use cultural-historical theory to outline a model for how IT is seen as a potential motivating artefact to mediate between teaching practice and learning activity. In this model, Vygotsky's distinction between everyday and subject-matter concepts and how they interact are combined with Hedegaard's conception of how children's meaningful motives can function as motivation for children to enter new activities and thereby develop motives for new knowledge and skills.

The model illustrates the idea that social goals for schools are reflected in subject-matter teaching and that children's activities in everyday home and community settings can be used to create children's motives in subject-matter teaching. In the next section we discuss how IT can support the relation between teaching practice and children's activities outside of school, as well as how children's acquisition of motives and engagement outside of school can create motivation and motives in school for subject-matter content.

THE RELATION BETWEEN KNOWLEDGE FORMS, MOTIVATION, AND IT IN TEACHING PRACTICES

In the model presented in Figure 8.1, we have outlined how IT and mobile technology potentially can help to mediate between the motives drawn

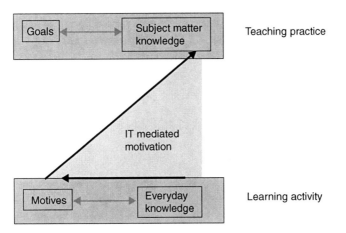

FIGURE 8.1. Using IT-mediated motivation to bridge everyday knowledge and subject-matter knowledge.

from everyday knowledge and subject-matter knowledge. We do extend our argument, however, and suggest that IT and mobile technology has the ability to bring subject-matter knowledge into the student's everyday life. We draw on 'the double move approach' (Hedegaard, 2002) to expand our model.

One of the overarching goals of school education is to get the students to comprehend subject-matter knowledge in such a way that it becomes personal knowledge that can be used in their everyday lives outside school. How everyday knowledge becomes related to academic knowledge depends on the form of academic knowledge and the motives in the teaching practice. The form of knowledge is important. Hedegaard points out that much school teaching draws on empirical knowledge which orients students to acquiring concepts from different subject domains which are not necessarily related to each other or to the children's local life world. To ensure that students can create cross-disciplinary relations, the teaching must help students to acquire subject-matter knowledge from theoretical core models through methods of investigation which enable the children to analyse and understand the complexity of different practices. Hedegaard (2002) provides a conceptual understanding of different forms of knowledge with strong focus on the theoretical foundations of each subject. Theoretical knowledge can be described as creating models of knowledge acquired by participating in practice.

ARTEFACTS AND PRACTICES

An important contributor to clarifying links between knowledge and practice was Wartofsky (1979). He distinguished between three types of artefact
by how and why they were used. Primary artefacts let people transform the
material reality; these can be, for example, a hammer, a camera or computer
(i.e. something which is used directly in an activity). Secondary artefacts
are representations of primary artefacts and can be, for example, a manual
for a camera whose purpose is maintaining communication and dissemination of knowledge about the primary artefact. Textbooks are therefore
secondary artefacts (Wartofsky, 1979, pp. 201–202). Tertiary artefacts are
representations of secondary artefacts. That is, they are based on general
representations and can include scientific theories and models (Wartofsky,
1979, pp. 208–209). Tertiary artefacts contain not only knowledge about
the practice, which the artefacts are included in and the artefacts themselves, but also invite their future use. Theoretical knowledge as formulated
by Hedegaard are tertiary artefacts.

Wartofsky's model of three types of artefact and the different ways in
which they mediate action in the world has implications for schools. A
school and the practices within it also mediate that engagement – a point
made clearly be Wartofsky in 1979 when he argues: 'Our environment is
changing throughout history in the form of various artifacts such as build-
ings, various infrastructures, and the clothes we wear, but the contexts are
also artifacts in themselves, linking up with different values (e.g. a dark
wood as dangerous, a large city as busy and smoky or a school as being
worn out and boring)' (Wartofsky, 1979, p. 206). If we follow that line, we
can see that schools will create certain kinds of associations and thought
patterns, although the physical environment, learning materials and teachers are replaced because the artefact 'school' consists of conceptual models
of interaction between the participants in this practice.

We draw on a research project called eBag. The vision behind eBag is
to use the student's everyday knowledge of mobile usage and at the same
time support the students knowledge sharing across different psychical
areas like the school environment, home and anywhere else the students
take their mobile phone. The eBag enables the students to take advantage
of the multimedia functions in their personal mobile phones posses – not
only in their spare time, but also in a teaching practice. The eBag was seen
as an IT solution to support the relation between the teaching practice and
children's everyday life, as well as utilising children's acquisition of motives

and engagement outside school to create motivation and motives in school for subject-matter content, as Figure 8.1 illustrates.

The eBag was presented as a school artefact, and the motivation for use outside school was thereby limited. The approach chosen for use and interaction with IT and mobile technology in a teaching practice is therefore essential to obtain the full potential that IT has as a mediator between everyday knowledge and subject-matter knowledge. The teaching practices themselves and how they are integrated with the IT and mobile technology are also important factors when presenting IT in a teaching practice. 'The double move approach' can be used to involve the teachers' and students' conceptions and understanding of IT to create a common model of how IT is used in different practices.

Teaching Practice and IT-Supported Engagement

We now have a theoretical understanding of how motivation can be created by drawing on existing motives from everyday activities, but the motives for using IT and the extent of IT use in both teachers and students' everyday activities can be very different. The use of models as a central part of learning subject matter can be found in Hedegaard's approach of the double move in teaching. This approach we use as a foundation to evaluate the eBag approach and to support us in formulating how to proceed.

'The double move approach' has four ground principles:

1. Use of a core model of the content area under investigation to guide instruction.
2. Use of research strategies in instruction in a way which is analogical to how researchers investigate problems.
3. Creation of phases in the teaching process reflecting qualitative changes in the child's learning process.
4. Formation of motivation in the class activity through creating tasks for investigation and through facilitating communication and cooperation between children (Hedegaard, 2002).

Hedegaard and Chaiklin's theory (2005) of radical local teaching and learning locate children's everyday knowledge in their community. Hedegaard and Chaiklin point out that one of the main barriers for further development in relating everyday knowledge to subject-matter knowledge is having adequate analysis of children's local knowledge. There is not a tradition for documenting local knowledge in relation to the life world of school children, and it is necessary to relate this knowledge to theoretical concepts in subject-matter traditions. The big advantage of 'the double move approach' is that offers a possibility for creating motivation for subject-matter knowledge by drawing on motives from everyday activities.

It cannot be expected that all teachers and students are equally motivated from the start, when new measures like implementation of IT are introduced in the teaching practice. Teachers and students can, however, gain new motives through new practices. In order for this practice to be successful, IT must provide the teachers with new motives. From our experience and talks with teachers, a number of teachers are not keen on using interactive whiteboards. This can be an expression of teachers not having experienced the interactive whiteboards inserted into a meaningful practice. The statement that follows is from a teacher who has not tried to work with interactive whiteboards and points out he cannot see any advantage introducing them into primary schools: 'I'll claim that almost all of the new learning effects caused by the integration of interactive whiteboards in teaching practices, could have been done by use of standard hardware such as a PC, a projector and a standard whiteboard' (Anders teacher and IT supporter from Vejle).

All people form opinions on things they have not tried from what they hear about them. We do not argue that all teachers will create new positive motives by engaging in a teaching context with interactive whiteboards. The point is that it is through practice that we have the opportunity to create new motives. Therefore, it is important to create a new teaching practice together with the teachers and not just give them an IT tool that does not align with the mediating context of the school, and central to that alignment are motives and motivation.

Developing a General Model of the Dynamics of IT-Supported Motivation

By reflecting on our development work with teachers through the prism of motives and motivation, we are now able to provide a more detailed description of how we see that IT can support the bridge between the school's subject-matter knowledge and children's everyday knowledge to motivate children to meet the goals of our education system. Figure 8.2 is a detailed version of Figure 8.1 and is a representation of IT as a possible mediator of this bridging.

The arrow between everyday knowledge and motives represents the fact that most children use a range of different forms of IT and mobile

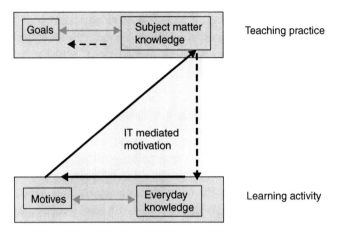

Pedagogical practice

FIGURE 8.2. Using IT-mediated motivation to qualify everyday knowledge through core models.

technologies to achieve their different goals – for example, to create and develop their social networks, profiling themselves and being entertained. In these cases, children acquire the understanding and skills in IT and become motivated and dedicated users based on their needs. The arrow between children's motives and the subject-matter knowledge represents the many opportunities to involve IT in the teaching and draw on, for example, mobile phones; the arrow also represents how IT can engage children in the professional knowledge by involving the everyday knowledge that children are engaged in. The rest of the arrows in the figure are dashed because the link is there but in a fluctuating stability, and this is were we argue to make an extra effort if IT should help to make the link between everyday knowledge and subject-matter knowledge better, thus ensuring children's engagement in the teaching and ensure that they can use the knowledge learned outside the educational setting.

The line between subject-matter knowledge and everyday knowledge is dashed because even if children have used technology to involve the everyday knowledge in the subject-matter knowledge and thus create engagement in the teaching, it is not a given that they know how to relate the subject-matter knowledge to their everyday knowledge. This is where we argue that children need to create models of the subject-matter knowledge they work with so they can benefit from it in other contexts. IT must therefore be able to support an understanding and creation of models in the subject-matter knowledge.

The line between subject-matter knowledge and goal is dashed because IT projects easily can include subject-matter knowledge without complying with the goals set for teaching. That means there are risks that IT can steal the picture from the subject-matter goals defined for the teaching and even if the focus remains of subject-matter knowledge, it is not certain that it fulfils the subject-matter goals defined for the knowledge.

The eBag Application

On the basis of our previous theoretical analysis, which resulted in a theoretical model (Figure 8.2) which outlined a possible linking of teaching practices and learning activities, we draw on a research project in which four classes tested new IT in the form of a software solution called eBag.

The eBag is a Web-based portfolio system with seamless proximity-based login from all interactive surfaces in the physical school environment, for example on mobile phones or on a traditional PC. Consequently, it serves as a link between different types of displays through which its contents can be accessed, and it allows the students to collect, carry, access and share digital information very easily. Thus, the eBag is the student's personal, digital repository in which they can place pictures, video, music, text documents and other digital material for use in and outside of school. With the eBag, the focus is on the ubiquitous aspects of Web support in learning environments that allows the digital information to travel seamlessly across technological platforms. Taking advantage of the current context when placing and retrieving information provides the teachers and students with a sense of seamless interaction with the digital material. The proximity-based login is based on a Bluetooth sensor network, and the eBag itself is 'tied' to a mobile phone with Bluetooth capabilities. The eBag works on almost any mobile phone, utilising the hardware platform that is already in the children's hands or pockets. Thus, whenever the students are within reach of a Bluetooth sensor, their eBags will appear on the display connected to that sensor. For more information about the eBag system, see Brodersen et al. (2005).

The eBag was developed as a part of the iSchool project. The iSchool project was a five-year research project with the vision of creating learning spaces wherein everyday cultural competences, the curiosity and the narrative skills and desires of children and adolescents meet the outside world that surrounds them, the teacher and the school (www.interactivespaces.net). The project aimed to develop an open and 'fluid' information technology with sufficient accessibility and robustness to support learning in and out-side the physical limits of the school, based on the development of software infrastructure, Graphical User Interfaces (GUI) and spatial concepts for new interactive school environments (Iversen & Brodersen, 2008). Using the eBag, teachers and students were provided with the means of experi-encing coherence between the use of digital and physical materials across school libraries, classrooms and on fieldtrips (Bouvin et al., 2005). The eBag was developed in collaboration with teachers, students and researchers (Iversen, 2006; Iversen & Brodersen, 2008).

eBag as IT-Supported Motivation

The preliminary evaluation of the eBag was conducted in the period between January 2006 and April 2006 at four Danish schools enrolling school clas-ses ranging from second to ninth grade. The evaluation consisted of thir-teen semi-structured interviews with students and teachers. Sixty-three students participated in the interviews. In addition, four focus interviews with six teachers were carried out. These qualitative data was supported by data deriving from a questionnaire which was handed out to every student in classes picked for evaluation. Seventy-three respondents answered the questionnaire (100 per cent response). For further information of the evalu-ation method and its results, see Stenild (2007).

All students were generally pleased to be able to use their mobiles in the classroom, and the use of mobile phones had a positive effect on student engagement. It proved effective both with students who did not usually have much experience in IT, and with the very IT-savvy students. Mobile phones' mere involvement was in line with Hedegaard's conception of the stimulating motive to engage students in the subject-matter knowledge acquisition.

The students were keen to make meaningful use of mobile phones in teaching and were generally motivated to find uses for both mobile phones and the eBag. The students were engaged through the stimulating motive: to be allowed to use mobile phones in the classroom, and together to create new meaningful motives for using IT in school.

Most surprisingly to the research team, students and teachers said that the eBag application did not make any difference regarding the students' motivation for school learning or portfolio building in their recess time. The students treated the eBag as school software – with no or only very limited relevance to their recess time activities. The students reported how the eBag software helped them to do their homework and supported the communication between school and home. However, the eBag only solved some practical problems and was only used as a PC application and not, as intended, as a mobile phone application. Thus, the vision of supporting the students' learning across and between institutions was not fulfilled.

DISCUSSION

In this section we will discuss the findings from the preliminary evaluation of the eBag research project. The students have a lot of narrative knowledge and experience with their mobile phones from their everyday lives. They possess comprehensive knowledge of how to operate their mobile phones and can be considered experts in using their own mobile phones. This everyday knowledge comes from motives created in a non-educational setting, and the preliminary evaluation indicated that the children had no trouble bringing this narrative knowledge into play in an educational setting and combining their narrative knowledge with subject-matter knowledge.

As our research has not focused on how students acquire theoretical knowledge, we cannot determine that mobile technology used in an educational setting will ensure theoretical knowledge, only whether or not the foundations are present. The mobile phones supported the students in drawing on their everyday knowledge when working with subject-matter teaching, and we argue that there is a positive effect in inviting this knowledge into the educational setting. We acknowledge that using everyday knowledge in an educational setting is indeed nothing new and that there are many great teachers who are combining everyday knowledge with subject-matter knowledge to help students to acquire theoretical knowledge.

We argue that mobile technology could be a valuable resource for these teachers if the focus is not only on using technology as motivation to involve the everyday knowledge in the subject-matter knowledge. The point we are making is that the focus should be on longer-lasting motives and creating models of the subject-matter knowledge that the students can work with so they can benefit from it in other contexts. The students should learn to use this generalisable knowledge in concrete interactions with different aspects of their worlds. To use the full potential of mobile phones in an educational practice, the learning practice needs to include a shared understanding on mobile phones use in a shared practice and what possibilities and limitations there are in different contexts. We believe that Hedegaard and

Chaiklin's conceptions within the radical local approach of students modelling their knowledge can be useful to further explore the full potential of
mobile phones in an educational setting.

The evaluation indicated that the students' usage of schools resources
(the eBag) was a motivating factor for the students and brought about a
range of new ideas concerning the use of mobile technology in school
context. Contrary to many IT artefacts presented to the students in an educational setting, the students' mobile phones were, seen from Wartofsky's
(1979) theory, not only primary artefacts introduced to help the student
in the subject-matter learning, but were already secondary artefacts to
the children because of their experience in their everyday life. Combining
the mobile phones and the educational setting led to an understanding
of the mobile phones as tertiary artefacts for many of the students. They
not only understood to use the mobile as a serious tool in the subject-
matter learning, but also themselves further developed the use of the mobile
phones within the educational setting. The preliminary evaluation did not,
however, focus on the student perspectives and understanding of mobile
technology before and after the evaluation, so we cannot evaluate whether
the students changed their perspective on their own mobile phones and the
possibilities for usages depending on the context they where in.

The eBag concept offers no specific theoretical knowledge in terms of
creating models of the usage of mobile phones and the implications of this
usage in different settings. From a radical local teaching and learning perspective, this is necessary in order to qualify the everyday knowledge that
the students possess concerning the use of their mobile phones so that it
transforms into theoretical knowledge. This argument can help us to explain
why the use of the students' personal mobile phones was successful. The
combination of the everyday knowledge that is brought into school context
by the student's personal mobile phone and the subject-matter knowledge
from school curriculum opens up the opportunity for theoretical knowledge to occur.

The students could easily combine their everyday knowledge from their
mobile phones with the eBag in an educational setting. They were, however, unable to see the possibilities the eBag had when combined with their
mobile phones in their everyday lives. They did not have an understanding of the eBag as mobile software set apart from the educational context.
The eBag was presented as an educational tool in an educational context by
teachers representing this context. The eBag was a success in the extended
context of the school. The students were excited to use the eBag for homework and sharing of school-related knowledge, but would leave the eBag – as

they would a normal school bag – when they were finished with their home assignments.

Our theoretical understanding of the link between teaching and learning, where IT is seen as a tool of mediation between everyday knowledge and subject-matter knowledge, as illustrated in Figure 8.2, focuses on three major areas:

1. How IT can engage children in subject-matter knowledge by involving the everyday knowledge that children are engaged in.
2. How IT can support the build-up of subject-matter knowledge so that it continues to meet the academic goals set for education.
3. How IT can help to connect subject-matter knowledge with the children's everyday knowledge, so they are able to use it outside of school.

We have argued that these three areas may be linked, starting with IT use in everyday life as the motivational element. We based our argument on the eBag research project and illustrated this linkage in Figure 8.2. By involving mobile phones in a teaching practice, the eBag research project built on the engagement that children had in their personal mobile phones, and thereby attempted to transfer this engagement to involvement in the subject-matter knowledge. For IT to function as mediator, it needs to be able to support children's use of subject-matter knowledge in everyday contexts and at the same time ensure that the goals set for a teaching practice are met through subject-matter knowledge.

We still believe that these three areas together allow an IT-supported mediation between children's learning and teaching practice by bridging their everyday knowledge within a spiral loop, where all parts of the spiral must be linked for a successful IT-supported mediation to take place.

CONCLUSION

We stress that the cultural-historical analysis we have undertaken can help to make the potential in IT and mobile technologies apparent for all and can help to make advantageous use of IT and mobile technology capabilities to bridge between everyday knowledge and subject-matter knowledge.

From the eBag research project we can conclude that IT and mobile technologies can, in fact, help to mediate between teaching practice and learning activity if children's everyday knowledge with these technologies is included in the practice of school teaching. IT and mobile technologies can be seen as teaching tools that can help to support 'the double move approach' if they are built to support theoretical knowledge in teaching practices. We also argue that IT and mobile technologies can support and generate motives for children to use subject-matter knowledge learnt in school in their everyday life.

Based on children's motives from their everyday lives, they acquire the understanding and skills in IT and become engaged and dedicated users. IT can motivate children to acquire subject-matter knowledge by involving the everyday knowledge that children are engaged in; however, it is not a given that IT can help the children to relate the subject-matter knowledge to their everyday knowledge. Drawing on the 'double move' learning theory, we argue that children need to create core models of the subject matter-knowledge they work with so they can benefit from it in other contexts. IT must, therefore, be able to support an understanding and creation of models in the subject-matter knowledge, that also support the goals set for the subject-matter knowledge.

REFERENCES

Bouvin, N. O., Brodersen, C., Hansen, F. A., Iversen, O. S., & Nørregaard, P. (2005). Tools of contextualization: Extending the classroom to the field. In *Proceedings of the 2005 Conference on Interaction Design and Children* (pp. 24–31), Boulder, Colorado, 8–10 June 2005.

Brodersen, A. C., Christensen, B. G., Grønbæk, K., Dindler, C., & Sundararajah, B. (2005). eBag: A ubiquitous Web infrastructure for nomadic learning. In *Proceedings of the 14th International World Wide Web Conference, Association for Computing Machinery* (pp. 298–306), Chiba, Japan.

Hedegaard, M. (2002). *Learning and child development.* Aarhus: Aarhus University Press.

Hedegaard, M., & Chaiklin, S. (2005). *Radical-local teaching and learning: A cultural-historical approach.* Aarhus: Aarhus University Press.

Iversen, O. S. (2006). Participatory design beyond work practices – designing with children. PhD dissertation, Dept. of Computer Science, University of Aarhus.

Iversen, O. S., & Brodersen C. (2008). Building a BRIDGE between children and users: A socio-cultural approach to child-computer interaction. *Cognition, Technology & Work, 10*(2), 83–93.

Leontiev, A. (1978). *Activity, consciousness and personality.* Englewood Cliffs, NJ: Prentice-Hall.

Ministry of Education (2006). The primary schools goals translated. Danish Ministry of Education homepage, available at http://pub.uvm.dk/2006/faellesmaal/folkeskolens_formaal.html

Stenild, K. (2007). IT I Folkeskolen – Hverdagslivsengagement som tilgang til implementering af IT I læringspraksis. Master thesis, University of Aarhus.

Vygotsky, S. L. (1982). *Om barnets psykiske udvikling – En artikelsamling [The psychic development of children – a collection of articles]*. Copenhagen: Nyt Nordisk Forlag Arnold Busck.

   (1987). *The collected works of L. S. Vygtosky: Vol 1. Problems of general psychology*. New York. Plenum.

Wartofsky, W. M. (1979). *Models: Representation and scientific understanding*. Dordrecht: Reidel.

9

Motivation for School Learning: Enhancing the Meaningfulness of Learning in Communities of Learners

WILLEM WARDEKKER, ANNOESJKA BOERSMA, GEERT
TEN DAM AND MONIQUE VOLMAN

INTRODUCTION: SCHOOL AND MOTIVATION

Teachers, especially in secondary education, report student motivation for learning to be their biggest problem (e.g. Del Río & Álvarez, 2002). This problem has, of course, long been present, but seems to have become more pressing over the last twenty years or so. Several changes in society may be identified as contributing to this development. The importance of school as a place for the acquisition of knowledge has gradually diminished since printed media became widely accessible, but the advent of Internet has accelerated the perceived function loss. The relevance of school has become unclear to students, whereas its socialisation function, given form as the 'transmission' of values and norms, is something young people have long been sceptical about, if not resistant towards.

A cultural-historical understanding of motivation and the associated problems in school is quite different from the two ideas that have dominated educational thinking on this subject: (1) that adequate teaching procedures will take care of motivation problems (see e.g. Thorndike, 1913; Oelkers, 1998), and (2) that motivation is part of the meta-cognitive skills a student needs to develop in order to be able to study properly (see e.g. Boekaerts & Cascallar, 2006). Cultural-historical theory, on the other hand (e.g. Davydov, 1999; Engeström, 1987; Fichtner, 1985; Lompscher, 1999; Lompscher & Hedegaard, 1999), interprets motivation as rooted in the dialectical relation between student and educational activity. Motivation may be understood as arising from the personal subjective meaning a student can attach to participating in the activity of school-going in the form that it takes at a given moment. Motivation in this sense is not the rather short-lived kind engendered by the experience of something unexpected, as when the chemistry teacher performs an experiment that ends with a bang. Nor is it the same thing as 'having a good time' in school, when that good time does not also challenge students to take a next step in their development. Motivation for school learning is, from this point of view, directly related to meaningful learning.

In this chapter, we discuss problems of student motivation in cultural-historical terms. We will maintain that motivation cannot be adequately understood in relation to educational goals and objectives alone; students have their own intended curriculum. As an empirical illustration of our theoretical position, we present some results of a study in which we tried to restructure part of a secondary pre-vocational curriculum in the Netherlands with the goal of reducing problems of motivation by realising meaningful education.

THEORY: MOTIVATION, EMOTION, VALUE

According to Leontiev (1978), motivation does not reside in the individual, but arises in a dialectic between the individual and features of the activities in which he or she participates. Through participation in activities a person's needs become concrete in actions on the 'object of activity', which in turn directs the motivation to act. Or to express this as Leontiev does, an activity is directed towards an object, and a person participates in that activity because this object orientation promises to satisfy this subject's need. The object of the activity, then, in fact can be said to motivate the subject's activity. In that activity, learning occurs through qualitative changes in the relationship between individual and object of activity arising from the learner's actions on the object.

As people participate in different activities, not only do their motivations change and develop, but also their needs are differentiated according to the possibilities afforded by the cultural practices in which they participate. Moreover, participating in an activity usually has multiple motivations. Thus a specific constellation of needs, goals and motivations develops for every individual, which Leontiev calls personality. In this context, Hedegaard (2002, p. 55) distinguishes between the terms *motivation* (referring 'to that dynamism and the actual goals that characterise a person's relationship to his surroundings in concrete activities and situations') and *motive* (referring to 'the goals that come to characterise a person's actions in different activities over a longer period of time' – such goals may be so persistent, that Hedegaard speaks of 'life motives'). The development of motives is thus related both to the activities a person engages in and to the gradual differentiation of that person's needs and character traits. It is, therefore, closely related to the development of personality or of personal identity. In a concrete situation, motivation and motives should ideally be connected or even coincide. This is a condition for the person to feel satisfied with participating. However, Leontiev and other writers do not always clearly distinguish between the two terms (at least not in the translations of Leontiev we used), or use them in different senses (e.g. motivation as the explicit account we give of the reasons for an action, while a deeper motive remains hidden: Leontiev, 1978, p. 122).

Given that participation is always multi-motivated, Leontiev distinguishes between two kinds of motivations: sense-forming motives that give participating in an activity personal sense (subjective meaning), and secondary or stimulating motives. The first kind is related to values:

> [T]he personal sense they [i.e. conscious phenomena] attain depends on what prompted the activity, that is, what motive was guiding the individual. Even to imagine a different motive for a particular action puts it and its internal psychical character into an entirely different light. A courageous deed carried out for one's people and country is a splendid thing and evinces a spirit of high morality. If, however, the principal motive of such a deed, and its sense for the acting individual, are more narrowly egotistical, then the act takes on a different character: it is morally less valued and evokes entirely different feelings. (Leontiev, 1993/1975, p. 24)

Stimulating motives are responsible for the emotional colouring of participating in an activity (van Oers, 1987, p. 104). Especially where stimulating motives clash with sense-generating motives, negative emotions occur.

Although interpretations differ, González Rey (2008; this volume) notes that Leontiev's theory focuses on the objective motivation-generating characteristics of an activity. Such a theory downplays the 'authorship' of the subject and interprets personality, and with that Hedegaard's concept of life motive, as the almost causal result of participation in activities. Leontiev emphasises the system of social relations and the person's position in this system rather than individual character traits and experiences. With González Rey, however, we think that more emphasis needs to be given to the subjective sense of participation. In this context, we want to give more weight to the conscious aspects of motivation, and of the process of deciding how to act in general. When motivations and personality aspects become conscious, they are put into words and structured in narrative-like self-concepts or 'identities' (Holland et al., 1998). These self-concepts are used when people try to govern their actions and their choices. There is, however, no one-to-one relationship between self-concepts and personality or motivations: self-concepts try to express how people understand themselves and their position in activities, but they may understand themselves incompletely or even incorrectly. Also, self-concepts do not determine action choices, but are used in a heuristic way. This implies that the relationship between motivations, emotions, and actions is more complicated than Leontiev's model suggests.

For Leontiev, emotions are indications of a relationship between motives and the perceived probability of success:

> The special feature of emotions is that they reflect relationships between motives (needs) and success, or the possibility of success, of realizing the action of the subject that responds to these motives. Here we are speaking not about the reflection of these relationships but about a direct sensory reflection of them, about experiencing. Thus they appear as a result of actualization of a motive (need), and before a rational evaluation by the subject of his activity. (Leontiev, 1978, p. 120)

However, the fact that needs, motives and participation in activities may be mediated by self-concepts puts the 'unreflected' quality of emotions into question. Negative emotions occur, for instance, when a person considers the attainment of the goal of an activity, given their conscious evaluation of their present competences, improbable. Such situations have been described by Meijers & Wardekker (2003) as 'boundary experiences' that call for revision of one's self-concept and/or for the acquisition of new competences. Thus, as a consequence of the mediating role of self-concepts, we need to interpret a person's actions and the account they give of their motives in a way that takes account both of the 'objective' realisation of needs afforded by their participation in an activity and of their subjective evaluations. This will turn out to be especially relevant in evaluating students' participation in educational settings.

Here it becomes significant that school-going is an activity related in a specific way to other activities: It intends to make it possible for students to participate in other activities. Student motivation in school therefore needs to connect to their wish to participate more fully and more centrally in societal activities. Our argument is that to engage young people's motivation, schools should make the relation of the curriculum to the students' experiences of practices outside the school explicit. This line of thought makes it necessary to pay more attention to the school as a setting in which motivation for learning can and must be *created*.

ANALYSIS: THE USE VALUE OF EDUCATION

School has historically developed as a solution to the problem of the growing complexity and abstractness of the instruments used in societal practices. Writing and arithmetic especially are instruments which are difficult to acquire in the context of acting within other activities: Learning them requires focused attention and the aid of others who have already mastered them. By creating a specific place for this attention, school has enabled the development of complex practices. This separation, however, has also had less desirable effects: School has separated learning and learners from the cultural practices for which it is supposed to prepare them. Firstly, school itself has become an activity setting, quite apart from the curricular content; therefore, students may develop both conscious and unconscious motivations for wanting or not wanting to participate in this activity itself. Secondly, students are often unable to see the relevance of the often abstract subject matter taught in schools – abstract in the sense that its relations to cultural practices that are experientially known to the students remain vague or non-existent for them. Only a few become interested in engaging with knowledge for its own sake. Many students become bored or reluctant, which relates to another source of negative emotions regarding school: the pressure of peers and of the culturally established idea that school is, or even ought to be, boring. Motivation problems in school are related to this fundamental contradiction in education in a complex way.

Engeström (1987, p. 95 v.) calls the dominant activity related to schools, described from the point of view of students, 'school-going'. According to his analysis, this activity (under the conditions of capitalism) is determined by a primary contradiction, that of schooling and the qualifications it offers as an instrument of 'content mastery' – which he labels 'use value' – versus as an instrument of 'societal success', which he labels 'exchange value'. Both lead to the student becoming a member of society, which is the object of the activity of schooling, although in different senses. An important consequence, however, is that students also have contradictory and competing motivations for participating: acquiring 'really useful knowledge' (related to the school's task of enabling students to participate in other practices) versus reaching the finish with as little effort as possible (related to the school being an activity setting in its own right). The way Engeström understands school-going from the perspective of students leads him to think that the exchange value motive has become dominant and the use value motive is underplayed. He sees schoolwork as working on texts that function as objects instead of as instruments or tools with which to understand and operate on the world:

> This object [i.e. the school text] is molded by pupils in a curious manner: the outcome of their activity is above all the same text reproduced and modified orally or in written form.... Since the dominant task is to reproduce and modify the given text, the role of the text in the societal practice, in the activity systems where it is created and used, is necessarily of peripheral importance. (o.c., p. 101)

This kind of engagement with texts can hardly lead to students becoming independent and creative thinkers, which for Engeström is necessary for schools to have the kind of use value he envisages. Indeed, one might suppose that this kind of education does not systematically satisfy students' need for learning in a way that helps them to make sense of the world, leading to negative emotions about school and consequent demotivation.

Engeström's analysis, although illuminating, is also quite one-sided. 'School-going' is an activity which is more diverse and has more internal contradictions than are apparent in Engeström's description. Most teachers, and most educational thinkers, are not satisfied with a form of education in which subject-matter content is only important for the selection function of education – which, by the way, does not imply that they share a common perspective on what exactly constitutes the use value of education (cf. Wardekker, 2004). Our point is that the cultural-historical perspective does allow a place for education which has use value, even though any educational setting will always have to contend with a tendency towards exchange value and with mixed motives (see the difference between sense-generating and stimulating motives) on the part of students.

The concept of 'learning activity' helps us to elaborate the use value of education. Learning activity, according to Lompscher and Hedegaard (1999), is

> a special kind of activity directed towards the acquisition of societal knowledge and skills through their individual re-production by means of special learning actions upon learning objects (subject matter methods and knowledge). Confronted with a certain subject matter area, learners can acquire skill and knowledge only by actively acting with the material according to its substance and structure (content and methods).... The coordination, communication and cooperation between learners, and with other people, is one of the most essential features of learning activity. (p. 12)

In the educational practices on which Hedegaard and others report, learners are given a culturally available model, schema or concept which they then use together in a specific kind of activity (learning activity) to elaborate phenomena in a certain disciplinary area, so they can make sense of them. Fichtner (1985) additionally points out that such learning brings about a transformation in the way students interpret the world and their position in it: In the process, their relationship with the world changes in qualitatively different ways, a transformation which is akin to that envisaged by the German tradition of Bildung.

However, this transformation does not always happen, and not always in the way intended by the school, the curriculum or the teacher. The previous quote looks at the process in the 'objective' tradition described by Leontiev, from the perspective of the activity as a whole. To understand the learning processes of individual students, we need to look at the practice of education from the perspective of the students, and examine how they work on and in it to create their social situations of development in a dialectical relationship with this institutional practice (Hedegaard, 2002). In other words, we need to take into account their self-concepts and the ways these are brought into play in the learning process. Students' engagement with educational practices, however well thought out these may be, is always mediated by their personal identities.

Here we need to remember that such learning activities take place in the institutional environment of the school, and students will always be aware of the specific properties of that environment. In other words, students are participating in two intertwined activities, that of 'school-going' and that of 'learning for use value', at the same time, with sometimes conflicting motives. Also, in actual school practice, not only the abstract concepts are derived from disciplinary sources, but often the problems to be worked on by the students as well, and thus not necessarily connected to students' personal identities as these mostly relate to social practices outside the school rather than to disciplinary ones. After all, it is actually one of the tasks of the school to make students acquainted with disciplinary practices, but this cannot fruitfully be done by just confronting them with such practices. This is where a more detailed analysis becomes necessary of what makes learning meaningful for students.

MOTIVATION AND MEANINGFULNESS

When we say that motivation is a problem, we do so from the cultural-historical point of view that motivation is directly connected with the object of an activity. The fact that students in school participate in at least two intertwined activities is significant here. In the activity of being in school, learning 'to be a student' occurs more or less unconsciously. It is what all students learn best and quickest – although it does not necessarily imply becoming a 'good' student as defined by the system. Participating in learning activity, however, has different properties. Here, learning becomes the object of the activity, and thus has to answer some need of the students. Moreover, learning in this sense is a conscious process requiring conscious effort. This means that learning activity is necessarily mediated by the students' identity (self-concepts). In learning activity, students need to be able to understand the relation between their own existence and the object of the activity. When a teacher's goal is unclear, or does not coincide with those of the students, students will either drop out of the activity or transform it into a different kind of activity. They may either revert to the kind of motivation connected with the exchange value of education or use the school space for quite different activities such as relating to classmates. Students are motivated to participate in learning activity directed at the use value of education only when engagement in classroom activities makes sense to them and is related to their prior, current, and (imagined) future existence.

Our argument is thus that a cultural-historical elaboration of education should explicitly try to create such relations for students. One way to do that is to engage students in activities as they occur outside the school, or in activities that are adapted to fit within the possibilities and limitations of the school. This 'natural' or 'authentic' learning takes its inspiration from forms of learning as they supposedly existed before schools became the only place for learning. Rogoff and Lave (1984), for example, have suggested that the medieval model of apprenticeship had advantages over modern-age schooling practices, in that for students it is easy to see the practical relevance of what they are doing.

The immediate meaningfulness created by 'authentic' situations is, however, not enough. The task of the school is to motivate students to go beyond the limits of what they can readily see as relevant to their own lives, as this scope may be limited by their cultural background and previous experiences. As Ziehe (2000, 2004) argues, the school should give students access to areas of culture that are not part of their everyday cultural consciousness. Also, it should show them that in every cultural activity system there are different roles, and they are not necessarily confined to the roles their social background deems suitable for them. Both these tasks for the school are important in the light of what Van Oers (2009) qualifies as the ultimate aim of education: to help students to develop agency in cultural practices.

The combination of elements of authenticity and 'transcending the constraints of the everyday' has been termed a 'second generation apprenticeship model' (we owe the term to Juan Daniel Ramírez Garrido, personal communication). In such a model, learning directly from a patron in the context of a practical demand is complemented by the availability of modern-age resources like books and other media, and by the distinctive quality of the school of providing space and cognitive instruments for reflection.

In such a system, students do not primarily participate with the goal of becoming 'central' or skilled participants, but as a 'community of inquiry' where participation and critical reflection – both on the nature of the practice and on their own relation to it – are balanced, with the ultimate goal of developing citizens who exercise what Dewey called 'a discriminating heart and mind'. Especially, the critical reflection should extend to those aspects of real practices (as found outside the school) which are boring, oppressive and supporting inequality (Ten Dam, Volman, & Wardekker, 2004, p. 71).

These ideas point in the direction of a cultural-historical revision of the concept of creating 'communities of learners', as we will now argue.

MOTIVATION IN COMMUNITIES OF LEARNERS

A concept of schooling that has attracted a lot of attention lately, and that explicitly tries to enhance student motivation, is 'community of learners' (Brown & Campione, 1990, 1994). Although this concept is often understood within a cognitive, socio-constructivist, paradigm, it may also be conceptualised from a cultural-historical perspective. In our view, such an interpretation is characterised by the following set of emphases (Ten Dam & Volman, 2009).

First of all, a meaningful setting is a key characteristic of cultural-historical communities of learners. This entails participation in social practices in the sense of historically and culturally evolved constellations of human activities that have a particular value and meaning within society (e.g. business, art, care). Thus, a motive in the sense of Leontiev's theory is provided. In a school context, activities organised in such a manner that students can learn something from them are of primary concern (e.g. having students run the school cafeteria in order to learn about business and logistics). Working with disciplinary 'big ideas' as advocated in Brown's original concept is just one example of meaningful settings which are worth exploring. Certainly for students in vocational education, meaningful roles may include the role of inquirer or researcher but also other roles one can take up in society, for example organiser, trader, caregiver and so forth. That is, as 'legitimate peripheral participants' (Lave & Wenger, 1991), students can assume a variety of roles that are meaningful in social practices.

Secondly, learning takes place in a social setting, which does not merely refer to the group of students involved in the collaboration but to the activity itself in which students are involved. The social setting encompasses knowledge, concepts, instruments (tools) and so forth. The resources that the students call upon are themselves social products and are meaningful within the activities of the community (Rogoff, Goodman Turkanis, & Bartlett, 2001). Students can master these tools by putting them to use within the relevant setting and with an image of the goal to be achieved ('prolepsis'). In such a social setting, the teacher or another, more capable adult or peer plays a critical role in the support of the participation of students. That is, teachers and learners together create a 'zone of proximal development' in which learning takes place. The social situations in which students participate are 'pre-arranged' to make them suitable for learning, but not fixed.

Thirdly, learning involves becoming a member of particular communities (Lave & Wenger, 1991; Wells, 2000). Student learning is not aimed at knowledge building as such, but at learning to participate in societal practices, for which knowledge is one requisite. Examples of such an outcome include being able to run a store with one's own products, organise a school trip to France or an exhibition. From the point of view of students, acquiring knowledge and skills is a by-product of these activities. Not only knowledge and skills undergo development, but also the manner in which the student participates in an activity and thus the identity of the student. Learning is identity building (Wells, 1999).

Finally, a cultural-historical interpretation stresses that the participants in an activity can and should learn to be critical participants. The focus of learning should be on transformation not only of themselves, but also of the practices in which they participate (Edwards, 2005; Engeström, 1999). This requires participants to build a sense of critical responsibility. Not only the rules for participation in an activity are thus of importance, but also, in particular, the degrees of freedom associated with participation in an activity (van Oers, 2010).

This wording of the argument mostly focuses on the 'objective' side of motives as emphasised in Leontiev's theory. The impression created is that motivation of students is, if not caused, then at least induced by measures that structure a learning situation. 'Meaningfulness' is a two-sided concept, however, the other side being that participation in such practices is ideally also experienced as personally meaningful by students themselves, so that they can see themselves as (potential) participants in such activities outside the school context (van Oers, 2009; van Oers & Wardekker, 1999). Students import their own lives into the school, and their motive structure is not wholly school-based. Neither is it the straight addition of all their experiences. Identity is a person's own construction and as such is not fully predictable. Educational situations should offer space, help and incentives for students to do this construction work. A focus on learning exactly what has been prescribed is counterproductive in this respect; rather one should encourage independent thinking and creativity. This also implies that even the best community of learners cannot be sure to engage all students – they always have a choice in the matter.

This suggestion has implications for how we organise student learning. 'Meaningful' should be interpreted not only as 'connected to societally relevant activities', but also as 'relevant to the image each student has of their own past, present and future existence', while acknowledging that the acquisition of knowledge and other artefacts as tools may lead to changes in that image. The students themselves change (Beach, 1999) and, as they become aware of this, they can also take their new selves into other contexts. In learning, they change their own 'social situation of development'. If made aware of this, they may also feel being taken seriously, that they can make a real contribution to the process, which in itself is motivating.

AN EMPIRICAL ILLUSTRATION

Despite the overwhelming number of articles on communities of learners, relatively few empirical studies of the effects on actual student motivation can be found. The majority of the relevant studies concern student achievement in various disciplines and subject areas (e.g. Engle & Conant, 2002; Shulman & Sherin, 2004). We have been unable to find relevant empirical studies from a cultural-historical point of view .

In the past few years, we have been struggling with the issue of motivation and engagement in a research project into learning in a community of learners, in which we built on a cultural-historical perspective. In this section, we will present an illustration of our theoretical discussion about student motivation from a cultural-historical perspective.

The project was conducted over two years in co-operation with two schools for pre-vocational secondary education, focusing on a Care and Welfare course (Boersma, Ten Dam, Volman, & Wardekker, 2010). Pre-vocational education aims at providing students with general competences and preparing students for advanced vocational education. It ideally involves making students aware of their own motives and the character of vocational practices, asking them to reflect on their own position. Here, we concentrate on one series of lessons that was designed in each school for ninth-grade students (ages fourteen to fifteen years). The subject was the so-called Make A Difference Day (MADD), modelled on the national volunteer day in the Netherlands. We wanted students to acquire competences in the context of their intended use (cf. Tuomi-Gröhn & Engeström, 2003). The idea was to allow students to experience being the provider of some form of care and by doing so to experience not being able to participate fully in these practices due to faulty or missing competences. The focus of the lessons was on introducing the students into Care and Welfare practices and providing basic knowledge, skills and attitudes necessary for students to be able to participate in a legitimate and peripheral way (Boersma et al., 2008). The students were asked to choose a volunteer activity from several options proposed by various Care and Welfare institutions. They could also come up with their own volunteer activity. The students prepared for the MADD-activity in teams of four-to-six students. The teachers offered special consultation hours, assignments (i.e. a small essay about the institution/target group, a preliminary visit to the institution/target group, the formulation of a plan of action), and non-compulsory workshops. The teams then went to the institutions to participate in the vocational practices with the employees on site. Afterwards, the students reported on their experiences during a presentation evening that they organised for their classmates and parents. The activity occupied a total of four full days. The lessons were analysed from the perspective of their societal as well as personal meaningfulness. We report here on some of the qualitative data gathered in the project.

Fien and Laura were in a team of four students who decided to volunteer in a retirement home for people with dementia. Some preparations were made at school. The teacher gave the group considerable freedom to prepare for the MADD-activity. The employees in the nursing home involved the students in each activity by letting them observe the conduct of affairs and join in the activity. Later on, as the employees saw that the students were doing well on their own, they left the students alone with the residents, requiring the students to assume the role of an activity leader.

The MADD days stimulated Fien and Laura to increase their efforts to live up to the expectations of the teachers, the employees at the institution and their parents. Furthermore, during and after the activity afternoon at the retirement home, they were able to show some competences necessary for working with people suffering from dementia. The students felt proud when a residence employee complimented their actions. Both Fien and Laura reported feeling that they were taken serious during the activity and treated as legitimate members of the vocational community. They may thus be seen to respond to the object-motive of the activity (in the sense of Leontiev) as designed by the school and the researchers. Even here, however, elements of use value and exchange value are intertwined: Living up to expectations is connected to school-going rather than to learning activity. However, when we look at the subjective reasons (motivations) the girls had, they differed in their reasons for increased effort.

Laura, previously known to be a persistent non-worker, appeared to appreciate the MADD days because of the liberty she was given. For example, Laura chose to join the girls team, not because she wanted to learn about elderly people with dementia, but because she wanted to be with her friend Jeanet. In fact, she was and remained convinced that she did not want to work with elderly people in the future at all. The goal of the MADD days' activity did not coincide with Laura's learning needs, so she found a motive in the activity that differed from what the school intended: having fun with her friends. Laura could not recognize the use value of the MADD days for her own acting and thinking; she participated for other reasons.

Fien appeared to have selected the activity because it was in line with her future work plans. The goal of the MADD days thus did match optimally with her motives. However, the MADD days' lessons could not add much to what Fien already knew about working with elderly people. She participated enthusiastically, but afterwards she was disappointed. The students were given considerable freedom for the conduct of the activities, the purpose of the community of learners project being for the students to *really* participate in actual vocational practice. But as the employees had had no time to meet with the students ahead of time, the students were not involved in the preparation of the activity afternoon. Consequently, the structure of the activity did not offer Fien enough opportunities to deepen her interest and knowledge.

Working as a community of learners therefore did not increase the motivation in the learning process of all students in the same way. Both students did recognize the use value of the MADD days. But they valued the MADD days subjectively in different ways, according with their learning needs. In both cases, there was a mismatch to some degree between the intended object-motive (preparation for the world of work) and the students' motives. The conclusion has to be that in a community of learners, as probably in any learning situation, the alignment between the intentions of the institution and the actual motives of the students is crucial.

CONCLUSIONS

Our analysis of the problem of motivation in education led us to believe that student motivation for learning is largely a question of meaningfulness, and requires the alignment of the object-motives contained in the curriculum with the identity-mediated motives of the students. The relevance (and thus the object-motive) of the normal curriculum is often difficult to understand for students. This problem does not disappear when teachers try to catch the attention of students by introducing new, exciting or popular elements into their lessons. Learning needs to be organised in such a way that students can relate educational content to their own past, present and imagined future, and are stimulated to do so. The concept of Communities of Learners, interpreted within a cultural-historical perspective, represents a possible form for this. In our empirical study, we found that working as a community of learners indeed motivated the students more than learning in a regular setting.

However, this does not take account of the individual motives of students. Our findings also suggest that not all students are motivated to participate in practices in similar ways. The students' own motivations play into creating different social situations of development for each participant. The alignment between the motives behind the curriculum and the personal motives of students for participating in the community (cf. Rogoff et al., 2003) requires having an eye for the differences in motives between students. Such differences, mediated by their identity and thus by previous experiences, may, globally speaking, be associated with, for example, gender or ethnic background (Holland, Lachicotte, Skinner, & Cain, 1998; Ten Dam, Volman, & Wardekker, 2004), but even such factors are experienced differently, so motivation is always related to individual differences in sense formation, as in the case of Fien and Laura.

Alignment of motives does not imply that teachers have to take the existing motivations of students as a given. Students play an autonomous, active role in their own education (see also Penuel & Wertsch, 1995; Volman & Ten Dam, 2007), but teachers can influence that role by helping students to recognise motives in practices and to align their motives with those of the practices. This dynamic between motives and practices is especially important in relation to the stated aim of education as endowing students with *agency* in cultural practices (van Oers, 2010). Agency implies being aware of your own position, role and competences, and being aware also that you can change these. The problems with realising this in schools are essentially related to the fact that for the students, a school situation can never be as 'real' as a cultural practice itself. Students would have to learn to build relationships between various elements of education and 'real' practices. This is a real challenge, even for Communities of Learners.

Discovering that one does not have the knowledge and skills to participate in an activity can be distressing, and it can lead to the student's withdrawal if he or she does not expect to be able to remedy the situation. Meeting this challenge may involve developing a new view of oneself, a (partially) new identity, and it is the task of the community, and especially of the teacher, to help students to make this transition. This, then, points at the importance of affective processes in education.

REFERENCES

Beach, K. (1999). Consequential transitions: A sociocultural expedition beyond transfer in education. *Review of Research in Education, 24*, 46–69.

Boekaerts, M., & Cascallar, E. (2006). How far have we moved toward the integration of theory and practice in self-regulation? *Educational Psychology Review, 18*(3), 199–210.

Boersma, A., Ten Dam, G., Volman, M., & Wardekker, W. (2008). *Motivation through activity in a community of learners for vocational education.* Paper for the ISCAR Congress, San Diego.

(2010). 'This baby... it isn't alive.' Towards a community of learners for vocational orientation. *British Educational Research Journal, 36*(1), 3–25.

Brown, A. L., & Campione, J. C. (1990). Communities of learning and thinking. In D. Kuhn (Ed.), *Contributions to human development* (Vol. 21), 108–125.

(1994). Guided discovery in a community of learners. In K. McGilly (Ed.), *Classroom lessons: Integrating cognitive theory and classroom practice* (p. 229–270). Cambridge, MA: MIT Press.

Davydov, V. V. (1999). What is real learning activity? In M. Hedegaard & J. Lompscher (Eds.), *Learning activity and development* (pp. 123–138). Aarhus: Aarhus University Press.

Del Río, P., & Álvarez, A. (2002). From activity to directivity: The question of involvement in education. In G. Wells & G. Claxton (Eds.), *Learning for life in the 21st century* (pp. 59–72). Oxford: Blackwell.

Edwards, A. (2005). Let's get beyond community and practice: The many meanings of learning by participating. *The Curriculum Journal, 16*, 49–65.

Engeström, Y. (1987). *Learning by expanding. An activity-theoretical approach to developmental research.* Helsinki: Orienta-Konsultit Oy.

(1999) Activity theory and individual and social transformation. In Y. Engeström, R. Miettinen & R.-L. Punamaki (Eds.), *Perspectives on activity theory.* Cambridge: Cambridge University Press.

Engle, R. A., & Conant, F. R. (2002). Guiding principles for fostering productive disciplinary engagement: Explaining an emergent argument in a community of learners classroom. *Cognition and Instruction, 20*(4), 399–483.

Fichtner, B. (1985). Learning and learning activity – two different types of learning in school and the historical-societal contexts of their development. In E. Bol, J. Haenen & M. Wolters (Eds.), *Education for cognitive development. Proceedings of the third international symposium on activity theory* (pp. 37–58). Den Haag: SVO.

González Rey, F. L. (2008). Subject, subjectivity, and development in cultural-historical psychology. In B. van Oers, W. Wardekker, E. Elbers, & R. van der Veer (Eds.), *The transformation of learning. Advances in cultural-historical activity theory* (pp. 137–154). Cambridge: Cambridge University Press.

Hedegaard, M. (2002). *Learning and child development.* Aarhus: Aarhus University Press.

Holland, D., Lachicotte, W. Jr., Skinner, D., & Cain, C. (1998). *Identity and agency in cultural worlds.* Cambridge, MA: Harvard University Press.

Lave, J., & Wenger, E. (1991). *Situated learning. Legitimate peripheral participation.* Cambridge: Cambridge University Press.

Leontiev, A. N. (1978). *Activity, consciousness, and personality.* (Trans. M. J. Hall). Englewood Cliffs, NJ: Prentice Hall.

(1993 [1975]). The development of the learning motive in children. (Trans. C. Tolman). *Multidisciplinary Newsletter on Activity Theory, 13/14,* 24–38.

Lompscher, J. (1999). Learning activity and its formation: Ascending from the abstract to the concrete. In M. Hedegaard & J. Lompscher (Eds.), *Learning activity and development* (pp. 139–166). Aarhus: Aarhus University Press.

Lompscher, J., & Hedegaard, M. (1999). Introduction. In M. Hedegaard & J. Lompscher (Eds.), *Learning activity and development* (pp. 10–21). Aarhus: Aarhus University Press.

Meijers, F., & Wardekker, W. (2003). Career learning in a changing world: The role of emotions. *International Journal for the Advancement of Counselling, 24*(3), 149–167.

Oelkers, J. (1998). Empirical research in progressive education. *International Journal of Educational Research, 27,* 715–722.

Penuel, W. R., & Wertsch, J. (1995). Vygotsky and identity formation: A sociocultural approach. *Educational Psychologist, 30*(2), 83–92.

Rogoff, B., Goodman Turkanis, C., & Bartlett, L. (2001). *Learning together. Children and adults in a school community.* New York: Oxford University Press.

Rogoff, B., & Lave, J. (Eds.) (1984). *Everyday cognition: Its development in social contexts.* New York: Oxford University Press.

Rogoff, B., Paradise, R., Mejia Arauz, R., Correa-Chavez, M., & Angelillo, C. (2003). First hand learning through intent participation. *Annual Review of Psychology, 54,* 175–203.

Shulman, L. S., & Sherin, M.G. (2004). Fostering communities of teachers as learners: Disciplinary perspectives. *Journal of Curriculum Studies, 36*(2), 135–140.

Ten Dam, G., & Volman, M. (2009). *Communities of learners; Why the concept deserves to be adopted in educational practice.* Keynote at 13th Biennial Conference, EARLI, August 25–29.

Ten Dam, G., Volman, M., & Wardekker, W. (2004). Making sense through participation: Social differences in learning and identity development. In J. van der Linden & P. Renshaw (Eds.), *Dialogic learning* (pp. 63–85). Dordrecht: Kluwer.

Thorndike, E. L. (1913). *Educational psychology, Vol. 2: The psychology of learning.* New York: Columbia University, Teachers College.

Tuomi-Gröhn, T., & Engeström, Y. (Eds.) (2003). *Between school and work. New perspectives on transfer and boundary crossing.* Amsterdam: Pergamon.

Van Oers, B. (1987). *Activiteit en begrip. Proeve van een handelingspsychologische didactiek. [Activity and conceptual understanding].* Amsterdam: VU Uitgeverij.

(2009). Developmental education: improving participation in cultural practices. In M. Fleer, M. Hedegaard, & J. Tudge (Eds.), *Childhood studies and the impact of globalization: Policies and practices at global and local levels. World Yearbook of Education 2009* (pp. 293–317). New York: Routledge.

(2010). Children's enculturation through play. In L. Brooker & S. Edwards (Eds.), *Engaging play* (pp. 195–209). Maidenhead: McGraw Hill.

Van Oers, B., & Wardekker, W. (1999). On becoming an authentic learner: Semiotic activity in the early grades. *Journal of Curriculum Studies, 31*(2), 229–249.

Volman, M., & Ten Dam, G. (2007). Learning and the development of social identities in the subjects Care and Technology. *British Educational Research Journal, 33*(6), 845–866.

Wardekker, W. (2004). Curriculum as vision. In J. Terwel & D. Walker (Eds.), *Curriculum as a shaping force* (pp. 1–15). New York: Nova.

Wells, G. (1999). *Dialogic inquiry. Towards a sociocultural practice and theory of education.* Cambridge: Cambridge University Press.

(2000). Dialogic inquiry in education. In C. Lee & P. Smagorinsky (Eds.), *Vygotskian perspectives on literacy research. Constructing meaning through collaborative inquiry.* (pp. 51–85) Cambridge: Cambridge University Press.

Ziehe, T. (2000). Debate article: School and youth – a differential relation. Reflections on some blank areas in the current reform discussion. *Young, 9*(1), 54–63.

(2004). *Pädagogische Professionalität und zeittypische Mentalitätsrisiken [Educational professionalism and contemporary mental risks].* Keynote address at the CSP Conference, Oslo, June.

PART THREE

CREATING CONDITIONS FOR CHILDREN'S ENGAGEMENT

10

Expertise in the Children's Workforce: Knowledge and Motivation in Engagement with Children

ANNE EDWARDS

MOTIVES AND EXPERTISE IN PROFESSIONAL PRACTICES

In this chapter the gaze turns to the work practices in settings which provide education and care and in which children create social situations of development. These practices are seen as historically formed, imbued with knowledge, freighted with emotion and shaped by the values and purposes of the institutions in which they are located. It is in these practices that the practitioner identities that mediate workers' engagement with children are formed. These practices are therefore part of, what Taylor (1995) has called, the 'background' from which people's engaged agency emerges. The very circularity of this account means that opening up the practices of educationally oriented work with children to conscious reflection (Flyvbjerg, 2001) is likely to be worthwhile. In the discussion that follows, the conscious reflection will focus on knowledge and motives in practitioners' work with children.

My use of the term 'motive' draws on the work of A. N. Leont'ev on the object of activity. Interweaving motives, goals and social conditions to overcome the dualism of contemporary mainstream psychology, he argued that 'society produces the activity of the individuals forming it' (Leont'ev, 1978a, p. 7). A key to the dialectic between people and activity in society was the object of activity, which gives rise to the object motive, that directs the participation of the actors in activities. He explained: 'The main thing that distinguished one activity from another, however, is the difference in their objects. It is exactly the object of activity, that gives it a determined direction. According to the terminology I have proposed, the object of activity is its true motive' (Leont'ev, 1978a, p. 17). However, for Leont'ev, the dialectic of person and object was crucial in the determining of direction: '[T]he object of activity is twofold: first in its independent existence as subordinating to itself and transforming the activity of the subject; second, as an image of the object, as a product of its property of psychological reflection that is realized as an activity of the subject and cannot exist otherwise' (Leont'ev, 1978a, p. 7). His recognition of the agency of the actor which realises the ideal of the object of activity reminds us that starting with practices in analyses of workplaces does not mean that we should expect to find that participants are simply swept along by the practices they inhabit. Instead, the understandings that are brought into play in realising objects in activities in practices have the potential to sustain a dynamic which ensures that practitioners engage and re-engage with the knowledge that matters in the practice. This expectation means that attention to professional knowledge and how it is engaged with needs to be part of the examination of workplace practices. The proposition is that the knowledge in professional practices is not static, but is part of what practitioners work on as they also work on the objects of their activity. What that knowledge is and what potential it holds for the development of a profession will, as we shall see, depend on the object of activity that is selected and the motives that are recognised in it.

Like Orlikowski (2002, 2006), I am taking a practice view of knowledge. From this perspective, knowledge is seen as 'not static or given, but as a capability produced and reproduced in recurrent social practices' and, potentially at least, 'always in the making' (Orlikowski, 2006, p. 460). It is a view which chimes with Leont'ev's admiration for the connection that Marx made between cognition and practice:

> A profound revolution brought about by Marx in the theory of cognition is the idea that human practice is the basis for human cognition; practice is that process in the course of whose development cognitive problems arise, human perceptions and thought originate and develop, and which at the same time contains in itself criteria of the adequacy and truth of knowledge. (Leont'ev, 1978b, p. 2)

However, Leont'ev's own development of the idea of the object of activity which not only objectifies what it is that is worked on in an activity, but also the needs, emotions and feelings associated with it, takes Marx's focus on practices much further. It recognises that objects of activity exhibit a motivating force which actors might recognise in different ways, and reminds us that the relationship between acting subject and object of their activity is never direct, but is always mediated by 'what matters' (Edwards, 2010, p. 67) in a practice.

Hedegaard's analysis of motives in institutional practices and their relation to the social situations of development created by young children

(Hedegaard & Fleer, 2008; Chapter 1 in this volume) captures the dynamics in which what matters – that is, motives – in practices shape how activities are experienced and in turn shape what matters. Using different terminology, Lave (1988, p. 181) has explained the cultural origins of motives is a similar way: 'priority, perspective and value are continuously and inescapably generated in activity'.

These analyses mean that identifying what matters in professional practices – the motivating forces that engage practitioners with the objects of activity in them – is a pre-requisite for a conscious reflection on the practices and the kinds of professional who is produced in them. Let us therefore turn to a cultural-historical account of expertise which will highlight connections between what matters in practices and expert engagement in these practices.

The starting point is Holland's analyses of the figured worlds in which identities are formed (Holland, Skinner, Lachicotte, & Cain, 1998). Holland and her colleagues explain:

> By 'figured world' then, we mean a socially and culturally constructed realm of interpretation in which particular characters and actors are recognized, significance is assigned to certain acts, and particular outcomes are valued over others. Each is a simplified world populated by a set of agents … who engage in a limited range of meaningful acts … these collective 'as if' worlds are sociohistoric, contrived imaginations that mediate behavior and so … inform participants' outlooks. (Holland et al., 1998, p. 52)

Figured worlds are made up of social practices where expertise is acquired, developed and exercised. Holland's analyses have included the practices that sustain the romantic lives of college students, and attempts by non-drinking alcoholics to create figured worlds where it is difficult to revert to drinking.

The dialectic of the figured worlds of practices and people's actions within them is central to an explanation of how people become expert within these worlds. Holland's account of expertise draws primarily on her study of how women college students in the southern United States developed and employed expertise in the world of romance. The analysis is, however, relevant to how specialist identities are formed and mediate expertise in the workplace.

Drawing on the Dreyfus and Dreyfus (1986) ladder of developing expertise, which runs in stages from novice through advanced beginner, competency and proficiency to expertise, Holland and her colleagues noted that in the final three steps in the ladder, there is a qualitative change in the relationship between individual and system. This change is marked by people moving from mainly following rules to devising their own moves. They suggested that individuals can eventually come to understand themselves in terms of an activity as it occurs in a cultural world – or, in the terms of the present chapter, in an activity in a practice. In this analysis, expertise is the ability to manipulate those practices to take forward one's intentions.

'Identification' with the figured world is the term preferred by Holland and colleagues. This they saw as 'the formation of a concept of self as an actor in a culturally devised system' (Holland et al., 1998, p. 120). Identification is evident when 'the figured world in which one has been acting according to the directions of others becomes a world that one uses to understand and organize aspects of one's self and at least some of one's own feelings and thoughts' (p. 121). Expertise is revealed in how the resources of the figured world are employed to carry out culturally appropriate intentional actions, where actions are given direction by the culturally valued motives which people appropriate as individuals. Motives and their cultural origins are therefore important.

Personal engagement, or identification with the motives embedded in activities in practices, appears to be a distinguishing aspect of expert work. For example, as a parent-support worker becomes expert in the activities in which she participates, she becomes less of a rule-follower and more identified with parent-support practice and its deeper and longer-term purposes. Motives are, therefore, neither simply internal nor only in the practices: They arise in people's engagement in activities in practices and their affiliation with what matters in those practices. Dreyfus discussed emotional engagement in activities as a sign of expertise:

> As the competent performer becomes more and more emotionally involved in a task, it becomes increasingly difficult for him or her to draw back and adopt the detached, rule-following stance of the beginner. If the detached stance of the novice and advanced beginner is replaced by involvement, and the learner accepts the anxiety of choice, he or she is set for further skill advancement. Then, the resulting positive and negative emotional experiences will strengthen successful perspectives and inhibit unsuccessful ones, and the performer's theory of the skill, as represented by rules and principles, will gradually be replaced by situational discriminations. (Dreyfus, 2004, p. 179)

Leont'ev's (1978a) view that taking 'activity' as the unit of analysis allows us to objectify 'needs, emotions and feelings' (p. 10) throws additional light on the Dreyfus insights into links between emotional engagement and expertise. Leont'ev elaborated the dialectic between the motives of acting subjects and objects of activity in terms of needs as follows: '[T]he process of development of objective content of needs is not one-sided. Its other side consists of the fact that the object of activity in itself appears to the subject as fulfilling one of his needs or another' (Leont'ev, 1978a, p. 10). Much is therefore revealed when researchers identify an object of activity, how it is interpreted, approached and acted on. Data of these kind offer windows onto what matters for practitioners in activities in work practices. A focus on the object of activity in practices is an analytic heuristic I have used in several studies of work with children. Examples include looking for changes in objects over time, in services supporting parents-as-educators (Evangelou, Sylva, Edwards, & Smith, 2008); and distinguishing between local authority service partnerships which were recognising and tackling the developmental challenges of preventing social exclusion and those which were not (Edwards, Barnes, Plewis, & Morris, 2006). In each study we elicited what Engeström has recently called 'action-level emotional experiences (as) an avenue to understanding activity-level motives' (Engeström, 2009, p. 308) to build a picture from a number of actors about what mattered in the practices of discrete work units such as children's centres and strategic partnership boards. In brief, what matters in practices is what creates motives.

WHAT MATTERS IN PRACTICES?

Attention to practice, as Cole (1996) observed, has been growing, in part at least to avoid the separation of mind and world that arises when 'context' is discussed. The shift has meant, as he notes, that we now recognise that it is 'in the territory of activity/practice that artifacts are created and used' (Cole, 1996, p. 138). However, despite accounts of the mediating function of identities formed in practices (Holland et al., 1998), how ways of categorising tasks in work-based talk both arise from and mediate engagement with those tasks (Mäkitalo, 2003; Mäkitalo & Säljo, 2002) and the development and importance of 'genre knowledge' in organisations (Russell, 2009, p. 46), too little attention has been paid to the production of mediating artefacts in practices and the relationships which obtain between these mediators and what is being worked on in activities in practices.

There is research on how these mediating devices, and particularly collective talk, shape the norms of practice – in other words, what language accomplishes (Mäkitalo, 2003; Mäkitalo & Säljo, 2002; Middleton, 2009). However, there is very little research on what the categories which are used in work talk tell us about what knowledge matters within particular practices.

I have recently argued (Edwards, 2010) that the practices in which expertise of the kind outlined by Dreyfus (2004) is enacted are the kinds of practices where problems, and the responses to them, are not routine. They therefore involve practitioners in engagement with knowledge as they make judgements. Analyses of professional work, I suggest, call for conceptual tools which can reveal knowledge, its use and its generation. We need to open up what Stehr (1994, p. 163) described as the 'black box' which is knowledge.

To find a strong emphasis on knowledge, I turn to the studies undertaken by Knorr Cetina on practitioners' engagement with what she termed 'epistemic objects'. These are not a simple equivalent to Leont'ev's object of activity. Rather, they are a feature of Knorr Cetina's description of the knowledge work which occurs when people are engaged with problems of practice and come to understand them better, shaping and reshaping new-for-them knowledge objects in the process. In an early study of the practices of research scientists, she described such engagement as forms of 'engrossment and excitement' (Knorr Cetina, 2001, p. 175), whilst they work on an unfolding knowledge or epistemic object as they carry out their research. In the terms of this chapter, they worked on what mattered for them as scientists.

I suggest that if expert knowledge in work with children cannot be seen as static or merely rule-following – for example, because new problems arise with different clients, and policies require revised responses with new configurations of resources – Knorr Cetina's notion of 'engrossment' with the needed knowledge should be an important part of professional practices. A similar point was made by Miettinen and Virkkunen (2005) who have observed a helpful co-existence between aspects of Vygotsky's legacy and the idea of epistemic objects. From their concerns with organisational change they argued that practice itself should be treated as an epistemic object and practitioners should focus on the institutional contradictions which become evident in it as practices change.

Knorr Cetina's work on epistemic cultures (1999) and on experts' engagement with epistemic objects in their practices opens up Stehr's black box. What she describes as the 'exteriorized theories of science and expertise', revealed in talk among research scientists (Knorr Cetina, 1997, p. 23), have much to offer to understandings of professional knowledge. In particular, her emphasis on the centrality of knowledge in practices and its potentially stabilising effect offers a way of capturing what makes practices distinct, recognisable and with consistent elements. She explains the function of epistemic objects as follows:

> [O]bjects serve as centering and integrating devices for regimes of expertise that transcend an expert's lifetime and create the collective

conventions and the moral order commutarians are concerned about. Object worlds also make up the embedding environments in which expert work is carried out, thus constituting something like an emotional home for expert selves. (Knorr Cetina, 1997, p. 9)

Here she is not talking about objects as instruments which are 'ready to hand' (p. 10); these should be seen as tools rather than knowledge objects. Epistemic or knowledge objects, in contrast, are problematic and need to be worked *on* to refine them, rather than worked *with* in routine tasks. Knowledge objects, she explains are 'the goal of expert work' (p. 12), where the expert self becomes bound to the knowledge object through a sense of 'lack' and the creation of a 'structure of wanting' (p. 16) which sustain the connection. The outcome is a 'state of subjective fusion with the object of knowledge' (p. 18).

The idea of engrossment is elaborated in her study of how traders in investment banks work with the market as an object of 'attachment' (Knorr Cetina & Brueggar, 2002). There the market is seen as a knowledge object which is unfolding and engaging those who work on it, not just to understand it, but also to test, move and manipulate it and be stimulated by its capacity to generate questions. Engagement arises through practitioners' need to continually work on the knowledge object and define it.

Knorr Cetina and Brueggar also describe this engagement in terms of 'lack' or incompleteness in the traders' understanding of the market and their desire to pursue a better grasp of what is there. Her work has been developed in relation to accountants, nurses, software engineers and teachers in the ProLearn project at the University of Oslo (Jensen et al., in press). Jensen, for example, has drawn on the notions of lack, desire and the binding power of knowledge to explain how seeking knowledge in research activities ties nurses to their concern with developing knowledge in and on nursing (Jensen, 2007; Jensen & Lahn, 2005)

I refer to Knorr Cetina's analyses because they alert us to the importance of knowledge in professional activities, such as responsive work with children, which are open-ended and which call for informed engagement with the problems which are revealed. However, knowledge is not forgotten in cultural-historical theory; the importance of mediation of what matters in a culture, through the use of cultural tools such as language, means that knowledge is a central element. But the idea of an epistemic object as an unfolding entity which is open to scrutiny and is made and re-made by practitioners in their work, that comes from Knorr Cetina, is useful when examining what matters in responsive work with children.

This brief overview of Knorr Cetina's work on epistemic objects inevitably raises questions for those who work with cultural-historical theory about what are the object motives for practitioners who work with children; what knowledge is brought to bear when working with them; and to what extent is the knowledge itself regarded as engrossing and stimulating further knowledge-seeking.

WHAT ARE THE OBJECT MOTIVES IN PROFESSIONAL WORK WITH CHILDREN?

This question needs to be asked afresh every time practices and the activities within them are examined, as the relationships between institutional practices and activities can be heavily shaped by local histories. In a study of pre-school settings, that were expected to shift from care towards education (Anning & Edwards, 2006), we drew on Engeström's (1999) developments of activity theory to examine the 'objects of activity' – that is, the focus of professional activity – in the settings. There we observed that practitioners found it difficult to reshape a practice led by a motive of care to one where the education motive dominated, unless the systemic contradictions which arose in the settings were tackled (Edwards, 2004). Work with young children as a practice of care is well documented. Cameron, Mooney and Moss (2002), for example, have observed that child-care work in England is closely associated with mothering, that in turn is leading to the development of services and workers 'as providers of substitute mothering' (p. 575) where around 98 per cent of the workforce are women and the levels of qualification are low, even when compared with the population as a whole.

An extended role for under-qualified staff was found a 2008 examination of an initiative aimed at developing the capacity of the Voluntary and Community Sector workforce to help parents, whose children were at risk of learning delay, to become educators of their own children (Evangelou et al., 2008). These practitioners, who were mainly women, found themselves in new activities inserted into established practices. To gain initiative funding they were required to model for parents what they could do to help their young children to learn. The initiative required all practitioners to shift the focuses of their practices: either from working in caring relationships with young children, as was the case for nursery nurses, or from giving practical and emotional aid to vulnerable adults, as was the situation for family-support workers, in order to work with parents to help them to support their children's learning. Practitioners interpreted the purposes of the new practices through what mattered in their previous work, with the result that their object motive was not always the parents' development as educator.

The new practices were complex, involving constant professional judgements. Practitioners were required to assess parents' readiness to engage as educators of their young children; parents' current understandings of what they might do; the practical possibilities of parents working with the ideas that were being passed on to them; the most appropriate material resources and ideas to use with them; and how to work with professionals from other agencies. The practitioners attended short training events of one day to a week in length, were given access to resources and, in the best situations, found themselves working at times alongside other practitioners who might support their learning.

There was considerable frustration about their lack of knowledge among staff, arising from their position as what Gunter (2007, p. 6) has described as a 'flexible and endlessly trainable' workforce. The workers demonstrated what we described as a 'thirst for knowledge' (Evangelou et al., 2008, p. 118). They knew that they did not know enough to work in the most beneficial ways with parents to help them to develop their children as learners and so experienced the 'lack', described by Knorr Cetina, once their appetites were whetted by the short doses of training they received. However, that lack was not met, as their engrossment with knowledge was not built into the development of the initiative.

The parents-as-educators project demonstrated just how dependent practitioners are on being able to access and engage with the knowledge which is regarded as powerful within a professional practice. They needed access to that knowledge in order to recognise what matters and so to work responsively with clients. In terms of the arguments made so far, practitioners' thinking arises in practices in which they demonstrate an expertise which involves some emotional engagement with the purposes of the practices. When engagement with clients occurs with limited access to the knowledge which matters in a practice, interpretations and responses are necessarily superficial.

Moving workers from one practice to another where the motives are potentially different – child as learner, parent as survivor, parent as educator – meant that the motives within the activities which gave direction to the new practices of developing parents-as-educators were quite general. Practitioners lacked the precision which arises through engaging long term with what matters. Consequently the new parent-as-educators practices embraced broad notions of well-being and social inclusion and involved the staff in being welcoming and encouraging. Their work was almost entirely relational, drawing on experiences they could generalise from other practices in their working and personal lives about being, for example, nice to clients. At the same time, the 'lack' of knowledge they discussed was a sign of their concerns about the level of generality at which they were working.

Colley, drawing on Hoschchild's accounts of emotional labour (Hochschild, 1979, 1983), examined how nursery nurses learnt to see their practice, initially at least, in terms of emotional work during their training (Colley, 2006). She documents how the students learnt to care *about* the children they cared *for*, both in college and in their work placements. Colley found that the strong emphasis on emotion as a resource for action in the nursery had its limitations, becoming something the students needed to keep under control in order to achieve a detachment that allowed them to cope with the children in their care. Ultimately their interactions were mediated by that detachment and they distanced themselves from the children.

In cultural-historical terms, the students' engagement with children as learners was not mediated by resources which would allow them to see children's learning as their motive as practitioners. Rather, led by motives of attachment, their focus was managing behaviour, and they were constantly let down. Their emotions were not objectified in the Leont'evian sense. Instead, emotions were the resources students used in their work with children. However, they reported that children could, as a consequence, 'wind me up'. As a defence they came to mediate their engagement with children with 'detachment'.

The purely relational aspects of the students' work were also highlighted in how they were expected to position themselves in workplace practices with colleagues. One of the team leaders on the training programme described the work of the nursery nurse as follows: 'It's the nature of the job. If you're working as an early years' worker, you're always going to work as part of a team, and you have to get on with people. You have to get on with adults, not just children ... I think the sort of hidden curriculum of the early years' course is getting to know people and working as a team' (Colley, 2006, p. ʃ8).

This emphasis on the 'know who' aspects of the relational was also clear in a study of how schools were adapting to the demands of inter-professional working (Edwards, Lunt, & Stamou, 2010). There we found that the pastoral demands of schooling, which were being amplified by inter-professional arrangements, were passed to practitioners, who we labelled 'welfare managers', who were a new role in schools. The teachers were then free to focus on children's progression through the curriculum. The motives in the teachers' focus on curriculum were, however, externally imposed. They were required by government performance indicators to ensure that children met curriculum 'targets', and by teachers' pay-scales, based on 'teaching and learning points', to relinquish their pastoral work. These externally imposed motives led to tensions for many of the teachers, as their experience told them that the cognitive and the affective could not be easily separated.

When we looked at the welfare managers, who were often former classroom assistants and had no job-related qualifications, we found that although they could often identify when a child needed help, they did not possess the specialist expertise necessary to respond. Instead we observed that they were highly dependent on being able to access the specialised professional knowledge which was available locally and could exercise 'know who', that operated as a substitute for 'know how and why'.

Welfare managers identified what they saw as the problems the children presented by drawing on their situated everyday knowledge of the children, their families and the neighbourhood; they then exercised their 'know who' by asking for help. These practitioners frequently described developing networks and the importance of 'know who' to how they operated: 'I've got the sort of rapport with social services that I can ring them up for advice ... now I would automatically ring them ... can you give me some advice. And if it is not you who should I go to?' The welfare managers were sometimes doing high-level, potentially risky work. However, they lacked an engagement with knowledge beyond their everyday understandings of the locality. Consequently, their engrossment was with specific children and their accounts of their practices were anecdotal, situated tales about children and families.

When we compare welfare managers with the traders studied by Knorr Cetina and Brueggar (2002), we find that the knowledge object in play in the schools was not at the more generalisable level of 'the prevention of social exclusions' or even 'the local system of support for children', but rather workers' everyday understandings of specific children. In cultural-historical terms, their object motive was each child's well-being, but their interpretations and responses of the child's strengths and needs – that is, the object of activity in the Leont'evian sense – were mediated by everyday understandings and not by the more powerful knowledge derived from experience of working across cases with well-founded and developing specialist knowledge. They had no distinctive professional knowledge to bring to bear; consequently they often found themselves assuming the role of a caring parent.

An alternative for all of the workers I have just described would be to conceptualise relational aspects of work with children without relying on emotion as a resource. Instead, I suggest, there is much to be gained by objectifying emotion in the properties of the object of activity as Leont'ev suggested, and, following Knorr Cetina, by attending to the knowledge which matters in practices and in so doing enriching the practices and the knowledge work within them.

RELATIONAL AGENCY IN WORK WITH CHILDREN

Elsewhere (Edwards, 2010), I have described a relational turn in expertise. The proposal was that complex problems of professional practice call for both the specific expertise to be found in discrete practices such as teaching or parental support and for an additional form of 'relational expertise'. The argument for relational expertise was premised on the observation that the more we recognise that specific expertise is located in practices which are distributed across social systems, and that complex problems call for complex interdisciplinary responses, the more we need to develop the capacity to work with the expertise of others.

Relational expertise is evident when people work with others to expand understandings of problems of practice, such as the difficulties accumulating for a vulnerable child, and attune their responses to these problems so that the specialist expertise available in different practices, such as health, education, social care and housing, can be brought to bear when best for the child. The distinct knowledgeable expertise of each practitioner is crucial, as the relational turn in expertise is not a plea for professional hybridity. Quite the reverse: It highlights the importance of the discrete knowledge that each practitioner can contribute to the distributed resources, whilst arguing that a relational expertise is also needed to recognise and work with what others offer.

The arguments for relational expertise were developed in research on inter-professional work (Edwards, 2005, 2009; Edwards, Daniels, Gallagher, Leadbetter, & Warmington, 2009). In brief, relational expertise within configurations of practices is developed as a two-stage process. First, understandings of 'what matters' in each practice are shared in meetings where the different practices intersect, such as inter-professional team meetings. When problems are discussed in these meetings, the categories employed in each practice to interpret and respond to the topics investigated reveal what is valued, that is, what matters in that practice (Edwards & Kinti, 2010).

This knowledge of what matters in other practices allows practitioners to recognise the standpoints of other professionals, that is, the background from which their engaged agency springs. Inter-professional discussions can therefore build common understandings which can mediate cross-professional interactions when working with vulnerable children. The importance of revealing what matters in practices is not unique to work with children. Studying how knowledge is mobilised between sub-units in the semi-conductor industry, Carlile (2004) found that knowledge held in common helped to mediate exchanges between sub-units within an organisation, so that knowledge could be managed across unit boundaries to provoke innovation. He made an important distinction between what he termed transfer, translation and transformation when knowledge enters new practices, and linked this distinction to how knowledge was mediated across unit boundaries by drawing on the knowledge which was held in common.

His argument was that what matters for knowledge mobilisation is the 'capacity of the common knowledge to represent the differences and dependencies now of consequence and the ability of the actors involved to use it' (Carlile, 2004, p. 557). He suggested that when the difference between what is known and what is new increases, the demands on the knowledge held in common – that is, recognition of what matters for others – also increases.

Accordingly, simple 'transfer' may be possible when new ideas are not too distant from existing specialist knowledge and object motives, such as when two early-childhood educators discuss a child's progress in mark-making; but translation may be needed when early-childhood educators talk to primary-school teachers about children's mark-making, as what matters in these practices differ. Accordingly, some transformation in parents' conceptions will be necessary when the conversation is with parents who cannot see mark-making as progress towards literacy. This argument suggests that building common knowledge which enables quick transfer or makes translation easy is an important pre-requisite to quick and responsive relational work across practice boundaries. Common knowledge, it seems, is comprised of knowledge of what matters in each practice and offers enough background insights to other practices to enable practitioners to recognise the motives of others when interpreting and responding to a task.

In the second stage of the development and use of relational expertise, the knowledge held in common mediates joint work in the field so that when practitioners need to work together to support a vulnerable child, they share enough common knowledge to understand each other and attune their responses. The offering and accessing of expertise in distributed systems has been captured in the idea of relational agency (Edwards, 2005, 2009, 2010). It is a capacity for working with others to strengthen purposeful responses to complex problems. The exercise of relational agency can be seen as a two-stage process within a constant dynamic, which involves:

1. working with others to expand the object of activity being working on, by recognising the motives and the resources that others bring to bear as they too interpret it; and
2. aligning one's own responses to the newly enhanced interpretations, with the responses being made by the other professionals to act on the expanded object.

Relational agency is an attempt to label what is involved in working with the object motives of other practitioners when both interpreting and responding to a complex problem such as a child's trajectory. Attention to the why, or motives, in collaboration arising from the idea of relational agency has implications for practitioners' professional identities in the object-oriented relationships which characterise it. There are three points here:

1. As practitioners work on objects of activity such as children as learners, the objects work back on them and impact on practitioners' subjectivities and how they then approach the object of activity. In this transactional relationship between subject and object, by transforming the object alongside other practitioners through contesting it and understanding it better, they also transform themselves – in other words, they learn (Edwards, 2005).
2. Working relationally involves being aware of one's own expertise and what matters as a practitioner and revealing these to others. This awareness can enhance practitioners' sense of themselves as knowledgeable professionals.
3. A capacity for working relationally with others can strengthen the actions of potentially vulnerable practitioners who are undertaking risky responsive work outside the safety of the social practices of their own organisations.

The exercise of relational agency is therefore premised on informed interpretations of, for example, a child as learner and the capacity to make those interpretations explicit. Importantly, relational agency requires that practitioners not only recognise and draw on the expertise which is distributed across local systems, but also contribute to it by bringing to bear their specialist knowledge – in other words, what matters – in interpretations and responses. It involves both a core expertise and a relational expertise, and the latter cannot be a substitute for the former.

MOTIVES AND KNOWLEDGE: THE IMPLICATIONS
FOR WORK WITH CHILDREN

The relational turn to be found in inter-professional work points to weaknesses in professional practices where the meditational means cannot be made visible to others, as was case with Colley's student nursery nurses, the welfare managers and the parents-as-educators staff. It also calls for attention to the knowledge which matters in practices. The knowledge which is made visible in the discussions which build common knowledge is the knowledge without which a profession could not function; it is what feeds the emotional connections of expert work described by Dreyfus (2004). The emotional ties of the nursery nurses and the 'know who' of the welfare workers are insufficient bases for the contribution of either group to the systems of distributed expertise, that are currently characterising much of the practices focused on children.

I agree with Hedegaard when she explains that '[c]ultural practice traditions and value positions connected to different traditions of practice are interwoven with daily activities in institutions and influence how communities within the institution are created' (Hedegaard, 2005, p. 187). I agree again when she highlights that how children develop needs to be seen in relation to the values and norms of society, so that development is recognised as an integration of competencies and values (Hedegaard, 2008). In this chapter I attempted to apply these precepts to the practices of the practitioners who inhabit the activity settings in which children create the social situations of development within which they dialectically articulate their connections with the world.

I have suggested the motives in practices should be seen as intertwined with the knowledge that matters for each profession. Knorr Cetina's attention to engrossment and her notion of how epistemic work in practices can give rise to and benefit from structures of wanting (Knorr Cetina, 1997) therefore provides useful connections between emotion, knowledge and motive. Consequently, as valuable as I find Leont'ev's work on objectifying emotion by locating it within the object of activity to which we respond, I am proposing increased attention to the knowledge which matters and which mediates interpretations of and responses to problems of practice. One way forward would be to build strong engrossment with the knowledge that mediates practices, into the values and norms of all the professions which work with children in education settings.

REFERENCES

Anning, A., & Edwards, A. (2006). *Promoting learning from birth to five: Developing professional practice in the pre-school.* 2nd ed. Buckingham: Open University Press.

Cameron, C., Mooney, A., & Moss, P. (2002). The child care workforce: Current conditions and future directions. *Critical Social Policy, 22*(4), 572–595.

Carlile, P. (2004). Transferring, translating and transforming: An integrative framework for managing knowledge across boundaries. *Organization Science, 15*(5), 555–568.

Cole, M. (1996). *Cultural psychology: A once and future discipline.* Cambridge, MA: Harvard University Press.

Colley, H. (2006). Learning to labour with feeling: Class, gender and emotion in childcare education and training. *Contemporary Issues in Early Childhood, 7*(1), 15–29 (available from www.mmu.ac.uk).

Dreyfus, H., & Dreyfus, S. (1986). *Mind over machine: The power of human intuition and expertise in the era of the computer.* New York: Free Press.

Dreyfus, S. (2004). The five stage model of adult skill acquisition. *Bulletin of Science, Technology and Society, 24*(3), 177–181.

Edwards, A. (2004). Understanding context, understanding practice in early education. *European Early Childhood Education Research Journal, 12*(1), 85–101.

(2005). Relational agency: Learning to be a resourceful practitioner. *International Journal of Educational Research, 43*(3), 168–182.

(2009). Relational agency in collaborations for the wellbeing of children and young people. *Journal of Children's Services, 4*(1), 33–43.

(2010). *Being an expert professional practitioner: The relational turn in expertise.* Dordrecht: Springer.

Edwards, A., Barnes, M., Plewis, I., & Morris, K. (2006). *Working to prevent the social exclusion of children and young people: Final lessons from the National Evaluation of the Children's Fund.* London: DfES Research Report 734.

Edwards, A., Daniels, H., Gallagher, T., Leadbetter, J., & Warmington, P. (2009). *Improving inter-professional collaborations: Multi-agency working for children's wellbeing.* London: Routledge.

Edwards, A., & Kinti, I. (2010). Working relationally at organisational boundaries: Negotiating expertise and identity. In H. Daniels, A. Edwards, Y. Engeström, & S. Ludvigsen (Eds.), *Activity theory in practice: Promoting learning across boundaries and agencies* (pp. 126–139). London: Routledge.

Edwards, A., Lunt, I., & Stamou, E. (2010). Inter-professional work and expertise: New roles at the boundaries of schools. *British Educational Research Journal, 30*(1), 27–45.

Engeström, Y. (1999). Activity theory and individual and social transformation. In Y. Engeström, R. Miettinen, & R.-L. Punamäki (Eds.), *Perspectives on activity theory* (pp. 19–38). Cambridge: Cambridge University Press.

(2009). The future of activity theory: A rough draft. In A. Sannino, H. Daniels, & K. Gutierrez (Eds.), *Learning and expanding with activity theory* (pp. 303–328). Cambridge: Cambridge University Press.

Evangelou, M., Sylva, K., Edwards, A., & Smith, T. (2008). *Supporting parents in promoting early learning*. London: DCSF Research Report 039.

Flyvbjerg, B. (2001). *Making social science matter*. Cambridge: Cambridge University Press.

Gunter, H. (2007). Remodelling the school workforce in England: A study in tyranny. *Journal for Critical Education Policy Studies, 5*(1), 1–11.

Hedegaard, M. (2005). Strategies for dealing with conflicts in value positions between home and school: Influences on ethnic minority students' development of motives and identity. *Culture and Psychology, 11*(2), 187–205.

(2008). A cultural-historical theory of children's development. In M. Hedegaard & M. Fleer (Eds.), *Studying children: A cultural-historical approach* (pp. 10–29). Buckingham: Open University Press.

Hedegaard, M., & Fleer, M. (2008). *Studying children: A cultural-historical approach*. Buckingham: Open University Press.

Hochschild, A. R. (1979). Emotion work, feeling rules and social structure. *American Journal of Sociology, 85*(3), 551–575.

(1983). *The managed heart: Commercialization of human feeling*. Berkeley and Los Angeles: University of California Press.

Holland, D., Skinner, D., Lachicotte, W., & Cain, C. (1998). *Identity and agency in cultural world*. Cambridge, MA: Harvard University Press.

Jensen, K. (2007). The desire to learn: An analysis of knowledge-seeking practices among professionals. *Oxford Review of Education, 33*(4), 489–502.

Jensen, K., & Lahn, L. (2005). The binding role of knowledge: An analysis of nursing students. *Journal of Education and Work, 18*(3), 305–320.

Jensen, K., Lahn, L., & Nerland (Eds.) (in press). *Professional learning in the knowledge society*. Rotterdam: Sense.

Knorr Cetina, K. (1997). Sociality with objects: Social relations in post-social knowledge societies. *Theory Culture Society, 14*(1), 1–29.

(1999). *Epistemic cultures: How sciences make knowledge*. Cambridge, MA: Harvard University Press.

(2001). Objectual practice. In T. Schatzki, K. Knorr Cetina, & E. von Savigny (Eds.), *The practice turn in contemporary theory* (pp. 175–188). London: Routledge.

Knorr Cetina, K., & Brueggar, U. (2002). Traders' engagement with markets: A postsocial relationship. *Theory Culture and Society, 19*(5–6), 161–185.

Lave, J. (1988). *Cognition in practice*. Cambridge: Cambridge University Press.

Leont'ev, A. N. (1978a). The problem of activity in psychology. In *Activity, consciousness and personality*. Upper Saddle River, NJ: Prentice Hall. Available online at http:Marxists.anu.edu.au/archive/leontev/works/1978) (April 29, 2004).

(1978b). Marxism and psychological science. In *Activity, consciousness and personality*. Upper Saddle River, NJ: Prentice Hall. Available online at http:Marxists.anu.edu.au/archive/leontev/works/1978) (April 29, 2004).

Mäkitalo, Å. (2003). Accounting practices as situated knowing: Dilemmas and dynamics in institutional categorization. *Discourse Studies, 5*(4), 465–519.

Mäkitalo, Å., & Säljö, R. (2002). Invisible people: Institutional reasoning and reflexivity in the production of services and 'social facts' in public employment agencies. *Mind, Culture, and Activity, 9*(3), 160–178.

Middleton, D. (2009). Identifying learning in inter-professional discourse: The development of an analytic protocol. In H. Daniels, A. Edwards, Y. Engeström, & S. Ludvigsen (Eds.), *Activity theory in practice: Promoting learning across boundaries and agencies* (pp. 90–104). London: Routledge.

Miettinen, R., & Virkkunen, J. (2005). Epistemic objects, artifacts and organizational change. *Organization, 12*(3), 437–456.

Orlikowski, W. (2002). Knowing in practice: Enacting a collective capability in distributed organizing. *Organization Science, 13*(3), 249–273.

(2006). Material knowing: The scaffolding of human knowledgeability. *European Journal of Information Systems, 15,* 460–466.

Russell, D. (2009). Uses of activity theory in written communication research. In A. Sannino, H. Daniels, & K. Gutierrez (Eds.), *Learning and expanding with activity theory* (pp. 40–52). Cambridge: Cambridge University Press.

Stehr, N. (1994). *Knowledge societies.* London: Sage.

Taylor, C. (1995). *Philosophical arguments.* Cambridge: Cambridge University Press.

11

Changing Situations and Motives

HARRY DANIELS

This chapter explores some of the personal motivational implications of the process of moving from one situation to another. In the cultural-historical phase of Vygotsky's writing, he strove to understand the development of psychological functioning in relation to the situation in which that development was taking place. This view is the point of departure for a consideration of the transformations which take place when a person moves from one institutional situation to another. I will discuss the ways in which institutions re-contextualise societal motives and thus mediate an individual's engagement with the social world. When viewed from this perspective, transitions between institutions may require engagement with new re-contextualisations of societal motives.

Alongside this emphasis on moving from one institutional setting to another, that may be thought of a movement in space, there is also the perspective of movement through time. On the one hand, institutions themselves change over time, and thus principles of re-contextualisation will also change over time. This may be viewed from a macro or micro perspective. At the macro level, changes over time, such as the change of headteacher of a school, will lead to changes in institutional form. At the micro level, as patterns of interaction within institutions change so will the ways in which societal motives come to inhabit the institution. As individuals change their forms of social relation over time so they also bring about changes in which the institution stands between society and the individual. This developmental perspective over time will be discussed alongside the implications of movement through. It is, of course recognised, that the forms of movement co-occur.

As Cole (1996) reminds, a central component of the cultural-historical tradition is the recognition of the importance of a non-dualist approach even if this is difficult to achieve both in theory and in terms of methodological features of research.

Vygotsky and his co-workers, notably Leontiev, gave rise to the inception of a tradition in which an understanding of the societal formation of motives was central to an overall thesis of the cultural-historical formation of mind. A weak point in this work has been with respect to the way in which specific institutions mediate societal motives, how they stand between society and the person. Although present in the latter stages of Vygotsky's writing, relatively little attention has been paid to the development of a non-dualist account of cognitive and affective features of human functioning, and these relate to the ways in which motives and goals arise in particular situations. When processes of institutional re-contextualisation are understood alongside such non-dualist accounts of functioning, then perhaps we will understand more about the personal challenges of moving from one situation to another. This is important both when situations change through movement in space and time and both carry developmental implications.

THEORISING THE NOTION OF SITUATION AND TRANSITION

In order to understand the implications of moving from one situation to another, it is first necessary to consider the accounts which are in circulation about the psychological implications of the setting in which human activity is situated. This section of the chapter will thus provide an outline of theories of situatedness before moving to discuss theories of transition from one situation to another.

As Suchman (1987) points out, the emphasis is on the often temporary and moment-by-moment activity which takes place in and with a particular situation. In her strong account of inseperability, the notion of what counts as a 'situation' becomes almost elusive given its ongoing reformulation. The calibration of 'situation' is not only unachievable; it is a task which is commensurate with the fundamental assumption of the approach. Similarly, durability over time and persistence or even transfer across contexts are either discounted or not placed in a prioritised position in the researcher's analytic lens. To the extent that some models of situated action privilege the emergent and that which is improvised, they consequently downplay a consideration of features, both of the situation and the person acting in the situation, which are routine and predictable.

The important common factor which links the writing of researchers such as Suchman (1987) and Lave (1988) amongst many others is that they take up a methodological stance which challenges the within person, insulated 'in the head' that either ignores the situation or context in which it is enacted or downplays the understanding of situated action. Suchman, Lave and others are directly challenging the insulated view of cognition which ignores these contextual factors. The social and individual are not connected in a mechanical manner by some device which acts much like the lead in an electronic system, as conduit of data from the outside to the inside, nor are the person and the situation simply different levels of analysis. The mutual constitution of person and situation in an ongoing, emergent dialectical interplay of inseparable co-formation is posited. As Lave (1991) notes: '"Situated" … implies that a given social practice is multiply interconnected with other aspects of ongoing social processes in activity systems at many levels of particularity and generality' (Lave, 1991, p. 84).

The struggle to articulate the notion of context or situation has been approached in a number of ways. Lave's (1988) formulation, that flows from the previously sketched argument, is that the focus of research must be the relations between the individual and the context or situation. Early-day research such as Lave, Murtaugh and de la Rocha (1984) had demonstrated the situation-specific nature of 'cognitive processes' in everyday situations. Consequently, Lave argued for a focus on what people were actually doing in particular situation. This anthropologically driven demand still calls for definitions of what counts as context or situation. Lave's (1988) answer is to distinguish between the stable institutional framework or 'arena' in which activity takes place and the way in which that arena is acted upon by participants in that activity and thence becomes the 'setting'. A central component of any setting is the social situation which obtains in that setting.

As Minick (1987, p. 29) notes, by 1933, Vygotsky began to argue that the social situation of play was one in which imagination frees thought and meanings from the perceptual field. This was a reversal of his earlier emphasis on the power of speech to bring this about.

> Thought is separated from the thing because a piece of wood begins to play the role of a doll, a stick becomes a horse; action according to rules begins to be defined from thought rather than things themselves.… The child doesn't do this suddenly. To tear thought (word meaning) from the thing is a terribly difficult task for the child. Play is a transitional form. At the moment the stick (i.e. the thing) becomes a pivot for tearing the meaning from the real horse … one of the basic psychological structures that defines the child's relationship to reality is changed.

> The child cannot yet tear the thought from the thing. He must have a pivot in another thing.… To think of the horse, he must define his action by this horse in the stick or pivot … I would say that in play the child operates in accordance with meaning that is torn from things but not

torn from real actions with real objects.... This is the transitional character of play. This is what makes it a middle link between the purely situ-
ational connectedness of early childhood and thinking that is removed
from the real situation. (Vygotsky, 1978, pp. 69–71)

This central emphasis on the analysis of the social situation of development
in connection with psychological development is reaffirmed throughout the
writing which Vygotsky undertook in the last two years of his life. Arguably
there are parallels with Gibson's (1986) notion of affordances which are not
properties of objects in isolation but of objects related to subjects in activity
or putative activities. However, this concept of affordance is open to many
interpretations alongside what might be thought of as a post-Vygotskian
version (Baerentsen & Trettvik, 2002). It should be noted that Gibson provides an account of person in the environment but does little to progress the
analysis of psychological formation within that which is afforded. The latter
is Vygotsky's distinctive contribution.

> The social situation of development, which is specific to each age, deter-
> mines strictly regularly the whole picture of the child's life or his social
> existence.... Having elucidated the social situation of development that
> occurred before the beginning of any age, which was determined by the
> relations between the child and his environment we must immediately
> elucidate how, new formations proper to (characteristic of) the given
> age develop from the life of the child in this social situation. (Vygotsky,
> 1998, p. 198)

This linkage between the social situation of development and psychological
development pervades his analysis in these crucial final years of his life.

The move that Vygotsky made during his work in psychology from the
analytic unit of the instrumental act through to the psychological system
and on to try and identify a unit compatible with his end of career thought
on psychological systems in social situations of development was brought to
an end at the point at which he was just starting to reflect on another extension to his project. Where, in the past, he had posited a dialectical unity of
thinking and speech, he now moved to understand experience as the unity
of personality and the environment as represented in development.[1]

> We have inadequately studied the internal relationship of the child to
> the people around him.... We have recognized in words that we need to
> study the child's personality and environment as a unity. It is incorrect,
> however to represent this problem in such a way that on one side we

---

[1] See Vygotsky (1998, pp. 289–296) for an extended discussion.

have the influence of personality while on the other we have the influence of the environment. Though the problem is frequently represented in precisely this way, it is incorrect to represent the two as external forces acting on one another. In the attempt to study the unity, the two are initially torn apart. The attempt is then made to unite them. (Vygotsky, 1998, p. 292)

Minick, Stone & Forman (1993) took this view and argued that the future of the Vygotskian tradition lay in acknowledging that the culturally specific nature of institutions demands close attention to the way in which they structure interactions between people and artifacts.

Yaroshevsky (1989) also points to the importance of understanding the complex inseparable relationship between situation, motive, emotion and understanding in Vygotsky's cultural-historical work. He suggests that Vygotsky turned to Stanislavsky's concept of 'understatement' for clarification of 'sense' understood as the local interpretation of more general societal meanings.

As Stanislavsky teaches us, underlying each line of a character's text in a drama is volition directed at achievement of certain volitional tasks – That is what understatement is – each line conceals volition or volitional task. It cannot be grasped from the meanings of these words themselves. It glimmers through the words, and can be understood if the motives of the behaviour of the speakers of those lines are known – Sense denoted the individual's emotional experience of the tense motivational attitude to the world, created by the volitional task. The hidden meaning of an action, including the generation of a word, can only be grasped if one knows the context out of which this task grows and the purpose for which it is solved. (Yaroshevsky, 1989, pp. 314–315)

It is suggested that, in this way, motives make actions meaningful in social situations. The motives that guide social action in situations are formative in the generation of meaning for the actor and the observer. Changing the social situation of action can bring change in motive, that in turn transforms the meaning of actions that may, on first observation, appear identical. Taken alongside Vygotsky's desire to understand affect and cognition in a non-dualist account, there is a need to understand action, emotions and motive in human activity.

ACTIVITY, ACTION, EMOTIONS AND MOTIVE

The argument outlined earlier suggests the need for theories that forge a link between situations (and the actions and activities which take place within them), emotions and motives. In this section of the chapter, an argument is advanced for a cultural-historical conception of motive which understands emotion and cognition in a non-dualistic frame. Despite the often espoused wish to create such a non-dualist account, it is perhaps not unfair to suggest that a surprisingly large amount of the research reported under the banner of the cultural-historical tradition remains overly cognitive. A reminder of some of the original assumptions of activity theory provides a useful point of departure in the quest for this non-dualist ideal. Through his formulation of 'object-motive', Leontiev (1978) presented the idea that human activities are always driven by an objective feature of the social world.

Leontiev (1978) provides examples of how motives can 'shift' onto goals and how social meanings are re-worked into personal senses; both accounts are indicative of his attempts – not always consistent and perhaps therefore often misunderstood – to overcome the dualism of social and individual levels (Stetsenko & Arievitch, 2003, p. 487). Engeström (1999) argued that motive can be collective but that goals are individual, and he explored the idea of partial and overall goals. The shifting and developing object of an activity is aroused by a motive individual (or group) action is referred to a conscious goal. Although actions are aroused by the motive of the activity, they seem to be directed towards a goal: '[T]he one and the same action can serve different activities' (Leontiev, 1978, p. 64):

> [A]part from its (the action's) intentional aspects (what must be dome) the action has its operational aspect (how it can be done), which is defined not by the goal itself, but by the objective circumstances under which it is carried out ... I shall label the means by which an action is carried out its operations. (Leontiev, 1981 [1972], p. 63).

Leontiev illustrates his proposed structure of activity with well-known examples of the activity of hunting in which, to understand why separate actions are meaningful, one needs to understand the motive behind the whole activity (Leontiev, 1978), and of learning to drive a car, that illustrates the movement from one level of the structure of an activity to another as actions become automatic operations, such as gear changing when learning to drive (Leontiev, 1978).

For Engeström (1987), activity is a collective, systemic formation which has a complex mediational structure. An activity system produces actions and is realised by means of actions. However, activity is not reducible to actions. Actions are relatively short-lived and have a temporally clear-cut beginning and end. Activity systems evolve over lengthy periods of socio-historical time, often taking the form of institutions and organisations.

Leontiev distinguished between the material objective and affective motives of activity, seeing the objective purpose as translating motive into a physical act, transforming the internal plane to the external world and driving activity through the formation of goals. After Hegel, he maintained that goals are determined in the course of activity (Engeström, 1999). Engeström (2004) notes a dual function in that an object can give coherence and continuity to the activity, but by virtue of its societal and historical nature it is also internally contradictory and thus a source of instability: 'The object is a heterogeneous and internally contradictory, yet enduring, constantly reproduced purpose of a collective activity system that motivates and defines the horizon of possible goals and actions' (Engeström, 2004, p. 17). If this position is adopted, there is a need to understand the relation between activity, social situation and the formation of motives.

There is a need to understand how practices are taken up and transformed in particular situations. Kozulin (1998) discusses relational changes in the child's position in relation to knowledge on entering school. He offers the example of changes in social relation from son/daughter/playmate to pupil/student. He links this change in social relationship to activities such as problem solving. In everyday situations, problems may be solved to achieve certain results, whereas in school, they may be solved in order to enhance the power of specific cognitive tools. Vygotsky discussed this difference in terms of the shift in position from communicating with words to communicating about words. Bernstein (1996) takes this issue much further in his discussion of re-contextualisation. His approach allows for a theoretical description and analysis of the ways in which knowledge is re-contextualised within the school and, importantly, the possibilities for learner positions within specific forms of pedagogic practice. Much of the early Russian work does not take account of such socio-institutional differences between institutions such as schools.

MOTIVE AND SITUATION: THE PROCESS OF RE-CONTEXTUALISATION

It has been established that the social relations which obtain in a particular setting may be related to different motives. In a study of teaching and learning art, Gearhart and Newman argued that, for the nursery school children they studied, learning the social organisation of a classroom and learning its curriculum could not be distinguished: 'What children know about drawing is intimately tied to what they understand of drawing activities undertaken in a particular social context' (Gearhart & Newman, 1980,

p. 183). They discussed the importance of the way the teacher spoke to the children about their drawings and also drew attention to the particular form of pedagogy in the classroom: '[D]rawing was also being learned from the teacher's efforts to teach the organizational independence of individual production tasks. Reflexively, this individual task organization was being learned from the teacher's efforts to teach independently planful drawing' (Gearhart & Newman, 1980, p. 183).

Whilst Gearhart and Newman's study is of interest in that it is suggestive of processes of re- contextualisation in a specific pedagogic context, it failed to undertake the comparative work needed to show the ways learning to draw differs under different forms of classroom social organisation.

In this section of the chapter, a theory of Bernstein's theory of re-contextualisation is introduced and discussed as a means of understanding the way in which motives may be transformed as social situations are changed in different institutional settings. Bernstein's (2000) model is one that is designed to relate macro-institutional forms to micro-interactional levels and the underlying rules of communicative competence. He provides a semiotic account of cultural transmission which is avowedly sociological in its conception. His work on the school shows his continuous engagement with the inter-relations between changes in organisational form, changes in modes of control and changes in principles of communication. His language of description is generated from an analysis of power (which creates and maintains boundaries in organisational form) and control that regulates communication within specific forms of interaction. Bernstein addresses these problems in the course of the development of his account of how pedagogic processes shape consciousness differentially. The evolution of his work was driven by three inter-related questions:

- How does a dominating distribution of power and principles of control generate, distribute, reproduce and legitimise dominating and dominated principles of communication?
- How does such a distribution of principles of communication regulate relations within and between social groups?
- How do these principles of communication produce a distribution of forms of pedagogic consciousness? (Bernstein, 2000, p. 4).

Bernstein's (2000, 1981) work on analysis and description focuses upon two levels: a structural level and an interactional level. The structural level is analysed in terms of the social division of labour it creates, and the interactional level in terms of the form of social relation it creates. Bernstein's (1981) general model speaks of classification and framing.

The social division of labour – classification – is analysed in terms of strength of the boundary of its divisions – that is, with respect to the degree of specialisation. When there is strong insulation between categories (i.e. subject, teachers), each category is sharply distinguished, explicitly bounded and having its own distinctive specialisation, then classification is said to be strong. When there is weak insulation, then the categories are less specialised and therefore their distinctiveness is reduced: Then classification is said to be weak. The interactional level emerges as the regulation of the transmission/acquisition relation between teacher and pupil – that is, the interactional level comes to refer to the pedagogic context and the social relations of the classroom or its equivalent. Framing refers to the regulation of communication in the social relations through which the social division of labour is enacted. The social relations generally, in the analyses, are those between parents/children, teachers/pupils, doctors/patients and social workers/clients, but the analysis can be extended to include the social relations of the work contexts of industry or commerce. From Bernstein's point of view, all these relations can be regarded as pedagogic relations through which cultural reproductions occur.

Bernstein (1977) made a distinction between instructional and regulative discourse. The former refers to the transmission of skills and their relation to each other, and the latter refers to the principles of social order, relation and identity. Both these aspects of pedagogic discourse may be described in terms of classification and framing. Descriptions of pedagogic practice may be made at the level of delicacy required in a particular empirical study. Pedagogic discourse is modelled as one discourse created by the embedding of instructional and regulative discourse. This model of pedagogic discourse provides a response to one of the many theoretical demands that have remained unfulfilled in the post-Vygotskian framework. It provides a way of theorising discourse as a tool within the activity theory, that incorporates both instrumental and moral/affective dimensions. Crucially it also allows the analysis and description of the discourse to be related to the relations of power and control, that obtain in the setting in which the activity is enacted. The move from the structural arrangements of classification and framing to the structure of the pedagogic discourse provides a way of attending to the critique of the notion of tool, that Bernstein outlined: 'The metaphor of "tool" draws attention to a device, an empowering device, but there are some reasons to consider that the tool, its internal specialised structure is abstracted from its social construction. Symbolic "tools" are never neutral; intrinsic to their construction are social classifications, stratifications, distributions and modes of recontextualizing' (Bernstein, 1993, p. xvii).

Vygotsky understood *perezhivanie* as the integration of cognitive and affective elements, that always pre-supposes the presence of emotions. Vygotsky used this concept in order to emphasise the wholeness of the psychological development of children, integrating external and internal elements at each stage of development. According to Bozhovich, for a short period of time, Vygotsky considered *perezhivanie* as the 'unity' of psychological development in the study of the social situation of development (Gonzalez-Rey 2002).

> The emotional experience (perezhivanie) arising from any situation or from any aspect of his environment, determines what kind of influence this situation or this environment will have on the child. Therefore, it is not any of the factors themselves (if taken without the reference of the child) which determines how they will influence the future course of his development, but the same factors refracted through the prism of the child's emotional experience. (Vygotsky, 1994, p. 339)

This idea of refraction 'through the prism of the child's emotional experience' has been largely ignored in the development of post-Vygotskian theory. In one and the same family, in one family situation, we find different changes in development in different children because different children experience one and the same situation differently (Vygotsky, 1998).

The rejection of the cognitive/affective dualism which Vygotsky (1994, 1987) announced was not followed by a model within which a unitary conception of thinking and feeling could be discussed and implemented within empirical research. Bernstein's formulation of pedagogic discourse as an embedded discourse comprised of instructional and regulative components allows for the analysis of the production of such embedded discourses in activities structured through specifiable relations of power and control within institutions.

Bernstein outlines his understanding of the pedagogic device which he posits as a set of rules and procedures which shape official pedagogic discourse, producing a curriculum and converting knowledge into classroom talk (Singh, 2002). For him, institutional discourse is produced through three main fields, which are hierarchically related: production, re-contextualisation and reproduction. New specialised and complex forms of knowledge are produced in certain institutions, such as universities and research institutes (the field of production). Specialised knowledge has to be interpreted and turned into pedagogical knowledge to be accessible and appropriate for the very different institutional context of schooling. This involves selection from existing forms of knowledge and converting it for use in a very different institutional setting from that in which it was formed. This 're-contextualising' work traditionally has been carried out by a different group of knowledge workers, found in government departments of education, curriculum bodies, teacher-education institutions, education journals, and by media gurus on education (the field of re-contextualisation). Reproduction – the teaching of these re-contextualised forms of knowledge – takes place in yet another social context and community of practice, the one found within schools, colleges and universities (the field of reproduction). As Bernstein explains in the case of schools: 'Pedagogic discourse is a principle for appropriating other discourses and bringing them into a special relation with each other for the purposes of their selective transmission and acquisition' (Bernstein, 1990, pp. 183–184).

Pedagogic discourse impacts the identities and practice of both teachers (and how they acquire and transmit knowledge which has been produced elsewhere) and pupils. Bernstein elaborates on the structure of the pedagogic device, stating that it

> provides the intrinsic grammar of pedagogic discourse through distributive rules, recontextualization rules, and rules of evaluation. These rules are themselves hierarchically related in the sense that the nature of the distributive rules regulates the nature of the recontextualizing rules, which in turn regulate the rules of evaluation. These distributive rules regulate the fundamental relation between power, social groups, forms of consciousness and practice, and their reproductions and productions. The recontextualizing rules regulate the constitution of specific pedagogic discourse. The rules of evaluation are constituted in pedagogic practice. The pedagogic device generates a symbolic ruler of consciousness. (Bernstein, 1990, p. 180)

When illustrating the differing nature of the criteria which the child is supposed to acquire in different teaching situation, reference is also made to the teaching of art. In what is termed the visible pedagogy with its strong classification and framing, the following example is given:

> What are the children doing? they are making facsimiles of the outside. They are learning a reproductive aesthetic code. They may be drawing or painting figures, houses, etc. The teacher looks at the product of one child and says, 'That's a very good house, but where is the chimney?', or 'There are no windown in your house,' or 'That man has got only three fingers', etc. Here the child is made aware of what is missing in the production and what is missing is made explicit and specific, and subject to finely graded assessment. (Bernstein, 1977, p. 119)

Whereas with the invisible pedagogy in the integrated-type curriculum realised through weak classification and framing:

> The children have a large sheet of paper, and not a small box of paints but an assembly of media whereby their unique visual imagination may be momentarily revealed. This is allegedly not a reproductive aesthetic code, but a productive aesthetic code. The teacher here is less likely to say, 'What's that?', is less likely explicitly to create in the child a consciousness of what is missing in the product: the teacher is more likely to do this indirectly, in a context of general, diffuse support. Where the transmission realises implicit criteria, it is as if the acquirer is the source of the criteria. (Bernstein, 1977, p. 119)

Bernstein (1993) argues that much of the work that has followed in the wake of Vygotsky does not include in its description how the discourse itself is constituted and re-contextualised. Within institutions motives, goals, emotions and ways of thinking are re-contextualised. Moving from one institution to another involves realignment and adjustment to re-contextualised object motives. Institutions may be analysed and described using the theoretical apparatus which Bernstein's theory supplies. Arguably it offers an alternative approach to the modelling of what counts as an activity system in activity theory. Engeström's (1987) formulation of rules, community and division of labour offers a powerful means of approaching the articulation of an activity system. Bernstein's formulation of pedagogic discourse as an embedded discourse comprised of instructional and regulative elements which may be re-contextualised in specific institutions which may be analysed in terms of the constitution of boundaries and social relations (classification and framing) offers an alternative, or perhaps an extension, to Engeström's formulation through the ways in which it seeks to connect structural and discursive features of institutions. Examples of the application of this approach may be seen, for example, in Daniels (2008, 2010).

CHANGING SITUATIONS THROUGH TIME AND SPACE

Activity systems do not exist in isolation; they are embedded in networks which witness constant fluctuation and change. Activity theory needs to develop tools for analysing and transforming networks of culturally heterogeneous activities through dialogue and debate (Engeström & Miettinen, 1999, p. 7). Bernstein's work has not placed particular emphasis on the study of change (see Bernstein, 2000). Activity could provide the tools with which to understand dialogues, multiple perspectives on change within networks of interacting activity systems all of which are underdeveloped in Bernstein.

The idea of networks of activity within which contradictions and struggles take place in the definition of the motives and object of the activity calls for an analysis of power and control within and between developing activity systems. The latter is the point at which Bernstein's emphasis on different layers and dimensions of power and control becomes key to the development of the theory.

Lemke (1997) suggests that it is not only the context of the situation that is relevant, but also the context of culture when an analysis of meaning is undertaken. He suggests that 'we interpret a text, or a situation, in part by connecting it to other texts and situations which our community, or our individual history, has made us see as relevant to the meaning of the present one' (Lemke, 1997, p. 50). This use of notions of inter-textuality, of networked activities or network of connections provides Lemke with tools for the creation of an account of ecosocial systems which transcend immediate contexts. Engeström and Miettinen recognise the strengths and limitations of this position. They imply they a need for an analysis of the way in which networks of activities are structured – ultimately for an analysis of power and control:

> Various microsociologies have produced eye-opening works that uncover the local, idiosyncratic, and contingent nature of action, inter-action, and knowledge. Empirical studies of concrete, situated practices can uncover the local pattern of activity and the cultural specificity of thought, speech and discourse. Yet these microstudies tend to have little connection to macrotheories of social institutions and the structure of society. Various approaches to analysis of social networks may be seen as attempts to bridge the gap. However, a single network, though inter-connected with a number of other networks, typically still in no way represents any general or lawful development in society. (Engeström & Miettinen, 1999, p. 8)

Leontiev (1981) explored this issue from the perspective of development through time. He suggested that in the study of human ontogeny, one must take account of the ordering of categories of activity which corresponds to broad stages of mental development. According to Leontiev:

> In studying the development of the child's psyche, we must therefore start by analyzing the child's activity, as this activity is built up in the concrete conditions of its life.... Life or activity as a whole is not built up mech-anically, however, from separate types of activity. Some types of activ-ity are the leading ones at a given stage and are of greatest significance for the individual's subsequent development, and other are less import-ant. We can say accordingly, that each stage of psychic development is

characterized by a definite relation of the child to reality that is the leading one at that stage and by a definite, leading type of activity. (Leontiev,
1981, p. 395)

This analysis of development in terms of stages characterised in terms of
particular dominant activities is often associated with the work of Elkonin.
In the terms of contemporary activity theory, this account is one of progressive transformation of the object through time. This could be termed a
horizontal analysis.

> [W]hen we speak of the dominant activity and its significance for a child's
> development in this or that period, this is by no means meant to imply
> that the child might not be simultaneously developing in other direc-
> tions as well. In each period, a child's life is many-sided, the activities of
> which his life is composed are varied. New sorts of activity appear; the
> child forms new relations with his surroundings. When a new activity
> becomes dominant, it does not cancel all previously existing activities: it
> merely alters their status within the overall system of relations between
> the child and his surroundings, which thereby become increasingly
> richer. (Elkonin, 1972, p. 247)

Griffin and Cole (1984) noted that in the course of a single session of an
after-school activity designed for seven-to-eleven-year-olds, there could be
fluctuations in what activity seemed to be 'leading'. This could be termed a
situated analysis. In Figure 11.1, an analysis of a particular moment in time
(A or B or C) considers the network of activity systems in which subjects
were located and seek to discern the shifts in dominance that take place in
short periods of real time in particular context. For example, at time A,
activity 1A assumes dominance, whereas at time B, activity 2B is represented as dominant or leading. This analysis could be pursued through the
application of Bernstein's model to several activities and systems (rather
than the one to which is usually referenced), and also could seek to apply
this analysis of power and control to the emergence of dominance (1A vs.
2A vs. 3A). This situated analysis would combine the strengths of AT with
its emphasis on networks of activity and the formation of objects of activity
with the analytical power and descriptive elegance of Bernstein's work. The
analysis is thus one in which the relational interdependence of individual
and social agencies is recognised. The historical analysis would focus on the
transformation of dominance through time.

The historical background of much of what is now termed activity theory posits 'networks' of activity systems in which dominance arises at particular moments in both long and short periods of time. The word 'network'

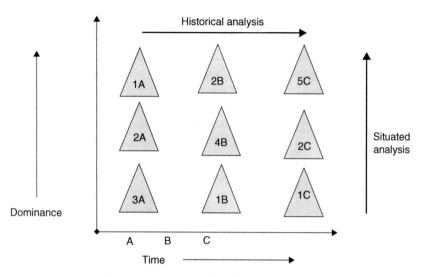

FIGURE 11.1. Dominance in networks of activity systems through time.

has been placed in quotation marks to signify a resistance to the notion of network as a connected system within which component parts share some function. Here concern is with the existence of multiple activity systems which may supplant each other and may be mutually transformed. By way of illustration I offer this rather crude example: Suppose a person is both a caregiver to their own child and a professional teacher. If that teacher has a need to collect their child from a nursery at the end of the school day, then the way that might respond to class disruption close to the final bell of the day may be very different to the way in which they might respond earlier in the day. Here two activity systems assume a different relationship to one another at particular times of the day. These fluctuations in dominance are rarely subjected to rigorous empirical scrutiny. Some of the empirical work which proclaims a CHAT orientation seems to constrain its analysis to one activity system, let alone a network of activity systems, and rarely strays into the analysis of shifts in dominance. Taken together, the implications of the work of Griffin and Cole, Lemke, Leontiev and Elkonin suggests that such an analysis should be deployed both at the levels of both long-term ontogenesis and short-term or even micro analysis. Makitalo and Säljö (2002, p. 75) argue that it is through the analysis of categories that 'people draw on the past to make their talk relevant to the accomplishment of interaction within specific traditions of argumentation'. They note, along with Sacks (1992), that categories are activity bound and that their use is inextricably bound up with a particular interactional and moral order (Jayyusi, 1984, p. 2). Such analyses would share the concern to explore the way in which subjects are shaped by fluctuating patterns of dominance from the perspective of those actors. However the emergence of categories is not explored in relation to the principles of regulation of the social setting in which they emerge. There may be some benefit in pursuing the Bernsteinian perspective in the context of the analysis of fluctuating patterns of dominance within networks of activity systems within this framework, but from the point of view of the pathway of the object-motive through networks of activity.

CONCLUSION

In this chapter I have argued that a recognition of the process of re-contextualisation of societal motives within specific situations provides an important window on the psychological implications of changing situations. The local arrangements of power and control within and between settings, such as institutions, give rise to specific modalities of discourse which constitute psychological tools which mediate the actions of persons located within these activity systems. It is from this base that I have argued that the development of the activity theory requires an understanding of the production of such tools and also requires an understanding of instrumental and affective/moral dimensions of these tools. A robust understanding of the complexity of networks of activity which have dimensions in space and time would then provide enhanced access to an understanding of the local formation of ways of thinking. My suggestion is that the sociology of cultural transmission developed by Basil Bernstein can do much to enhance current understanding of the local formation of motives and the implications of changing situations.

REFERENCES

Baerentsen, K. B., & Trettvik, J. (2002). An activity theory approach to affordance. NordiCHI, October 19–23, 51–60.
Bernstein, B. (1977). Class, codes and control, Vol. 3: *Towards a theory of educational transmissions*. 2nd rev. ed. London: Routledge & Kegan Paul.
    (1981). Codes, modalities and the process of cultural reproduction: A model. *Language in Society 10*, 327–363.
    (1990). *The structuring of pedagogic discourse, Volume IV: Class, codes and control.* London: Routledge.
    (1993). Foreword. In H. Daniels (Ed.), *Charting the agenda: Educational activity after Vygotsky*. London: Routledge.
    (1996). *Pedagogy, symbolic control and identity: Theory, research and critique.* London: Taylor and Francis.

(2000). *Pedagogy, symbolic control and identity: Theory, research, critique (revised edition)*. Lanham, MD: Rowman & Littlefield Publishers.

Cole, M. (1996). *Cultural psychology: A once and future discipline.* Cambridge, MA: Harvard University Press.

Daniels, H. (2008). *Vygotsky and research.* London: Routledge.

(2010). The mutual shaping of human action and institutional settings: A study of the transformation of children's services and professional work. *The British Journal of Sociology of Education, 31*(4), 377–393.

Elkonin, D. B. (1972). Toward the problem of stages in the mental development of the child. *Soviet Psychology, 4,* 6–20.

Engeström, Y. (1987). *Learning by expanding,* Helsinki:Orienta-Konsultit Oy.

(1999). Innovative learning in work teams: Analysing cycles of knowledge creation in practice, In Y. Engeström, R. Miettinen, & R. Punamaki (Eds.), *Perspectives on Activity Theory* (pp. 307–406). Cambridge: Cambridge University Press.

(2004). New forms of learning in co-configuration work. *Journal of Workplace Learning, 16*(1/2), 11–21.

Engeström, Y., & Miettinen, R. (1999). Introduction. In Y. Engeström, R. Miettinen, & R.-L. Punam äki (Eds.), *Perspectives on activity theory* (pp. 1–18). Cambridge: Cambridge University Press.

Gearhart, M., & Newman, D. (1980). Learning to draw a picture: The social context of an individual activity. *Discourse Processes, 3,* 169–184.

Gibson, J. J. (1986). *The ecological approach to visual perception.* Hillsdale, NJ: Lawrence Erlbaum.

Gonzalez-Rey, F. (2002). L.S. Vygotsky and the question of personality in the cultural-historical approach. In D. Robbins & A. Stetsenko (Eds.), *Voices within Vygotsky's non-classical psychology: Past, present, future* (pp. 24–37). New York: Nova Science.

Griffin, P., & Cole, M. (1984). Current activity for the future: The Zo-ped. In B. Rogoff & J. V. Wertsch (Eds.), *Children's learning in the zone of proximal development: New directions for child development* (pp. 45–63). San Francisco: Jossey-Bass.

Hegel, G. W. F. (1977). *The phenomenology of spirit* (A. V. Miller, Trans.). Oxford: Oxford University Press. (Original work published 1807).

Jayyusi, L. (1984). *Categorization and the moral order.* London: Routledge & Kegan Paul.

Kozulin, A. (1998). *Psychological tools. A sociocultural approach to education.* London: Harvard University Press.

Lave, J. (1988). *Cognition in practice: Mind, mathematics and culture in everyday life.* Cambridge: Cambridge University Press.

(1991). Situating learning in communities of practice. In L. B. Resnick, J. M. Levine, & S. D. Teasley (Eds.), *Perspectives on socially shared cognition* (pp. 63–84). Washington, DC: American Psychological Association.

Lave, J., Murtaugh, M., & de la Rocha, O. (1984). The dialectic of arithmetic in grocery shopping. In B. Rogoff & J. Lave (Eds.), *Everyday cognition: Development in social context* (pp. 67–94). Cambridge, MA: Harvard University Press.

Lemke, J. (1997). Cognition, context, and learning: A social semiotic perspective. In D. Kirshner (Ed.), *Situated cognition theory: Social, neurological, and semiotic perspectives.* New York: Erlbaum.

Leontiev, A. N. (1978). *Activity, consciousness and personality*. Englewood Cliffs, NJ: Prentice Hall.

(1981). The concept of activity in psychology. In J. V. Wertsch (Ed.), *The concept of activity in Soviet psychology* (pp. 121–145). Armonk, NY: M.E. Sharpe.

Makitalo, A., & Saljo, R. (2002). Talk in institutional context and institutional context in talk: Categories as situated practices. *Text*, *22*(1), 57–82.

Minick, N. (1987). *The development of Vygotsky's thought: An introduction*. In R. W. Rieber & A. S. Carton (Eds.), *The collected works of L.S. Vygotsky*, 17–38, New York: Plenum Press.

Minick, N., Stone, C. A., & Forman, E. A. (1993). Introduction: Integration of individual, social and institutional processes in accounts of children's learning and development. In E. A. Forman, N. Minick, & C. A. Stone (Eds.), *Contexts for learning: Sociocultural dynamics in children's development* (pp. 3–16). Oxford: Oxford University Press.

Sacks, H. (1992). *Lectures on conversation*. Oxford: Blackwell

Singh, P. (2002). Pedagogising knowledge: Bernstein's theory of the pedagogic device. *British Journal of Sociology of Education*, *23*(4), 571–582.

Stetsenko, A., & Arievitch, I. (2003). The self in cultural-historical activity theory: Reclaiming the unity of social and individual dimensions of human development. *Theory & Psychology*, *14*, 475–503.

Suchman, L. (1987). *Plans and situated actions. The problem of human-machine communication*. Cambridge: Cambridge University Press.

Vygotsky, L. S. (1978). *Mind in society: The development of higher psychological processes*. In M. Cole, V. John-Steiner, S. Scribner, & E. Souberman, (Eds. and trans.), Cambridge, MA: Harvard University Press.

(1987 [1933–1934]). *The collected works of L.S. Vygotsky: Problems of general psychology*. (Vol. 1). New York: Plenum Press.

(1994 [1930]). The socialist alteration of man. In *The Vygotsky reader* (pp. 175–184). Oxford: Basil Blackwell.

(1998 [1928–1931]). *The collected works of L.S. Vygotsky: Child psychology* (Vol. 5). New York: Plenum Press.

Yaroshevsky, M. (1989). *Lev Vygotsky*. Moscow: Progress Publishers

12

A Conceptual Perspective for Investigating
Motive in Cultural-Historical Theory

SETH CHAIKLIN

It is useful to have an explicit theoretical conception about motive. In this volume, *motive* refers to a theoretical concept in cultural-historical theory. As used by researchers here, motive is not located solely in a person, nor solely in a situation or condition external to a person. It describes a general relation which must be discovered analytically in the particular substantive relations in which persons are engaged. These relations transcend the individual, even whilst the individual is necessarily involved. Motives are embedded in a societal practice, not simply emerging or arising transitorily, appearing and disappearing. The concept must be studied in conjunction with other theoretical concepts, perhaps most importantly with some account of societal or 'macro-social' aspects. Concepts like practice, institution, tradition, values become important (see Hedegaard). In relation to a single person, motive is understood as a relation, where a person's experience is related to, but not definitional of, motive. One could continue to rehearse these general statements, but understanding the theoretical concept of motive (in general) is only a prelude to the important scientific work of analysing motive (in specific).

The chapters in this volume are focused on understanding persons acting in their everyday situations in a particular meaningful societal practice, whether at home (Hedegaard; González Rey; Zinchenko), in preschool (Fleer; Kravtsova & Kravtsov; Sanchez & Martinez; Winther-Lindquist), school (Daniels; Stenild & Iversen; Wardekker, Boersma, van Tem, & Volman) or at work (Edwards). Most of them include analyses that discuss specific events or aspects within the practice, where the motive concept is part of the analysis for understanding either how particular forms of acting have developed or for understanding how to influence the development of concrete actions in these specific situations. In other words, the motive concept is used as part of analysing specific instances of human practices, rather than starting with the concept and seeking situations in which to apply it. This approach is consistent with the wholistic orientation of cultural-historical theory.

The chapters also draw on many other concepts from cultural-historical theory, (e.g. consciousness, meaning, sense, will, emotion, psychological function, voluntary action, activity) and include discussions of general theoretical perspectives about activity and development found in the works of Leontiev, Vygotsky, El'konin, and Bozhovich, among others. This focus on a system of concepts and general theoretical perspectives is to be expected in a wholistic perspective.

The *wholistic* orientation in cultural-historical theory arises from its theoretical and ontological assumptions (such as the role of societal practices in the development of psychological characteristics) and methodological orientations (such as Vygotsky's discussion of 'analysis by units' and 'analysis by elements', or Leontiev's discussion of the dialectical theory of knowledge, with focus on internal relations, and an essence/appearance distinction).

The wholistic perspective has important implications for studying the emotional aspects of the development of action. Several chapters referred to the idea of the unity of intellect and affect (Daniels; González Rey; Kravtsova & Kravtsov; Zinchenko) and/or the importance of emotional experience in relation to motives (Edwards; Hedegaard; Wardekker et al.).

Two important aims of this volume are to bring the concept of *motive* more fully into ongoing cultural-historical research, and to highlight the idea of individual experience (which includes emotional aspects) and its role in the theoretical understanding of motive.

Draft chapters were discussed among most of the chapter authors in a workshop (March 2010). It was apparent from that meeting that there was general agreement about several theoretical issues in relation to the motive concept. For example, no one disputed the need to engage with a motive concept in the analysis of children's development, or analyse actions in relation to a societal perspective. All were oriented to having a dynamic understanding of the concept, which was seen as providing a way to understand how individual action is integrated with or related to institutional/societal practices.

No one wanted a motive concept that was a kind of cause or agent for human action, but there was uncertainty about how to use the motive concept in a satisfactory way. Two themes that arose repeatedly in the workshop discussions were (1) the meaning of concepts (e.g. difference between motive and motivation) and which concepts should be taken into account in making these analyses (e.g. role of intentions, agency); and (2) the analytic relationship between individuals and collective or societal concepts. These two themes are addressed in this chapter. Some orienting perspectives for thinking about the concept of motive are presented and interpreted in relation to the chapters. Thereafter, some implications and consequences for further productive investigation of the motive concept are highlighted.

MOTIVE IN CULTURAL-HISTORICAL PERSPECTIVE

In cultural-historical theory, there is no common or standard theoretical view about how to elaborate each concept or to understand their place in the system of ideas. Many fundamental concepts in cultural-historical research are not readily accessible, both in textual and conceptual senses, where *motive* is one of them. No single or key text can be identified as the initial or definitive statement about *motive*. One cannot go to the library to get an instruction manual for how to work with the motive concept. It is necessary for the individual authors to draw upon different aspects from the theoretical sources to formulate their interpretation of motive and motivation concepts.

The concept of motive is central in cultural-historical theory. The concept must necessarily be understood as part of a system of concepts, particularly the concept of *activity*, and related concepts such as *societal need*, *goal*, and *action*. This necessity reflects the standard understanding that the meaning of theoretical concepts comes from their relationship in the system rather than from absolute or universal definitions. If one does not have some understanding of the system of concepts in which *motive* is embedded, then there is a tendency to fall back to an everyday meaning, or seek a formal definition of *motive*, followed by a hermeneutic attempt to decode the words in the definition. Textual exegesis and formal definition will not be sufficient to achieve this purpose. An adequate, productive understanding of the motive concept (within cultural-historical theory) requires engagement with conceptual questions about the construction of scientific arguments.

Why a Motive Concept Is Needed: Conceptual and Historical Background

Human action is sometimes mysterious or incomprehensible, but rarely random or pointless. It would be impossible to study human action scientifically if it were without structure or reason. Whilst one may accept the assumption that human action is organised or structured in systematic ways, the principles by which this structuring or organisation operates are difficult to establish, and which phenomena may allow for systematic analysis are difficult to delimit.

The analysis and explanation of action is particularly important in cultural-historical theory, both because of a focus on individual development of psychological capabilities, which are often understood in terms of self-control of action, and a basic premise that psychological capabilities and characteristics are formed as a consequence of acting in structured practices.

In the history of psychology, it has been common for theorists to pursue the idea that human action can be explained or understood from a few underlying principles (e.g. pursuit of pleasure or reward, avoidance of pain or punishment) or a small set of underlying characteristics (see discussions in Hedegaard; Kravtsova and Kravtsov). A contemporary example asserts: 'Motives are the motors of behavior, energizing purposive behavior that serves a function for the individual' (Fiske, 2010, p. 14), where *motive* is used informally to characterise basic principles that underlie human action in social situations, and *belonging* is proposed as a main organising principle (with a suggestion that this can be grounded in evolution), along with understanding, controlling, trusting and so on as general motives for realising this belonging.

In effect, these kinds of approaches locate motive or motivation as a property of the person, or as a person's attempt to realise an abstract characteristic that transcends the content of practical situations. Whether intended or not, appeal to one or more general underlying principles tends to incline one to interpret substantive details of practical situations in relation to these overall principles. For example, explanations of a schoolchild's orientation to doing homework or a preschool child's choice of play themes would appeal to these general underlying principles as the 'motivating' or 'driving' forces that are manifested in the child's actions.

An Ontological Shift Gives a Different Explanatory Logic

Cultural-historical approaches pursue a qualitatively different theoretical conceptualisation for explaining these situations. The concept of motive is used to refer to relationships that organise a person's action in the situations in which they are acting. As a simple rule of thumb, one might speak about action that is oriented or related to a motive, where further specification of that relation is an analytical problem. Concepts like *motive* and *motivation* are not a property of a person, or something that 'drives', 'causes' or 'determines' action.

This shift in explanatory logic (from property to relation) has been observed historically in other sciences (e.g. the shift in explaining displacement of physical objects as the loss of the property of impetus to Newton's relational account in terms of unequal balance of forces). This seemingly small shift has many implications and consequences for how to use the motive concept in scientific investigations. For example, now, rather than being an object of investigation in and of itself, a motive (or motivation) concept becomes an auxiliary concept, used as part of an analysis or explanation of other phenomenon.

Focus on Development of Psychological Functions

The development of a science depends on having a clear vision of its object of investigation, with specific phenomena chosen in relation to that object. In the cultural-historical tradition, the original or initial object was the formation of psychological functions. Many of the chapters in this volume can be understood from this point of view, even if they are not formulated in this original terminology. The cases discussed in the chapters reflect such formation processes as acquisition of word, the formation of interest in play materials, the formation of self-conception, engagement with school activities, theoretical thinking, resolution of conflicts in play situations and knowledge in professional practice. The interest is to understand the origin or formation of a psychological capability. Recognising this aspect is important for engaging with the general conceptions in cultural-historical theory about formation of psychological capabilities. For example, capabilities are formed as a consequence of acting in structured practices, where these practices are developed historically, reflecting traditions of action in relation to societally-valued goals. Accordingly, acting is organised in relation to demands and expectations in societal traditions of action (rather than determined by innate characteristics), and motives must be understood in relation to these societal traditions of action. In this way, motive is part of an analysis of development of psychological functions, which is illustrated in the chapters.

Relation between Individual Action and Societal Practice

The problematic issue about the relation between individual action and societal practice is not unique to the cultural-historical tradition. Any sociologically-oriented tradition confronts the same problem, and major twentieth-century social theorists (e.g. Durkheim, Weber, Parsons,

Bourdieu) are still consulted regularly for their views on how to conceptualise these relations, which appear under a variety of oppositions like micro-
macro relations or agency-structure.

The classic form of this problem is how local, singular actions can collectively be taken to reflect or produce societal structure, and conversely
how societal structures are manifest in the individual interactions. These
problems arise in part because they presuppose that a separation between
individual and collective is meaningful.

This form of the classic problem does not arise in cultural-historical
theory because of an ontological assumption that rejects the split between
person and historically-structured societal practices. A striking example of
this rejection can be found in Zinchenko's argument that *word* is already
embedded in the physical interactions between newborn infant and
caretaker – not just in the sounds uttered, but in the physical interactions
themselves. Word is present before there is word.

To explain how the relations between individual actions and societal (or
cultural) structures can be understood in a cultural-historical perspective, a
few relevant points about theory of activity must be elaborated, with a focus
on the object-oriented character of activity. Thereafter, implications for the
motive concept can be discussed.

Excursus on Activity
As a historical fact, the concept of *activity* emerged from scientific efforts
to understand the development of psychological functions, where there
was a special concern to find a way to explain these functions without
resorting to a mechanistic or behaviourist view in which environmental
features (e.g. stimuli) were the cause or source of action. If one rejects the
hypothesis that human behaviour can be understood solely as responses
to environmental conditions, then another concept is needed to explain
the process by which psychological capabilities are formed. The notion of
activity was this concept. For example, activity is understood as 'a unit of
life, mediated by psychic reflection, the real function of which is that it
orients the subject in the objective world' (Leontiev, 1978 [1975], p. 50). An
important implication of that notion is that action (and its explanation)
must be understood in units of life (i.e. as part of meaningful practice).
Another implication is the 'totality' of activity. That is, action is always
activity, because persons are always orienting in the objective world.
Activity is manifest in actions, where the concept of activity refers to the
structural relations in which the action occurs, and where this structure

is integral to the action, not simply background or a mediator between person and other persons and things (p. 51).

Theoretical Implications

A consequence of interpreting all meaningful practices in terms of activity is that it is necessary to understand action in relation to objects. This idea is sometimes expressed as *object-oriented activity*, where this term is redundant, given that activity is defined as 'object-oriented', but scientists often introduce a term to emphasise something that has not been commonly or previously recognised. In this case, the object-oriented aspect serves to avoid an idealist position that there are aspects of human psychology that can be understood independently of objects. This necessity of understanding action in relation to objects is critical for understanding how cultural-historical theory handles the relation between individual action and societal practice. Societal conditions are embedded in the objects and practice in which a person is acting.[1] (Consider the examples of the mobile phone in Stenild & Sejer Iversen, or the word in Zinchenko.) In such a conception, it becomes impossible to speak about action as separate from activity, or to speak about an action level that is distinct from an activity level (see Chaiklin, 2007, pp. 183–184, for further explanation). Individual action is always activity, where activity always has a societal dimension.

The scientific task is to analyse the internal systemic connections in activity (Leontiev, 1978 [1975], p. 67). The analytic work is oriented by a complex of interdependent assumptions, namely that all actions have a societal meaning, that individual acts are always organised in relation to the societal practices and that action is always oriented in relation to objects (i.e. object-oriented character of activity). Given that motive is what arouses action, then this complex provides a way to understand motive as embedded in societal practice. Accordingly, cultural-historical research is oriented to understanding the development and transformation of action (i.e. development of psychological functions) rather that describing individual interactions themselves. Together with the wholistic assumption, one can see that the main focus of many chapters in this volume is to analyse the actions of individual children in relation to the practices in which they are engaged.

[1] This kind of idea can be understood as an elaboration of Vygotsky's genetic law of development, where its philosophical roots were introduced by Marx (e.g. 1964 [1844], pp. 139–140) and developed subsequently by Wartofsky (1976), independently of Leontiev.

Practical Consequences

Some chapters are focused on the variations observed by participants in the same situation (Wardekker et al.; Winther-Lindquist), whereas others focus on how different children in the same situation act in relation to cultural resources in their local circumstances (Fleer; Hedegaard; Sanchez & Martinez). Especially the latter three chapters interpret (rather than describe) children's interactions in terms of the societal interactions, and one could read Wardekker et al. and Winther-Lindquist in this way (even if they did not emphasise these aspects explicitly). This is not a simple (vague) appeal to cultural or societal influences. All these chapters 'take the lid off' the processes by which cultural differences are manifest, seeking to explain specific processes by which societally-grounded motives are expressed in individual action.

In pursuing these questions, it can be meaningful to draw on ideas and concepts that have been developed among researchers who have not been working self-consciously in relation to the cultural-historical theory. This can be seen in several of the chapters in this volume that propose or draw on other concepts.[2] The introduction of such concepts reflects partially the consequences of putting whole persons in meaningful practices as the centre of investigation, and the need to understand the empirical material theoretically. One can discuss whether adequate (or potentially adequate) concepts already exist within cultural-historical theory for some of the concepts introduced here, but the important point is that the whole person in meaningful practice is the starting point of the analysis rather than the promotion of particular concepts.

DIFFICULTIES

"Besides vision, there must be work' (Zinchenko, 2004 [2001], p. 57). Zinchenko's pithy expression was formulated to summarise his argument that internalisation and externalisation differ from acts of perceiving the world. Zinchenko's point is that an individual cannot simply master new ideas by being able to see or identify them. One must also be able to externalise them as part of their free action. This point also provides an excellent (literal) image of the task that confronts the researcher who wants to use the concept of motive in cultural-historical theory.

---

[2] Daniels proposes the use of Bernstein's concepts; Edwards draws on Knorr-Cetina's concept of *epistemic object*; Hedegaard draws on Alfred Schutz; Wardekker et al. draw on Holland's concept of personal identity; Winther-Lindquist introduces the social identity concept from the social representation tradition; Zinchenko draws on Florensky and Bernshtein; and so forth.

As a historical fact, many cultural-historical researchers do not have their initial scientific training within this theoretical tradition, acquiring it largely through reading (with occasional conversations with others). Through this mode of acquisition one usually gets a vision but not an idea of how to work. Perhaps this is why so much research that is self-described as socio-cultural or cultural-historical is largely descriptive of phenomena in a new terminology. In Mikhailov's (2006) sharp judgement: 'Many psychologists use the terminology of L. S. Vygotsky to create an elegant impression, while formulating their personal scientific problems in the logic of patent empiricism' (p. 21). Presumably these shortcomings are not intentional; however, Mikhailov's observation indicates the challenge involved in understanding the implications and consequences involved in cultural-historical theory for research. During the workshop discussions, participants noted several times how easy it is to fall into positivist and mechanistic language for describing and discussing these problems.

Many authors in the present volume noted in conversation that it was difficult to write a chapter with a focus on motive, which may explain, in part, why this concept is not highlighted in the published cultural-historical research literature, even if the concept has been under discussion for almost seventy-five years. One possible reason for this difficulty is the ontological shift from motive as reason or cause to motive as one concept within a system of concepts. Another is the wholistic assumption which orients one to look at meaningful life practices, which broadens the prerequisites for working with the concept. That is, just to get to the 'beginning', where one can work with motive, it is necessary to have an analysis of a societal practice and a focus on the development of some psychological capability, which in turn may be understood in relation to some larger meaningful actions. This need to make preliminary analysis could be illustrated with most of the chapters, but to take just one example, consider that Stenild and Sejer Iversen needed to analyse goals of school practice and activities in everyday practice, and the theoretical structure of subject-matter concepts, as part of using the motive concept.

RESEARCH WITH MOTIVES: POSSIBILITIES

In further work with the motive concept in a cultural-historical perspective, it is important to keep three interrelated perspectives – wholistic, developmental and activity – in the foreground, where a main objective for cultural-historical research is to account for the development of psychological processes (which has also been a main focus in the present volume).

Important to Keep a Wholistic, Developmental, Activity Perspective

In the late 1970s, an edited volume on children's thinking had the stimulating subtitle: What develops? (Siegler, 1978). This question can be usefully revived in relation to the problems addressed in this volume. One answer to this question, from a cultural-historical perspective, is personality, emphasising that a general research problem is to explain development of the whole person, not just specific psychological functions. This wholistic focus is present in Vygotsky and continued in the analyses from El'konin and Leontiev, where motive is a central part of their analysis of what develops (with capabilities for action in relation to societal practices being another part).

Attention to whole persons brings forward the issue of personality, which leads theoretically to a focus on motives and actions (see Kravtsova & Kravtsov).[3] Hedegaard's focus on actions in relation to practice can also be understood in terms of personality and the development of motives, even if not framed explicitly as such. If the research focus is on development of whole persons, and not on psychological functions or motive per se, then the task is to explain the development of psychological functions in relation to the demands of institutional practice, where it will be necessary to understand the role of motives in this process.

This idea does not contradict the suggestion that development of psychological processes is a main research objective in cultural-historical research, nor suggest that motive is the 'key' or 'solution' to the theory of development. It only highlights the need to understand the development of psychological processes in relation to the practices in which a person is engaged, which will necessarily require an engagement with motive.

Whilst motives are part of the analysis of development, they must also be understood in a developmental perspective. It is meaningless to speak about motives alone (i.e. as if universal or general), without relating the person's situation and capabilities in the societal practice in which they are acting. One cannot write about motives in a general or universal way. For example, the motives for eight-year-old children (in one historical tradition of practice) are not likely to be the same as those for eighteen-year-old children. Hence statements about 'motives to learn' (as a general property or

---

[3] González Rey also appeals to the personality concept, but wants to replace 'motive' in the theoretical structure with 'subjective configuration' as a way to bring a subjective dimension which he thinks is missing from the motive concept.

quality) do not give much meaning, unless they are related to the practices in which a person is engaged, and the person's capabilities are related to the demands of these practices. If one accepts that motive must be understood as part of a system of relations, then it cannot subsequently get a singular position in the theoretical analysis. In other words, as part of a wholistic account, and with a focus on development of psychological capabilities, one must clarify the meaning of motive in relation to developmental character-istics, which are often changing with experience and related to age/time.

This wholistic perspective has similar implications in relation to the con-cept of agency, which some want to introduce because of the belief that the theory of activity has ignored the subjective aspects of action (e.g. González Rey's chapter could be read in this way). Does introducing a notion of agency (or subjective configuration) lead to a new superseding concept (to replace motive) in which action can be explained through agency? The question here is about the role of this concept within the theoretical analysis, and not a rejection of the idea of agency per se. Subjective or intentional aspects (see also Hedegaard) may be serving as indicators but not revealing the full structure of conditions in relation to which a person is acting. A focus on 'agency' alone loses a wholistic focus, so that one examines a person's action through the keyhole of their intentions, without understanding how and why the intentional keyhole was formed as it was.

Motive is both an individual and collective concept. Individuals can have motives, but the individuality of motives is always within the fabric of soci-etal practice. Accordingly, it can be meaningful to speak abstractly about motives as reflecting a general or collective form that a concrete individual is likely to acquire in a particular sociohistorical practice. The activity con-cept helps to understand why one can expect to find these general forms (because of the relations between motive and action).

These general forms are not completely determined for all individuals, nor do all individuals acquire exactly the same form (e.g. consider per-sonal sense), and other forms can also develop, but this attention to general forms gives a sharp contrast to the implicit assumptions in the locutions of psychologists who speak about 'a person in the world' or 'a person going around in the world'. This way of speaking reflects a conception of a per-son as separate from the world (perhaps with their own agency) and acting in relation to a context or surroundings. From a common-sense perspec-tive, it would appear as if there are two different kinds – psychological processes and societal processes, where it is tempting to separate the two. Within cultural-historical theory, such expressions are ontologically mean-ingless, because a person is always engaged in activity. The object-oriented character of activity implies that one cannot conceive of a person as separable from the context. This is the same point as was discussed previously in relation to the problem of relating individual action and societal practice, where the 'solution' is to avoid creating the problem by ontological assumptions that separate persons from societal practices. This is not to say that all is easy thereafter. The theoretical conception simply opens new problems and challenges, grounded in different assumptions about what must be explained, where the main focus is on the development of psychological capabilities through action within societally meaningful practices.

May be Useful to Consider Intervention

Another way to address the main research objective in cultural-historical theory is to make interventions into human practices, with the aim of developing psychological capabilities. The cultural-historical theory is focused on what can be rather than what is (cf. oral history about the 1966 Gal'perin/Piaget interchange).

The idea of intervention was an explicit focus in Stenild and Sejer Iversen and in Wardekker et al., and it can be seen lying just below the surface in Fleer, Hedegaard, Kravtsova and Kravtsov, and Winther-Lindquist, where one sees comments about implications for intervention.

There is a well-known phrase within different scientific communities, that if you want to understand the nature of something, then try to change it. This perspective can be an important technique for organising studies in relation to motive.

Appropriate Methods of Motive Investigation Must Reflect the Concept's Relational Nature

Is it meaningful to speak about 'measurement of motives'? If motive is viewed as a property of a person, then one might expect that an interview or paper-and-pencil test will be sufficient to identify or 'reveal' a person's motives. If motive is understood as a relation between persons and possibilities of action, where the substantive meaning of motive arises as a relation between concepts, then an idea like 'measuring' a motive does not make much sense. If motives are understood as a system of relations, then analysis must focus on this system and not just the motive itself, which implies the need for analyses of practices, production in relation to those practices, and personal sense of these practices. Interviews and questionnaires, at best, help to give some insight into personal sense, but it is still necessary to interpret the interview statements in relation to societal demands and meaning.

If one wanted to use the subjective configuration concept (González Rey), then presumably the configuration available to a schoolchild in an interview may not be the same as the subjective configuration for this child in the playground, the classroom, and the family breakfast table. It may be relevant and necessary to see persons in action in relation to their every-day situations (as shown in this volume by the many chapters that examine children acting in their everyday settings) – and not remain only with self-aware descriptions.

If motive is understood as an 'energizer' or 'initiator' of action, then it could be tempting to see if there is a correlation between 'amount of motiv-ation' and 'amount of action'. Such attempts reflect a view of motives as a property rather than an account of systematic relations. This is not to deny that one can observe differences in the intensity of action, but this aspect is theorised so far in terms of resolutions of conflicts in a motive hierarchy (e.g. Leontiev, 1978 [1975], p. 136). If motives are understood as hierarchic-ally related, then focus on one motive alone may not always be sufficient for understanding action in meaningful practices. At the very least, one should be seeking to uncover a system of motives in relation to a practice (see Chaiklin, 1999, pp. 203–204 for a simple example). Studies of motive conflicts and their resolution may require data collection procedures that involve looking at a person's actions across several different kinds of situations.

Important to Engage with the Classical Texts

The authors for Chapters 2 through 4 in this volume were all educated in the Soviet Union. They necessarily encountered Leontiev's ideas, maybe not always voluntarily. It is notable that these three chapters in particu-lar mark a clear distance from Leontiev's ideas. Given that these authors are well-respected researchers, one might conclude that there is nothing further to be learned from Leontiev's texts. More generally, one can hear discussions in the research community that characterise his theory as being determinist, or only focusing on objective aspects. It might simplify matters to place Leontiev's theory into a 'determinist' or 'objective-only' classifica-tion – so that one does not have to read or engage with his arguments. This would be unfortunate. Leontiev's texts are still worth reading – both for the sophistication in their presentation of the research problems and for many ideas that deserve further critical evaluation in relation to contemporary issues and concerns. No doubt Leontiev's ideas need to be clarified, revised and extended, which Leontiev himself would presumably endorse (see first sentence in the introduction to Leontiev, 1978 [1975]), but it would be a mistake to believe that contemporary thinking has surpassed many important issues and hypotheses that he raises.

STATUS AND THREE OPEN PROBLEMS

The broad outlines of motive as a theoretical concept in cultural-historical theory are clear, even if many fine details are still problematic and difficult to control adequately. In abbreviated form, the concept arises as part of theory of activity, with at least four important aspects that should be highlighted. First, it refers directly to an object that is lacking but wanted (as part of a societally meaningful practice). Second, the meaning of motive cannot be reduced to the object alone (i.e. no object is, by itself, intrinsically motivating). Rather, an object has the motive quality when it serves in a special relationship between the state of a person (who wants the object) and the state of a situation (i.e. where the person lacks the object and has possibilities to produce it). Accordingly, an individual can lose a motive if this special relationship disappears (e.g. in achieving the object permanently, or in losing a want for the object). This special relation also implies that motive is not a property of a person, or as something for which one has more or less. In the theoretical structure of the psychological theory of activity, motive is understood as arousing action, where action is oriented to producing the lacking object, and where this object cannot be produced through a single action. Activity arises as a process for producing the motive (i.e. the object that satisfies the need), where the motive serves as the object towards which action is oriented. This way of conceptualising motive implies that motive cannot be studied by itself, but only as part of a study of human action, including processes of development. Third, individual activities can have more than one motive. Fourth, a person lives in multiple institutional relationships (see Hedegaard). The last two points emphasise that one must study relationships among motives. It is not meaningful to study a single motive.

Three Open Problems

There are reasons to believe that more societal interpretations of the activity concept were never developed adequately (see Hedegaard; also Gal'perin, 1992 [1977], pp. 43–49; Zaporozhets, 2002 [1990], p. 48). The object-oriented character of activity may still be preserved, but the societal aspects of those objects may be more salient now. This historical condition leaves many important scientific problems in relation to motive. The following three problems reflect a view about what is crucial to address.

The relation between actions, goals, and motives in the theory of activity continues to be a devilish problem. In part, there is a theoretical position that goals can become motives (an idea used by Winther-Lindquist). The importance is to clarify actions in relation to the structure of activity and to psychological functions. My own guess is that motive should be defined and limited more rigorously in relation to societal needs. This step will require that many motives will have to be re-described as goals. Does this make any difference? From one point of view, the observed physical movements are the same, regardless of the theoretical description, but conceptualising them as actions opens a new challenge to characterise motives to which they are related.

Understanding the dynamics of the resolution of motive conflicts and the dynamics of motive hierarchies seems like an important issue for a cultural-historical theory of development. This issue will depend directly on the analytic and definitional issues just mentioned. If one is uncertain what should be identified as a motive, then it is necessarily difficult to form a hierarchy of motives.

Given that motives must be understood in relation to activity, and given that activity has not been developed adequately from a theoretical point of view, then there is an issue about the role of practices and institutions. Hedegaard has raised the issue of institution, which Daniels also notes with approval. Kravtsova and Kravtsov mention Arsen'ev's idea of community. Some may think of Engeström's 'activity system'. The notion of practice may also be meaningful (Chaiklin, 2011). The research goal is to understand how to use these concepts in relation to development of psychological capabilities. It is not simply a problem of formulating new definitions, but of elaborating the life processes through which psychological capabilities are developed. If one only introduces the societal or collective aspect without understanding its relation to activity (see preceding discussion), then one recreates to the micro-macro problem, nominally (but falsely) within the theoretical perspective.

REFERENCES

Chaiklin, S. (1999). Developmental teaching in upper-secondary school. In M. Hedegaard & J. Lompscher (Eds.), *Learning activity and development* (pp. 187–210). Aarhus: Aarhus University Press.

(2007). Modular or integrated? – An activity perspective for designing and evaluating computer-based systems. *International Journal of Human-Computer Interaction, 22*, 173–190.

(2011). The 'practice' of cultural-historical science. In M. Kontopodis, C. Wulf, & B. Fichtner (Eds.), *Children, development, and education: Cultural, historical, anthropological perspectives* (pp. 227–246). Dordrecht: Springer.

Fiske, S. T. (2010). *Social beings: Core motives in social psychology*, 2nd ed. Hoboken, NJ: Wiley.

Gal'perin, P. I. (1992 [1977]). The problem of activity in Soviet psychology. *Journal of Russian and East European Psychology, 30*(4), 37–59.

Leontiev, A. N. (1978 [1975]). *Activity, consciousness, and personality* (M. J. Hall, Trans.). Englewood Cliffs, NJ: Prentice-Hall.

Marx, K. (1964 [1844]). *Economic and philosophical manuscripts of 1844* (M. Milligan, Trans.). New York: International Publishers.

Mikhailov, F. T. (2006). Problems of the method of cultural-historical psychology. *Journal of Russian and East European Psychology, 44*(1), 21–54.

Siegler, R. S. (Ed.) (1978). *Children's thinking: What develops?* Hillsdale, NJ: Erlbaum.

Wartofsky, M. (1976). Perception, representation and the forms of action: Towards an historical epistemology. In J. Manninen (Ed.), *Aisthesis: Essays on the philosophy of perception* (pp. 19–43). Helsinki: The Philosophical Society of Finland.

Zaporozhets, A. Z. (2002 [1990]). Problems in the psychology of activity. *Journal of Russian and East European Psychology, 40*(4), 47–52.

Zinchenko, V. P. (2004 [2001]). The psychological theory of activity: 'Remembrances of the future'. *Journal of Russian and East European Psychology, 42*(2), 30–68.

INDEX

CPSIA information can be obtained at www.ICGtesting.com
Printed in the USA
BVOW051102171011

273579BV00005B/3/P